eople whose children
the coop ("post-kid"),
ling on the parks with
otions that are vastly
om those of the
suasion.

, unlike *Birnbaum's
ide to Walt Disney*
no means compre-
ther, it skips the kid
elivers the goods on
nusements Disney
. And because this
dated every year,
ent the past twelve
ating which of the
hotels, and restau-
new and old—
merit special atten-
lts. Final decisions
d after making
ips to Florida and
ything to the test.

research aplenty,
ould never have seen
not for the assistance

of many other people. To begin,
we owe a thank-you to the
people who run Walt Disney
World. It is their willingness to
explain operations in the most
accurate way possible that makes
this the Official Guide. However,
it is important to note that while
the folks at Walt Disney World
help us to ensure factual accura-
cy, they do not determine what
we do and do not cover in the
guide. *All editorial decisions are
made by the editor.*

In the listing below, I've tried to
acknowledge Disney staffers who
contributed their time, knowledge, and experience to this edition. In addition, I want to extend
a deep bow to Linda Warren,
Darlene Papalini, Laura Simpson,
Jeff Titelius, and Dave Herbst for
the care and effort they've put
into this project.

For their key roles behind the
scenes, we salute Duryan Bhagat,

ln't Have Done It Without . . .

rhill	Janice Hilliard	Anna Rivera
arroll	Mike Nesmith	Mary Roche
:olquitt	Lee Kitchen	Laura Simpson
Cook	Kristi Koester	Rick Sylvain
ezern	Tim Lewis	Jeff Weber
rennen	Brad Much	
laynes	Rosely Priaino	

Birnbaum's
Walt Disney World

WITHOUT KIDS

Wendy Lefkon
EDITORIAL DIRECTOR

Jill Safro
EDITOR

Elliot Kreloff
DESIGN DIRECTOR

Rob Eberhardt
DESIGNER

Lois Spritzer
CONTRIBUTING EDITOR

Jody Revenson
CONTRIBUTING EDITOR

Alexandra Mayes Birnbaum
CONSULTING EDITOR

THE OFFICIAL GUIDE

Disney EDITIONS

Other 2004 Birnbaum's Official Disney Guides

Disneyland

Walt Disney World

Walt Disney World For Kids, By Kids

A Word from tl

When you stop to think about it, a Walt Disney World guide for grown-ups makes a lot of sense. After all, how many kids do you know who have been there alone? As it happens, Disney has been catering to grown-up sensibilities for a long time; the most obvious example is one entire theme park, namely Epcot.

But don't think for a moment that the rest of the World is the exclusive domain of small fry. Grown-up glee can be experienced at every bend in the road (or safari trail) in each of the parks. In keeping with the spirit of the World that Walt built, there are no age limits here. The Disney-MGM Studios is a veritable haven for movie buffs. The Magic Kingdom sprinkles guests with pixie dust and transports them to the giddy, fantasy-filled days of their youth. Disney's Animal Kingdom, a lush celebration of all creatures great and small, is sure to lure the nature lover out of even the most buttoned-down sophisticate. Add to the above a hopping nightlife district and an all-out sports complex and you have proof

Editor
and N
Worl

posit
expa
tion.
resta
cours
ment

Bu
subtl
Disn
appe
refer
visu
ping
them
Disn
cros
side
both

and older
have flow
are descen
needs and
different f
parental pe

This boo
Official G
World, is h
hensive. R
stuff and c
the adult a
has to offe
guide is up
we have sp
months de
attractions
rants—bot
continue tc
tion by adv
were reach
countless t
putting eve

Even wit
this book v
print were

Jim Bc
Mike C
Bobbi
Stacey
Craig
Mark
Karen

Jill Newman, Diane Hodges, Sue Cole, Janet Castiglione, William Feik, Bob Rohr, Frieda Christofides, and Michelle Magenheim.

Special kudos to those for whom doing Walt Disney World research is truly a labor of love (as in no financial compensation whatsoever). The class of 2004 includes Irene Safro, Roy Safro, Joy Safro, Amy Safro, Margaret Verdon, Linda Verdon, Trace Schielzo, Judith Lagano, Donna Sabino, and Suzy Goytizolo.

Of course, no list of acknowledgments would be complete without our founding editor, Steve Birnbaum, as well as Alexandra Mayes Birnbaum, who continues to be a guiding light and a careful reader of every word.

Finally, it is important to remember that Walt Disney World is constantly changing and growing, and with each annual revision, we refine and expand our material to serve your needs even better. For the present edition, though, this is the final word.

Have a great visit!

Don't Forget To Write

No contribution is of greater value to us in preparing the next edition of this book than your comments on what we've written and on your own experiences and discoveries at Walt Disney World. Please share your insights with us by writing to:

Jill Safro, Editor
Birnbaum's Walt Disney World Without Kids 2004
Disney Editions
114 Fifth Avenue, 12th Floor
New York, NY 10011

Table of Contents

9 Planning Ahead

First things first: Lay the groundwork for an unforgettable vacation by timing your Disney visit to take advantage of the best weather, crowd patterns, and special goings-on. We set forth information about package and ticket options, offer time- and money-saving strategies, and present the keys to the World's transportation system. Our custom-designed sample schedules will help you plan your days and nights. And a round of specialized advice offers the promise of a hassle-free trip.

39 Checking In

Whether it's elegant, rustic, whimsical, or romantic digs you're seeking, you'll find them among Walt Disney World's 22 resorts—including the new Pop Century Resort and Saratoga Springs Resort & Spa—and two island-bound cruise ships, themed as only Disney knows how. Choose from hotels whose architecture and ambience evoke such locales as Africa, New Orleans, Martha's Vineyard, Polynesia, or an early 1900s mountain lodge. Within our listing we explain the big draws of and grown-up appeal of all the resorts located within Walt Disney World borders.

81 Theme Parks: The Big Four

Enchanting, engaging, entertaining . . . overwhelming. The Magic Kingdom, Epcot, Disney-MGM Studios, and Disney's Animal Kingdom can rekindle even the most sluggish sense of wonder. But where to begin? Right here: We've devised strategies to help you make the most of each day. We've also provided detailed theme park walking tours that highlight the most alluring stops for adults; a primer on Fastpass, Disney's time-saving service; and lists of touring priorities that rank every attraction. From "Don't Miss" to "Don't Knock Yourself Out," we've scoped out the grown-up fun quotient.

141 Diversions: Sports, Shopping, & Other Pursuits

Because the World's attractions extend way beyond the theme parks, so does our guidance. Here, discover the options, including five first-rate 18-hole golf courses, tennis, boating, fishing, and biking. Shoppers will have a field day checking out our favorite shopping spots. For those who prefer soaking and sliding, we dive into the water parks. Our in-depth report on romantic (and private) sunset and fireworks cruises reveals the creative essence of this adult-minded retreat. We also visit the natural realms of Fort Wilderness, and indulge in the sinful splendor of Walt Disney World's three spas.

183 Dining & Entertainment

Here's your insider's guide to adult best bets for full-service restaurants and casual eating spots in the theme parks, resorts, and elsewhere in Walt Disney World. We've found dining rooms with prime views, cheap eats, sweet treats, afternoon tea, wines by the glass, and hearty microbrews. After dark, you'll know where to go to watch the big game, hear cool jazz, join in a rollicking sing-along, and dance the night away (disco, country, or hip-hop), as well as how to navigate the newest Downtown Disney hot spots, find a dinner show or a comedy club, or catch a theme park spectacular.

Anyone can have a magical time at Walt Disney World with advance planning.

Planning Ahead

There are plenty of hotels, restaurants, and theme park attractions for everyone at Walt Disney World. So why sit down with a book to plan ahead? Because a little attention to detail beforehand—we like to think of it as shopping for fun insurance—pays big dividends once you arrive. Just ask the couple who had the foresight to book a table at the deluxe Victoria & Albert's dining room before they left home. Or the friends who arrived with tickets in hand and avoided the line at the entrance to Epcot (they also saved money by purchasing tickets in advance). Or the golfers who were able to snag a coveted mid-morning tee time during their Easter visit.

Our point: You can't be assured of the vacation experience you want without knowing which of the gazillion ways to enjoy Disney World most appeal to you—and how to make sure these potential highlights don't become missed opportunities.

This first chapter not only provides the framework for a successful visit but also establishes a vital awareness that helps the information in subsequent chapters fall right in line.

On the following pages, you'll find insight on when to visit; advice on tickets, packages, reservations, and how to save money; information on how to get around the World; flexible adult-oriented touring schedules; and tips for older travelers, couples, singles, and guests with disabilities. In short, it's a handy guide to all the magic of Disney—and a whole lot more.

This chapter is a straightforward planner that you'll return to again and again—no doubt with greater purpose than the first time through, when you're still eager to learn about Disney's hotels, theme parks, dining, and nightlife. So go ahead and give it a quick skim if this is your first read, but don't forget to come back.

WHEN TO GO

Much tougher than the (rhetorical) question of if you want to visit Walt Disney World is the prickly matter of when. In addition to your own schedule, there is the weather to consider; you would also like to avoid the crowds, although you'd love to get a gander at the Christmas parade or that flower festival you read about in the newspaper. You want to experience Disney World at its best. But when?

Weather and crowd patterns are charted in this section, along with other factors, such as extended park hours, so you can see how possible vacation dates stack up. Timing your visit to meet all expectations may be impossible, but our experience does suggest certain optimum times. Mid-January through early February, late April through late May, September through early November, and the week after Thanksgiving through the week before Christmas stand out as particularly good times to find oneself in the World.

Taking things one step further, we like to underline the period from the Sunday after Thanksgiving to the week before Christmas as the ultimate timing

for a WDW visit. This is a chance to savor Walt Disney World during one of its least crowded and most festive times of year. The place is wrapped in wonderful holiday decorations, and there are scads of special goings-on, from parades to parties.

WDW WEATHER

Average:	High (F)	Low (F)	Rain (inches)
January	71	49	2.3
February	73	50	3.0
March	78	55	3.2
April	83	59	1.8
May	88	66	3.6
June	91	72	7.3
July	92	73	7.2
August	92	73	6.8
September	90	72	6.0
October	85	66	2.4
November	79	58	2.3
December	73	51	2.2

If your travel dates fall outside the above-mentioned ideal, don't despair. Walt Disney World makes a spectacle of itself year-round. This listing highlights holidays and happenings that—for their fanfare, crowd-drawing potential, and, in some instances, accompanying package deals—are worth factoring into your vacation plans.

NOTE: We've provided 2004 dates when available, but specifics are apt to change.

For current details about listed events, call 407-824-4321, or visit *www.disneyworld.com* up to three months before your visit. For more information about package offerings, turn to "The Logistics" later in this chapter.

Holidays & Special Events

WALT DISNEY WORLD MARATHON (January): Marathoners lace up for a 26.2-mile race through scenic areas of Walt Disney World. Live bands, Disney characters, and hot-air balloons inspire some 15,000 runners to stay the course. For details, call 407-939-7810. Vacation packages are available.

MARDI GRAS (February 28, March 1, and March 4): New Orleans' traditionally grand celebration comes vividly to life at this three-night celebration at Downtown Disney's Pleasure Island. Expect live bands, stilt-walkers, and Cajun cuisine.

ATLANTA BRAVES SPRING TRAINING (March): Some of Major League Baseball's greatest gather at Disney's ballpark to get a jump on the upcoming season. Packages (407-938-7810) and single-game tickets (407-839-3900) are available.

ST. PATRICK'S DAY (March 17): Impromptu shindigs sprout like shamrocks in the more spirited corners of the World, while Epcot's United Kingdom offers a tiny taste of Emerald Isle traditions.

All in the Timing

Consider the following WDW trends before settling on vacation dates. For details on park hours and attraction refurbishments, call 407-824-4321.

Shortest Lines, Smallest Crowds: The second week of January through the first week of February; late April through late May; the week after Labor Day until Thanksgiving; the week after Thanksgiving through the week before Christmas.

Longest Lines, Biggest Crowds: Presidents' week; the third week of March through the third week of April, especially Easter week; June through Labor Day, particularly the Fourth of July; Christmas through New Year's Day.

Potential Pitfalls: The water parks and certain WDW attractions sometimes close for renovations (most often during winter months). Spring break (between February and mid-April) lures many students, as do Grad Nites (weekend events in late April and early May).

Extended Hours: The two weeks surrounding Easter; summer; Thanksgiving week; Christmas through New Year's Day.

EASTER (April 11): Extended hours—and monumental crowds—at the parks make for a hopping Magic Kingdom. It's one of the busiest times of the year.

EPCOT INTERNATIONAL FLOWER & GARDEN FESTIVAL (late April– early June): This flowery, annual event—a fragrant affair featuring some 30 million blossoms—not only makes a glorious perfumery of Epcot, but also allows garden- ers to learn a trick or two from the folks who care for 10,000 rosebushes and then some.

In addition to character topiaries and elaborate display gardens, guests can take part in workshops, behind-the-scenes tours, dining, and entertainment events.

STAR WARS WEEKENDS (May– June): Galactic good times can be enjoyed as Disney-MGM Studios salutes the ever-popular *Star Wars* saga with celebrities and characters from the movies, autograph and photo opportuni- ties, trivia contests, and more.

FOURTH OF JULY CELEBRATION (July 4): Double-fisted fireworks at the Magic Kingdom, Epcot, and the Disney-MGM Studios are a glorious salute to our nation's birthday. The parks often have extended hours to mark the occa- sion. But you pay a price: it's the busiest day of the summer.

What to Pack

- Comfortable shoes (2 pairs)
- Sunglasses and sunscreen
- A bathing suit
- Insect repellent
- T-shirts and shorts for day
- Casual separates for evening (jeans are okay)
- Lightweight sweaters or jackets for summer evenings and air-condi- tioned rooms; warmer clothing for evening (and often daytime) from November through March
- A jacket for men and a dress or comparable outfit for women for dinner at Victoria & Albert's
- Suitable togs and equipment for tennis, golf, fishing, jogging, or gym workouts (racquets, clubs, balls, golf shoes, and poles are available for rent)
- Lightweight rain gear and a folding umbrella

FUNAI CLASSIC AT WALT DISNEY WORLD RESORT (October): In this tournament, now in its 35th year, top PGA Tour players compete alongside amateurs on two Walt Disney World venues: the Palm and Magnolia courses. The drama builds until the final day, when the Magnolia's fickle 18th hole has been known to twist the fates of more than a few players. For information, refer to the "Golf" section in the *Diversions* chapter, or call 407-824-2250. Vacation packages are available.

EPCOT INTERNATIONAL FOOD & WINE FESTIVAL (October–November): The temptation to eat and drink your way around World Showcase is intensified by cooking demonstrations (past years have brought such notable chefs as Julia Child to the table), plus samples of a host of exotic specialty dishes, international wines by the glass, and worldly desserts ($1 to $4.50 per taste). Special five-course dinners sponsored by various vintners are also a highlight (to book the aforementioned dining experience, call 407-WDW-DINE).

ABC SUPER SOAP WEEKEND (November): Soap fans will think they've died and gone to Port Charles at this Studios event. Meet actors from the ABC daytime dramas *All My Children*, *General Hospital*, *One Life to Live*, and *Port Charles*.

Question-and-answer sessions give die-hard fans the chance to interact with the stars. For more information, contact the Super Soap Hotline at 407-397-6808 or visit *www.abc.com*. Note that this is a popular event.

FESTIVAL OF THE MASTERS (November): One of the South's top-rated art shows, the three-day event at Downtown Disney draws upward of 150 award-winning exhibitors from around the country.

Hot Tickets

Here are a few numbers to add to your pre-vacation Rolodex.

- Consider that a recent month brought such acts as Aretha Franklin and the Black Crowes to House of Blues, and call 407-934-2583 a good month ahead to reserve your seats.

- To make a sure thing of witnessing Cirque du Soleil at Downtown Disney, call 407-934-7639 for tickets up to six months ahead.

- Advance planning also pays off when Disney's Wide World of Sports complex hosts, say, the always popular Atlanta Braves. Call 407-939-4263.

It tends to be least crowded on Friday and Sunday mornings during the festival.

DISNEY'S MAGICAL HOLIDAYS

(December): The whole wide World is positively aglow with holiday spirit, and it doesn't stop at decorations: Tree-lighting ceremonies are held in three theme parks.

The Magic Kingdom celebrates the season with Mickey's Very Merry Christmas Parade and Mickey's Very Merry Christmas Party, a special-ticket event held on several nights during the first three weeks of December that includes hot chocolate and holiday cookies, plus a dusting of snow over Main Street.

Epcot invites guests to enjoy a candlelight procession and a choral celebration of holidays around the world (inquire about dinner and show packages).

The Disney-MGM Studios mesmerizes with the Osborne Family Spectacle of Lights—an enveloping display featuring some five million twinkling lights. Vacation packages are available; for details, call 800-828-0228.

Cost-Cutting Tips

- Consider accommodations with kitchen facilities to save on food costs, or rent a refrigerator (available at WDW resorts for a $10 nightly fee).

- Compare lunch and dinner menus. The same dishes are often available for less at midday. Also ask about early-bird dinner specials.

- Buy a WDW resort mug good for unlimited refills (of soft drinks) at the hotel's food court, snack shop, and pool bar during your stay; save time, too—just swipe the bar code on your mug past the reader at the self-service dispenser and fill 'er up.

- Keep a refillable water bottle with you on steamy summer days.

- When choosing a place to stay, don't break the budget for a resort packed with amenities you won't have time to enjoy. Also realize that often the only difference between the least and most expensive rooms in a hotel is the view, and decide how often you'll be looking out that window.

- If you plan to stay at Walt Disney World for more than a week, or make multiple visits within a year, get an annual pass. Ownership nets many discounts, including savings on merchandise and room rates.

- Membership in organizations such as AARP and AAA often come with a few Disney perks as well. Check with your member representative to see if there are any special privileges for you to take advantage of.

NEW YEAR'S EVE CELEBRATION

(December 31): The theme parks are open after midnight, attracting huge throngs and presenting high-spirited fun.

Though all of the theme parks are decked out in full holiday regalia, Animal Kingdom does not offer pyrotechnic displays (for obvious reasons). Many of the resorts have special celebrations. Double-size fireworks are launched in the skies over the Magic Kingdom, Epcot, and the Disney-MGM Studios.

Pleasure Island unleashes its own New Year's Eve spectacular in a special-admission blowout.

THE LOGISTICS
Should You Buy a Package?

Travelers who like the convenience of paying for their vacation in one lump sum that includes accommodations, transportation,

Extra Magic Hour

If you're staying at a WDW resort hotel, set your alarm an hour early. Why? On select days, one theme park opens its doors early for guests bearing a resort ID (and a park ticket). It allows you to visit some of your favorite attractions and hobnob with Disney characters before the park officially opens. Check with your hotel's guest services desk for Extra Magic Hour locations.

and park admission have a wealth of choices when visiting Walt Disney World.

Vacation plans put forth by Disney tempt with such extras as unlimited golf, spa treatments, meals, and admission to Walt Disney World's bounty of attractions.

Specifics vary, but Disney's package offerings range from the economical Dream Maker Package to the top-of-the-line Platinum Plan. Additional packages are built around the needs of golfers or honeymooners, and still others are tied to a season or special event. Featured accommodations include hotels on and off WDW property; some deals incorporate discounted airfare or meal plans.

The Disney Cruise Line can combine a visit to Walt Disney World with a cruise vacation.

For details about packages offered by the Walt Disney Travel

Company, call 800-828-8101 or go to *www.disneyworld.com.* Note that you must pay for vacation packages in their entirety up front. Cancellations must be made at least 45 days in advance in order to receive a full refund.

Other operators with plans featuring Walt Disney World include American Airlines Vacations (800-321-2121), Southwest Vacations (800-243-8372), and the Walt Disney Travel Company (800-828-0228). Online tour operators offering a variety of WDW vacation packages include GoGo

Tours (*www.libertytravel.com*), Travelocity (*www.travelocity.com*), and Vacation Outlet (*www. vacationoutlet.com*; or call 800-690-2210).

Because the value of any vacation package depends wholly on your needs, we have provided a checklist to help you quickly narrow the choices. If you think you might be interested in buying a package, call for brochures. Then use these guidelines to help determine which plan, if any, suits you.

The right package: (1) saves you money on the type of lodging, transportation, and recreation you want; (2) includes meaningful extras (meals at restaurants of your choice, for example), as opposed to fluff like welcoming cocktails or so-called privileges that are actually services available to all WDW guests; (3) fits like a glove; no matter what the sale price, you wouldn't buy gloves that were two sizes too big, nor should you buy a package that encompasses more than you can reasonably expect to enjoy.

Keep in Mind

- All admission tickets and passes are non-transferable.
- When we say that any unused days on a ticket may be used on a future visit, we mean that these days don't expire until you do.
- At the end of your visit, note the number of unused days on a multi-day ticket. Write it on the ticket itself.
- As long as you have at least one day left on a multi-day ticket (except the Ultimate Park Hopper Ticket), you can upgrade to the next level within seven days of first use by paying the difference.
- If you want to spend the day in the Magic Kingdom and then head to Epcot for dinner, you need either one of the Park Hopper Tickets, or an annual pass.

Money Matters

A few points of interest related to green matter and its plastic counterparts: Traveler's checks, American Express, Visa, MasterCard, Discover Card, Diners Club Card, JCB, and the Disney Visa Card are acceptable for most charges at Walt Disney World. While restaurants in the parks accept credit cards, some refreshment stands operate on a cash-only basis.

WDW resort guests who leave a credit card imprint upon check-in may use their hotel ID card to charge meals at all restaurants and some food carts, purchases at shops and lounges, and recreational fees. These guests also receive the benefit of Express Check-out—an itemized bill is slipped under their door on the day of departure—a much appreciated perk when that morning rolls around and last-minute to-dos await.

As for banking services, there are a slew of ATMs accessible for a $2 service fee. Locations include Main Street, Frontierland, and Tomorrowland in the Magic Kingdom; the entrances to Epcot, the Studios, and Animal Kingdom; Germany and the walkway between Future World and World Showcase in Epcot; the Toy Story Pizza Planet Arcade in the Studios; the Transportation and Ticket Center; Pleasure Island; Downtown Disney Marketplace and Disney West Side; and the lobbies of all WDW resorts.

That's the Ticket

Admission tickets may be purchased at Disney's stores at the Orlando International Airport, theme park entrances, Guest Relations at Downtown Disney, any WDW resort, any hotel on Hotel Plaza Boulevard, and the Transportation and Ticket Center (offerings vary at each location). WDW resort guests may charge tickets to their rooms. Cash, traveler's checks, personal checks (with presentation of driver's license and major credit card), Visa, MasterCard, American Express, Discover Card, Diners Club Card, JCB, and Disney's Visa Card are also accepted.

Multi-day tickets can be bought at the Disney Store; by phone at 407-824-4321 or online at www.disneyworld.com (allow two to three weeks for processing); or via mail order (allow three to four weeks). Get annual passes at theme park entrances, through WDW's website, or by mail. To get tickets by mail, send a check or money order (including $3 for handling) payable to the Walt Disney World Company to: Walt Disney World; Box 10140; Lake Buena Vista, FL 32830-0000; Attention: Ticket Mail Order.

For full-service banking, there is a SunTrust branch opposite the Downtown Disney Marketplace, at 1675 Buena Vista Drive (407-828-6118 or 800-786-8787); hours are 9 A.M. to 4 P.M. weekdays (until 6 P.M. Thursdays), with drive-in teller service from 8 A.M. to 6 P.M.

Admission Options

Thankfully, Disney has made the name game a little easier to play: Nearly all forms of admission media are now called *tickets*. (The exceptions are annual admission media, which are still called *passes*.)

NOTE: For the purposes of this section, the term *parks* means the Magic Kingdom, Epcot, the Disney-MGM Studios, and Animal Kingdom. Prices quoted include sales tax and were correct at press time, but may very well go up in 2004.

Call 407-824-4321, or log onto *www.disneyworld.com* for current prices. Keep in mind that it may be more cost-effective to purchase tickets in advance, prior to arriving at Walt Disney World.

ONE-DAY TICKET ($55.38): Good for one-day admission to one theme park only. (It does not allow for park-hopping.)

FOUR- AND FIVE-DAY PARK HOPPER TICKETS ($221.52 and $254.54, respectively): Valid in all four parks (Magic Kingdom, Epcot, Disney-MGM Studios, and Animal Kingdom) for four or five (not necessarily consecutive) days; include unlimited use of Walt Disney World transportation. Unused days may be used on a future visit.

FIVE-, SIX-, AND SEVEN-DAY PARK HOPPER PLUS TICKETS ($286.50, $318.45, and $350.40, respectively): Valid in all four theme parks for five, six, or seven (not necessarily consecutive) days; includes two, three, or four "plus" options, which may be used for admission to Typhoon Lagoon, Blizzard Beach, Disney's Wide World of Sports, or Pleasure Island; allows unlimited use of WDW transportation. Unused days or "plus" options may be used on a future visit.

ULTIMATE PARK HOPPER TICKET: Available to Walt Disney World resort guests only. Valid for the duration of a guest's stay for admission to the four theme parks, as well as the water parks, Disney's Wide World of Sports complex, DisneyQuest, and Pleasure Island; ticket includes unlimited use of Walt Disney World transportation.

Prices are $179.99 for two days, $241.76 for three days, $289.68 for four days, $323.76 for five days, $356.78 for six days, and $392.99 for a seven- day pass.

THEME PARK ANNUAL PASS ($392.99; $350.39 for renewal): Valid for unlimited admission to all four theme parks for one year; includes unlimited use of WDW transportation and free theme park parking.

PREMIUM ANNUAL PASS ($520.81; $467.56 for renewal): Valid for admission to the four theme parks, the water parks, Disney's Wide World of Sports complex, Downtown Disney Pleasure Island, and DisneyQuest for one year; includes unlimited use of Walt Disney World transportation and free theme park parking.

NOTE: Both types of annual passes provide savings on theme park admission; they may also net discounts on Walt Disney World resort rooms (depending on the season and availability), dinner shows, and more.

Medical Matters

Although medical care is readily available at WDW, travelers with chronic health problems are advised to carry copies of prescriptions and ask their physicians to provide names of local doctors. Diabetics should note that Walt Disney World resorts will provide refrigeration for insulin. More generally:

Report emergencies to 911 operators or to Sandlake Hospital (407-351-8550).

Each of the theme parks has a First Aid Center staffed by a

Tips for Drivers

- Florida state law requires use of headlights in the rain or fog and at dusk.

- Gas stations opposite Pleasure Island and near BoardWalk are open 24 hours; another, in the Magic Kingdom Auto Plaza, stays open until two hours after the park closes.

- Be alert to slippery roads when it rains, as a fine layer of oil accumulates between drizzles.

- It's legal to turn right at a red light anywhere in Florida, unless a sign is posted.

- Call 407-560-7959 for free AAA towing at WDW. The Auto Plaza's AAA Car Care Center provides service (407-824-0976). Off-property, call Riker's Wreckers for 24-hour towing (407-855-7776) and repairs (407-238-9800), or call AAA if you're a member.

- For traffic, news, and weather reports, tune to 580 AM.

registered nurse. In the Magic Kingdom, the center is next to Crystal Palace; at Epcot, it's in the Odyssey Center; at the Studios, it's by Guest Relations; and in Animal Kingdom, it's near the Creature Comforts shop, on Discovery Island.

For non-emergency medical care, CentraCare (407-238-2000) offers 12-hour-a-day house calls. Doctors On Call Service (407-399-3627) offers 24-hour house-call-only medical service.

Another non-emergency medical care option is CentraCare Walk-In Medical Care (407-238-2000), located at 12500 South Apopka-Vineland Road, open 8 A.M. to midnight weekdays and 8 A.M. to 8 P.M. weekends.

For referral to a pharmacy or to find out how to have medication delivered, call Turner Drugs: 407-828-8125. (It's located next door to CentraCare.)

GETTING AROUND

Before you can find your way around WDW, you must have a firm sense of where you are (and where you are not). Disney World is actually about 22 miles southwest of Orlando in a much smaller community called Lake Buena Vista.

The most important (and congested) highway in the Orlando area is I-4, which cuts through the southern half of Disney World. All the area's other major highways intersect I-4.

Among the more frequently traveled is Route 435 (or Kirkman Road), a route that links I-4 to the major hotel and

business thoroughfare called International Drive, known locally as I-Drive.

Should You Rent a Car?

Will you need a car during your stay? It's a tough call. Most area hotels offer buses to and from Walt Disney World. Disney's own resorts and parks are serviced by buses, monorail trains, and boats, which provide efficient (though time-consuming) means of traveling within WDW borders.

This transportation is available to visitors staying at WDW resorts and those with a multi-day park ticket or an annual pass. If reliance on mass transit will cramp your style, by all means rent a car. It'll often get you from point A to point B in a fraction of the time (provided that you're familiar with the terrain).

Disney's transportation is reliable (departing from most areas every 15 to 20 minutes), but it can accommodate only limited spontaneity and can take up a bit of time. If you decide to drive, note that parking at any of the theme parks costs $7 per day (it's free for WDW resort guests).

We find it's easiest to rent a car from one of the airport's on-site companies (Avis, Budget, Dollar, and National). You can rent a car after you've arrived at WDW, too. Inquire at your hotel's front desk.

Once you're inside the resort, you can rely on an array of options—bus, monorail, boat, or, in some cases, your own two feet—to get you wherever you're going. Be aware that not all destinations can be reached directly; you may have to transfer several times, which can add extra minutes to your commute.

Detailed transportation information is available at WDW resorts. Schedules coordinate with park hours (service begins about one hour prior to park opening and continues until one hour after closing), so there is little chance of being stranded. Call 407-824-4321 to confirm routes.

Our Take on Taxis

Disney's transportation system is vast and cost-efficient. That said, it can also chew up time and, at times, can be flat-out confusing.

Getting from a Walt Disney World resort to any theme park is a no-brainer. It's also relatively easy to "hop" from park to park. The options always include buses (usually direct) and often choices such as monorail or ferry. However, as we've traveled the World over, we have come across a few trouble spots. In each case, we've solved our transportation woes simply by hailing a cab. The only drawback? It'll cost ya.

Traveling between resorts usually involves at least one bus transfer. If you ask bell services to call a cab (making sure it's authorized, with regulated fares), you'll get to your destination in a fraction of the time. Trips generally cost about $5–$15 plus tip.

Buses to and from Downtown Disney are plentiful. However, when all is said and done (often in the wee hours of the morning), it's nice to forego the wait for the bus and hop into a waiting cab. The trip shouldn't set you back too much (in the $10–$18 range), depending on the destination.

Cabs are an efficient means of getting to and from Orlando International Airport. Taxis can take up to 9 passengers. Rates are one-way. Trips to Magic Kingdom resorts cost $50, Epcot resorts $43, and Hotel Plaza Blvd. resorts $37 (plus tip and tolls). The wait for taxis here is shorter than for the Mears Shuttle and the trip is direct.

Getting to WDW from Orlando Airport

During rush hour take the airport's South exit, and follow the Central Florida Greeneway (Route 417) to State Road 536, which leads right to WDW; tolls total $2. The distance is about 22 miles. For the shortest route, take the airport's North exit, head west on Route 528 (aka the Beeline Expressway) to I-4 west, and turn off at the appropriate WDW exit; tolls are $1.25.

- **Exit 68:** Resorts on Hotel Plaza Boulevard

- **Exit 67A:** Epcot, Typhoon Lagoon, Old Key West, Caribbean Beach, Swan, Dolphin, BoardWalk, Yacht and Beach Club, Port Orleans Riverside and French Quarter, or Downtown Disney

- **Exit 64A:** Magic Kingdom, Disney-MGM Studios, Animal Kingdom, Blizzard Beach, Fort Wilderness, Disney's Wide World of Sports complex, Pop Century, Grand Floridian, Contemporary, Polynesian, Wilderness Lodge, All-Star resorts, Coronado Springs, Animal Kingdom Lodge, Palm and Magnolia golf courses, or Celebration

- **For those without wheels:** Florida Towncars offers direct service to Disney resorts for $85–$95 round-trip for up to five people. Call 407-277-5466 or 800-525-7246. A Selective Limousine, Inc. will transport up to four passengers in a Town Car starting at $40 per person; call 407-351-1533 or 800-854-7503. Mears Motor Shuttle, though time-consuming, is efficient and economical. Operating 24 hours, Mears serves area hotels at $16 one way or $28 round-trip, per person. Taxis are also a viable option. For info, call 407-423-5566. (For details on taxi transport, turn to page 21.)

DAY-TO-DAY SAMPLE SCHEDULES

A Day at Disney's Animal Kingdom

- Arrive about a half hour before the park's posted opening time, and prepare to bond with others waiting to enter.

- Pick up a guidemap and times guide and check schedules for shows you may want to see, such as Tarzan Rocks! or Festival of the Lion King. Arrive about 45 minutes before the Lion King show begins, and up to 30 minutes for Tarzan.

- Resist the urge to conduct an informal wildlife census in the Oasis and head straight for the bridge to Discovery Island (the path on the right offers the most direct route). The animals will be here all day. Minimal lines for your biggest priorities, Dinosaur, Kali River Rapids, and Kilimanjaro Safaris, won't be around for long.

- Give The Tree of Life a quick once-over, but don't stop to inspect it now. Instead, head to the first brachiosaurus skeleton on your right. In DinoLand U.S.A., make the thrilling acquaintance of Dinosaur. Also swing over to Tarzan Rocks! if the show is starting soon.

- Next, go to Asia and ride the drenching Kali River Rapids. Afterward, walk through the Maharajah Jungle Trek and explore the tiny village of Anandapur. While you're in the area, consider taking in Flights of Wonder (check your times guide for the schedule).

- Grab a quick bite along the way to Africa (we suggest Tusker House, in Harambe). Then make tracks for Kilimanjaro Safaris. Afterward, dally on the Pangani Forest Exploration Trail to watch the gorilla family at play.

- When afternoon crowds descend, hop on the Wildlife Express to Rafiki's Planet Watch, and get your fill of all the interactive exhibits at journey's end.

- Make your way to Camp Minnie-Mickey in time for the next Lion King staging.

- Now it's time for It's Tough to be a Bug! in The Tree of Life. Be sure to check out the amazing animal carvings on the tree

- No fireworks here (imagine the stampede). As an alternative, experience dinner as entertainment at Rainforest Cafe (or, hop to Epcot for IllumiNations).

A Day at the Magic Kingdom

- Plan to be in the parking lot at least 30 minutes before the park is scheduled to open.

- If you haven't booked a table in advance, make priority seating arrangements at City Hall. (We recommend Cinderella's Royal Table or Crystal Palace for an early lunch.) Get a guidemap here.

- If you haven't had breakfast, stop at the Main Street Bake Shop.

- When the park opens, grab a Fastpass (see page 83) for your personal "must-sees." Don't miss Splash Mountain, Big Thunder Mountain Railroad, and Pirates of the Caribbean. After exhausting Adventureland, head for The Haunted Mansion, followed by a

cruise on the *Liberty Belle* Riverboat. Resist the urge to sprint through the park and move at a comfortable pace.

- Pausing for lunch when your priority seating time arrives or hunger calls, begin a second sweep of the park, targeting such attractions as Mickey's PhilharMagic and the Country Bear Jamboree. Check out any shops and entertainment en route that catch your eye.

- About 20 minutes before the afternoon parade (daily at 3 P.M.), either camp out on Main Street or skip the parade and head for Fantasyland to see as many key attractions—Peter Pan's Flight, The Many Adventures of Winnie the Pooh, Mickey's PhilharMagic, and It's a Small World—as possible before the crowds swell back to normal.

- Phobic about long lines? The Walt Disney World Railroad, Tomorrowland Transit Authority, and The Hall of Presidents all tend to keep wait times to a relative minimum. And take advantage of Fastpass as much as possible!

- Breeze through Mickey's Toontown Fair. Then head over to Tomorrowland and experience one of the biggest thrills the Magic Kingdom has to offer—Space Mountain—before taking a jaunt through toyland on the zany Buzz Lightyear's Space Ranger Spin.

- Spend the rest of the day tying up loose ends on your touring checklist and perusing the shops on Main Street.

- Consider having dinner at a restaurant accessible via monorail (perhaps California Grill or Narcoossee's). Return to the park in time to watch the evening parade. If there are two runnings of the parade, aim to see the later one, when the crowds are apt to have dwindled and better viewing locations can be had.

A Day at Epcot

- Guests are often permitted to enter the park a half hour before the opening time, though the attractions may not be up and running.

- Stomach growling? If you haven't had breakfast or need a quick java jolt, slip into Fountain View Espresso and Bakery.

- If you don't have priority seating arrangements for dinner (see page 185), you can stop at Guest Relations or Innoventions Plaza to book a table at one of the restaurants of World Showcase. We enjoy Les Chefs de France, in the France pavilion, and Germany's Biergarten.

- Fight the urge to see Spaceship Earth (the lines are lighter later) and head to Test Track, followed by Mission: SPACE, and Wonders of Life (your priorities: Cranium Command and Body Wars), the Imagination! pavilion (if you miss Honey, I Shrunk the Audience, you will probably live to regret it), and finally, The Land.

- This should take you up to (at least) noon, which is about the time World Showcase opens. Consider grabbing a bite at The Land's Sunshine Season Food Fair before crossing over into World Showcase.

- View *O Canada!* at the Canada pavilion. Then wander through the shops, gardens, and pub at the United Kingdom before fully exploring France. (There's a lovely movie here, too.)

- Work your way toward The American Adventure to catch the extraordinary live performers and the star-spangled audio-animatronics show, stopping to take in the sights along the way.

- Don't forget about priority seating arrangements for dinner. Keep in mind that most restaurants can accommodate walk-ins.

- After dinner, pop into Mexico and then hightail it back to Future World to visit Spaceship Earth and Innoventions.

- Plan to get to the World Showcase Lagoon at least 30 minutes ahead to secure a spot to watch the evening's performance of IllumiNations.

A Day at the Disney-MGM Studios

- Arrive before the posted opening time, as doors often open early.

- Pick up a complimentary guidemap and times guide; many attractions have set showtimes, and some don't open until later in the morning. Study the layout of the park—it has been known to confuse even the most skilled navigators.

- Haven't had breakfast yet? Consider stopping by the Starring Rolls Bakery for a quick croissant.

- If you were unable to book a table for dinner before leaving home, just stop at the kiosk at Hollywood Junction (the corner of Hollywood and Sunset boulevards) and make priority seating arrangements for the 50's Prime Time Cafe, Sci-Fi Dine-In Theater, Mama Melrose's, or the Hollywood Brown Derby. This plan assumes a quick lunch taken whenever your personal lunch bell rings (good bets include Sunset Ranch Market and ABC Commissary).

  - If you're up for some early-morning thrills, head to The Twilight Zone Tower of Terror, but be sure to do so before you eat. For something much tamer, you might try the Great Movie Ride, followed by Magic of Disney Animation and Walt Disney: One Man's Dream.

  - Stroll over to Mickey Avenue where you'll go behind the scenes via the Disney-MGM Studios Backlot Tour. Afterward, try your luck at Who Wants to Be a Millionaire—Play It! Note: The Disney Stars and Motor Cars parade passes through each afternoon.

- Make time for Jim Henson's Muppet*Vision 3-D and Sounds Dangerous starring Drew Carey. The Indiana Jones Epic Stunt Spectacular and Star Tours both merit a look-see. As do the Voyage of the Little Mermaid and Rock 'n' Roller Coaster (provided that you're comfortable being flipped and shaken like James Bond's martini.)

- Between attractions, check out the shops on Sunset and Hollywood boulevards. For a relaxing breather, slip into the Tune-In Lounge.

- Note when the Beauty and the Beast—Live on Stage takes place and be sure not to miss it.

- Get a spot for Fantasmic! at least 60 minutes before showtime. This evening spectacle wraps up the day nicely. (Though the bleacher-style seating can be tough on tired backs.)

A Day at a Water Park

- Choose between Typhoon Lagoon, themed as a tropical paradise with one of the world's largest wave pools, and Blizzard Beach, Walt Disney World's biggest water park, themed as a ski resort.

- Blizzard Beach's relative novelty makes it extremely popular with visitors of all ages. Expect lots of company and ask an attendant to point out any quiet zones.

- Tyhpoon Lagoon's breezy tropical ambience and ever-so-slightly smaller crowds make it the more appealing choice for swimmers who've long since shed their water wings.

- Typhoon Lagoon and Blizzard Beach each feature a lazy waterway that's perfect for a cool respite from the water-slide traffic. Grab one of the inner tubes and settle in.

- The wave pool at Typhoon Lagoon elicits more raves than its Blizzard Beach counterpart, while daredevils are drawn to the latter's water slides in droves.

- Whichever you visit, be at the gate when the park opens, as these places fill up before noon during the warmer months. When the parks reach a certain capacity, only guests arriving via WDW buses are admitted until crowds subside, usually about 3 P.M. When they hit peak capacity, no one gets in until the throngs ease up.

- Guests may bring a picnic lunch and nonalcoholic beverages into the water parks, but coolers are not allowed. While fast food is available, it can be fun (and cost-efficient) to bring your own.

- Surf clinics are offered on select mornings at Typhoon Lagoon. For information, call 407-939-7873. Keep in mind that you need some serious upper-body might to hoist yourself up onto the board. And it helps to be an early riser—as the clinics are done in the wee hours of the morning, long before the park opens.

CUSTOMIZED TIPS
Guests with Disabilities

Walt Disney World has long earned praise from guests with disabilities because of the attention paid to their special needs. Still, familiarization with the World as it relates to one's personal requirements is essential, and to this end, the comprehensive *Guidebook for Guests with Disabilities* is required reading. The guide is available at all wheelchair rental locations (as well as City Hall in the Magic Kingdom and Guest Relations at Epcot, Disney-MGM Studios, and Animal Kingdom). However, we recommend getting this publication before you leave home to become familiar with procedures and accessibility. To receive a free copy of the *Guidebook for Guests with Disabilities*, send a written request, well in advance, to Walt Disney World Guest Communications, Box 10000, Lake Buena Vista, FL 32830, or call 407-939-6244.

Those interested in guided tours should note: The Society for Accessible Travel & Hospitality (347 Fifth Ave., Suite 610, New York, NY 10016; 212-447-7284; *www.sath.org*) can provide a list of travel agents who are knowledgeable about travel for people with disabilities. To receive the listing, send a check or money order for $5.

If you prefer to connect directly with a tour operator who specializes in travel for the disabled, consider Flying Wheels Travel (507-451-5005 or 800-535-6790) or Accessible Journeys (610-521-0339 or 800-846-4537). While we defer to the *Guidebook for Guests with Disabilities* for its comprehensiveness, the following advice is an indication of WDW facilities and services:
• Accessible parking is available at the theme parks (inquire at the Auto Plaza upon entering).
• All monorail stations are accessible to guests in wheelchairs. Most WDW (but not all) buses are equipped with wheelchair lifts.
• Life jackets for guests with disabilities are available at the water parks.
• Most theme park attractions are accessible to guests who can be lifted to and from their wheelchairs with the assistance of a member of their party, and many can accommodate guests who must remain in their wheelchairs.

Consult the *Guidebook for Guests with Disabilities* or a theme park guidemap, or check in with a host or hostess for additional guidance.

Note that all hotels listed in the *Checking In* chapter offer rooms specially equipped for guests with disabilities. Walt Disney World resorts are easily explored by wheelchair. While guestroom and bathroom configurations vary from hotel to hotel, lending themselves better to guests with certain needs, all resorts offer roll-in showers.

For assistance in selecting a Disney hotel whose public areas and rooms best serve your specific requirements, ask to speak to someone in the Special Reservations Department when you call Central Reservations (407-934-7639 voice; 407-939-7670 TTY). Confirm any special requests before you arrive.

Most Disney resorts provide a limited number of free wheelchairs (with a $250 refundable

In the Evening Hours

Here's more than a week's worth of activities for your consideration. For more information on after-dark amusements, refer to Dining & Entertainment.

- Attend a dinner show. All require reservations, and the Hoop-Dee-Doo Musical Revue calls for more forethought than any other.

- For a relatively cheap thrill (about $8 per person) and an early night, take a wagon at Fort Wilderness. Or enjoy a slightly more extravagant carriage ride for about $30 for four people.

- Grab a partner and play the coolest tennis at Walt Disney World. There are a few courts lighted for night play. The courts at Swan and Dolphin are open 24 hours a day.

- For dining as a special event, book a table at Artist Point, California Grill, Cítricos, Shula's Steakhouse, Victoria & Albert's, or Flying Fish Cafe.

- If ready-made nightlife appeals, go club-hopping at Pleasure Island—one stop, many different venues (check out the Jazz Company, the Adventurers Club, or 8TRAX). Or swing by Downtown Disney West Side, Pleasure Island's neighbor, to see who's playing at the House of Blues.

- Take a wine tour. California Grill at Disney's Contemporary resort and Cítricos at the Grand Floridian take crushed grapes seriously and pour wines both by the glass and in pairings suggested by the sommelier.

- Prefer the grain to the grape? Beer lovers' hangouts include BoardWalk's ESPN Club; Crew's Cup lounge at the Yacht Club resort; and The Laughing Kookaburra Good Time Bar at Wyndham Palace Resort and Spa.

- For a nostalgic evening, stroll the boards at BoardWalk, where everything from saltwater taffy to a dance hall and a sing-along piano bar awaits.

deposit). Request one when reserving your room and call to confirm it before you arrive. You may use the wheelchair across Walt Disney World property for your entire length of stay.

Wheelchairs are available for rent at each of the theme parks, as are Electric Convenience Vehicles (ECVs). At the Magic Kingdom, the rental area is inside the entrance on the right; at Epcot, rentals are available inside the entrance plaza on the left, at the shop to the right of the ticket booths, and at International Gateway; at the Disney-MGM Studios, rentals are handled at Oscar's Super Service, just inside; at Animal Kingdom, the site is Garden Gate Gifts near the entrance.

Wheelchair rentals cost $7 per day plus a $1 refundable deposit. Guests planning to visit more than one park on the same day may get a replacement at the next park with no extra charge or deposit (save your receipt and return the wheelchair by the end of the day). ECVs can be rented at the parks

Know Before You Go

- If you want to see a dinner show—especially the Hoop-Dee-Doo Musical Revue, one of the World's tougher tickets—reserve a table when you book your hotel. Reservations are taken up to two years ahead; call 407-939-3463.

- Arrange for priority seating at WDW restaurants (up to four months in advance) by calling WDW-DINE. Refer to page 185 for details.

- Plan on attending a Magic Kingdom E-Ride Night. Call up to a month ahead for exact dates. (See page 85 for the E-Ride lowdown.)

- Call 407-824-4321 or visit www.disneyworld.com to confirm park hours in effect during your visit, and use the schedules provided in this chapter.

- If you're a golfer, reserve tee times as far in advance as possible. Golf reservations may be made 90 days ahead if you've purchased a golf package or if you're staying at either a WDW resort or a resort on Hotel Plaza Boulevard, 30 days ahead if you're not, to secure your preferred time(s) and venue(s). Lessons may be reserved up to 90 days ahead. Call 407-WDW-GOLF (939-4653). Also see "Sports" in Diversions.

- Note that tennis lessons and guided fishing trips may be booked up to 90 days in advance. Call 407-WDW-PLAY (939-7529).

- A few days before you leave home, make a quick round of calls to confirm all arrangements and reservations.

- You must dial the area code for all local calls.

for $30 (plus a $10 refundable deposit) per park per day.

Due to the limited number of ECVs, they usually sell out soon after the parks open. To avoid disappointment, consider renting from ScootAround (888-441-7575), which provides standard and electric wheelchairs as well as scooters; pickup and delivery is available to all hotels in the Walt Disney World area. Wheelchair Getaways (800-242-4990 or 407-292-7614) and Rainbow Wheels of Florida (800-910-8267) both rent wheelchair-accessible vans and offer pickup and delivery for most hotels in the area.

Certain spots along most parade routes and at nighttime show areas are marked for guests using wheelchairs. Arrive early, as these areas are filled on a first-come, first-served basis. See park maps for locations.

For guests with visual disabilities, the theme parks offer audiocassettes designed to accentuate enjoyment of each park through detailed description. A $25 refundable deposit is required for use of a tape recorder.

Pay phones equipped with Text Typewriters (TTYs) are available throughout the Disney World Resort. For more information,

call 407-824-4321 (voice) or 407-827-5141 (TTY).

Assistive Listening devices, which amplify attraction sound tracks, are available (with a $25 refundable deposit) at City Hall in the Magic Kingdom and at Guest Relations in Epcot, the Studios, and Animal Kingdom. Scripts are also available for guests with hearing disabilities at most attractions. For live performances, guests may request sign language interpretation; to make arrangements, call 407-824-4321 (voice) or 407-827-5141 (TTY) at least two weeks in advance.

Also, Reflective Captioning devices that project dialogue onto a panel placed in front of guests are available for use in some theater shows. Inquire at Guest Relations.

Older Travelers

Walt Disney World is a friendly and welcoming place, but its

disneyworld.com

Log onto *www.disneyworld.com* to receive an interactive preview or update of WDW's offerings.

Among its more valuable features: ticket sales, customized resort recommendations, a reservations desk, maps, details about special events, and park hours during your stay.

sheer enormity and energy level, and its mere heat, particularly during the summer, have the potential to overwhelm.

While knowing what to expect is half the battle, planning accordingly is just as important. The keys to an enjoyable, relaxed visit apply to everyone. Our suggestions:

Plan your visit for one of the

Important Numbers

AMC Theatres: 407-298-4488

Behind-the-Scene Tours: 407-WDW-TOUR (939-8687)

Central Reservations: 407-W-DISNEY (934-7639)

Disney's Wide World of Sports Complex: 407-828-3627

Florida Hospital Celebration Health: 407-303-4000

Golf Reservations / Lessons: 407-WDW-GOLF (939-4653)

Lost and Found: 407-824-4245

Priority Seating: 407-WDW-DINE (939-3463)

Recreation: 407-WDW-PLAY (939-7529)

Sandlake Hospital: 407-351-8550

Walt Disney Travel Company: 407-828-8101

Walt Disney World Information: 407-824-4321

Weather: 407-824-4104

less crowded times of year. That will make for shorter, less harried days. In the parks, eat early or late to avoid mealtime crowds.

Florida residents may net discounts on selected dates. Call 407-824-4321 for details. Also, some off-property hotels offer discounts to AARP members.

Take frequent rest stops in the shade (for the best locales in each park, see the "Quiet Nooks" lists in the margins of the *Theme Parks* chapter). Know that if you are overcome at any point, each park has a first aid station with a friendly and certified staff.

Don't underestimate the distances to be covered at Epcot and Animal Kingdom. These parks are huge, and visitors often log a few miles in a full day of touring. Lots of older travelers who enjoy walking around the other parks choose to rent a wheelchair or Electric Convenience Vehicle at these two (they're available at the park entrances).

No matter how you're getting around, take it slowly. Broken into small increments with plenty of air-conditioned and shaded breaks, it's not so tiring. The *FriendShip* launches that cross World Showcase Lagoon in Epcot provide a nice break for weary feet.

Not all of Pleasure Island's clubs are inundated with exuberant twenty-somethings. Stop in for some smooth sounds at the Pleasure Island Jazz Company and eavesdrop on tall tales told by weary world travelers at the Adventurer's Club. Don't rule out the Comedy Warehouse, either. It's always good for a hearty yuk or two.

Don't miss the four-star tribute to Hollywood's heyday that is the Disney-MGM Studios. The Art Deco architecture, retro restaurants, and Technicolor tributes to Tinseltown make for a day of nostalgic amusement.

Single Travelers

While Walt Disney World may not exactly be the last word for singles, the fact is, unattached guests and independent travelers can have an absolute blast here.

Some ideas:

Pleasure Island's clubs typically attract lots of locals on weekends. The restaurants and lounges at Downtown Disney West Side, particularly the concert hall at House of Blues, also attract a fun-loving crowd.

Try eating at the Teppanyaki Dining Rooms and the Biergarten restaurant at Epcot, where smaller parties are seated together, creating a social setting.

At all of Walt Disney World's 18-hole golf courses, company is a given; players are assigned to a foursome when tee times are allotted.

Some of the World's more compelling restaurants have an area with counter seating, which helps take the sting out of dining solo. These noteworthy spots include Flying Fish Cafe, Narcoossee's, Cítricos, Fulton's Crab House,

For Woofers & Meowers

No pets other than service animals are permitted in the parks. Travelers may lodge Fluffy or Fido in one of WDW's five air-conditioned Pet Care Kennels: near the TTC; at the entrances to Epcot, the Disney-MGM Studios, and Animal Kingdom; and at Fort Wilderness. WDW resort guests pay $9 for overnight pet stays, including food; others pay $11. Day rates are $6 and include one feeding. Pets must have proof of vaccinations. Accommodations are available on a first-come, first-served basis. Guests must walk their pets several times a day, as the animals are not otherwise sprung from their cages. For hours and other information, call 407-824-6568.

Wolfgang Puck Cafe (the sushi bar) and Portobello Yacht Club.

The casual atmosphere along the BoardWalk makes it a fun place to people-watch, and the eateries, shops, and clubs provide interesting diversions. The Jellyrolls' piano bar never fails to entertain.

Another favorite, and a great destination for sports fans, is ESPN Club. The environment is conducive to frenzied rooting for your home team, as well as calmer discussions about the

intricacies of the game with fellow fans.

If you're a tennis player sans partner, consider the player-matching program at Disney's Racquet Club (407-824-3578). Tour programs are engaging alternatives to exploring Epcot solo (see page 116 for details).

Couples

There is a place for lovebirds at Walt Disney World. Actually, there are many spots in the World perfectly suited to those with romantic intentions.

The Magic Kingdom's carousel-and-castle combo invokes enchantment in true fairy-tale tradition. Epcot's World Showcase has the aura of a whirlwind tour (and inspiration for a future trip?), with countries as exotic and far-reaching as Japan and Morocco. The Disney-MGM Studios recaptures an era of starry-eyed elegance. And what could be more titillating than sharing a surprise-filled safari through Africa at Animal Kingdom?

By day, there is romance in the theme parks for couples who are already inclined to hold hands; by night, the parks sparkle with an intensity that inspires sudden mushiness in those who never

---

Rainy-Day Advice

The sun will come out tomorrow (or maybe in a few hours). In the meantime, here are some great ways to pass the time.

- See a movie with all the comforts in the 24-screen AMC Theatres at Downtown Disney.

- Sink into a sofa in the lobby of the Grand Floridian and listen to the graceful music. Or curl up by the fireplace at Wilderness Lodge.

- Pick up a rain poncho (about $6) and head for Epcot, which has more places to escape rain than any other park.

- Experience the high-tech interactive arcade games at Downtown Disney's DisneyQuest.

- Get a massage. Disney spas offer myriad treatments that can be blissful excuses to stay dry.

- Take afternoon tea at the Grand Floridian's Garden View lounge.

considered themselves the type, and that's before the fireworks.

As the themed resorts of Walt Disney World go about transporting guests to various times and places, they make quite a few passes through settings straight out of everyone's fantasy textbook.

From the endearing Victorian charms of the Grand Floridian to the exotic island getaway that is the Polynesian, it's safe to say that Disney definitely has romantic notions (if not in the form of heart-shaped tubs).

You won't find a more inspiring backdrop than that at the wondrously rustic Wilderness Lodge, marked by geysers, waterfalls, steamy hot springs, and the grandest stone fireplace you've ever seen.

At the nostalgic BoardWalk resort, unique surrey bikes are available for romantic rides along the waterfront. You can pedal all the way to Epcot's International Gateway. And a romantic stroll around Crescent

The Most Romantic Places in the World

RESORTS

Animal Kingdom Lodge

BoardWalk

Grand Floridian

Polynesian

Port Orleans Riverside and French Quarter

Wilderness Lodge

Yacht and Beach Club

RESTAURANTS

Artist Point

Bistro de Paris

California Grill

Cinderella's Royal Table

Cítricos

Le Cellier Steakhouse

San Angel Inn

Victoria & Albert's

LOUNGES

Belle Vue Room at BoardWalk

Martha's Vineyard at the Beach Club

Matsu No Ma at Japan

Pleasure Island Jazz Company

THEME PARK SPOTS

Magic Kingdom's *Liberty Belle* Riverboat

All of Epcot's World Showcase

Lake is an undoubtedly lovely way to cap off the day.

For those too lovestruck to think about taking pictures themselves, there's the Romance Photographic Session. For $295, a photographer follows you and your sweetheart around the park of your choice, clicking away. For more information, call 407-827-5029.

Couples with bigger things in mind, like perhaps tying or re-tying the knot, might consider "I do"-ing it here. Each year, more than 2,300 couples flock to Disney to exchange their vows.

Why this place? For some couples it's a matter of mutual Disney admiration; for others it's a convenient answer to the dilemma posed by the bride being from one area of the world and the groom from quite another (why not make a vacation of it for everyone?)

While no one yet has likened Mickey Mouse to Eros, newlyweds have beaten such a path to Mickey's doorstep over the years that Disney World rates as one of the most popular honeymoon destinations in the country.

WEDDINGS: In these parts, the sky is truly the limit. Intimate weddings for up to eight guests start at about $3,300; for larger affairs, figure $7,500 minimum during the week, $10,000 on Fridays, Saturdays, and Sundays. Coordinators work with couples from three months to a year in advance to create a wedding tailored to their needs—from elegant affairs without a hint of Disneyana to the sort in which the bride arrives in Cinderella's coach and Goofy "crashes" the reception. These wedding gurus can handle any detail and a litany of unimaginables.

Nuptials in the theme parks (which range from $7,500 in Epcot to $45,000-plus in the Magic Kingdom) take place before and after park closing and allow couples to take their vows in front of Cinderella Castle in the Magic Kingdom or in an English courtyard in Epcot's World Showcase, among other places. For an extra $15,000, a free-spending couple gets pixie dust and a personal fireworks show.

Then there's the Wedding Pavilion, a structure reminiscent of a Victorian summerhouse, which sits on a landscaped island between the Grand Floridian and Polynesian resorts. Surrounded by roses, palm trees, and beaches, the pavilion seats 250 and offers a prime view of Cinderella Castle, which is framed in a window behind the altar. Picture Point—a trellised archway set among the pavilion's gardens, with the castle in the background—is also available for intimate ceremonies.

For couples in the planning stages, the on-site wedding salon—known as Franck's Bridal Studio—is like a three-dimensional bridal magazine.

Ceremonies can be held at many WDW resorts; the garden gazebo at the Yacht Club, Sunset Point at the Polynesian, Sea Breeze Point at BoardWalk, and Sunrise Terrace at Wilderness Lodge are all popular spots for weddings or vow renewals.

Packages vary depending upon the type of ceremony and reception and can include discounted tickets and rates at certain resorts for guests attending the wedding. When booking a package, the bride and groom get a complimentary room for the first night. For more information about Disney weddings, call 407-828-3400; *www.disneyweddings.com*.

Did You Know?

Walt Disney World encompasses 47 square miles, an area about twice the size of Manhattan.

HONEYMOONS: Most Disney resorts have designated suites for just-marrieds. Special honeymoon packages offer keepsakes and pre-arrival services. For information, call 877-566-0969; *www.disneyhoneymoons.com*.

Religious Services

Protestant services are held on Sundays at 10:30 A.M. at River of Life Presbyterian at 83 Sand Lake Rd. (407-351-4333) and at 11 A.M. at Lake Buena Vista Baptist Church at 11551 County Rd. 535 (407-239-6030). Catholic masses are held at Mary, Queen of the Universe Shrine at 8300 Vineland Ave. (407-239-6600; call for mass times).

Jewish visitors may attend Conservative services at Temple Ohalei Rivka at 11200 Apopka-Vineland Rd. (407-239-5444), or Reform services at the Congregation of Liberal Judaism at 928 Malone Dr. (407-645-0444). Muslim services are at Jama Masijid at 11543 Ruby Lake Rd. Call 407-238-2700.

At Walt Disney World, there's a hotel to suit every taste, budget, and mood.

Checking In

Like a photograph whose mood changes depending upon the frame in which it is displayed, a Walt Disney World vacation is colored by the context in which it is experienced. Guests have quite a variety of frames—rather, resorts—from which to choose, and each yields a unique perspective on the World.

Some hotels imbue the mousedom with surprising elegance; others render it especially whimsical, homey, or romantic. Looking for grand seaside digs or a home base straight out of New Orleans? They're here. Something Polynesian? No problem. From campsites to villas, economy-priced rooms to suites, there are accommodations in Cinderella's neighborhood to suit most every taste and billfold.

If you're the sort who favors a gilded frame for your vacation, you'll find the chandelier quotient you're seeking—and a rich Victorian aura—at Disney's turreted Grand Floridian Resort & Spa.

If rustic romance is more your style, your ultimate roost is the Wilderness Lodge, which patterns its grandeur after National Park Service lodges of the early 1900s.

To stretch your vacation dollar, do try the All-Star and Pop Century resorts. Starting at $77 a night and augmented by three-story cultural icons, they're the brightest dwellings you'll ever call home.

If you're not quite sure what you want, that's fine, too. We've covered all of the Disney-owned resorts and their favored siblings, the Swan and Dolphin, plus the Disney Cruise Line.

When it comes to the resorts that line Hotel Plaza Boulevard (seven properties that are within Disney's borders but independently managed) we've included our top three choices for adults.

So think about what's important to you in Walt Disney World resort. Then read on for all the information you'll need to choose the perfect frame.

WALT DISNEY WORLD RESORTS

As an example of the meticulous theming that is a hallmark of the Disney resorts, consider Port Orleans French Quarter, a moderately priced resort designed to evoke the Big Easy's most famous neighborhood. As you check in, you might catch the aroma of fresh beignets wafting over from the resort's food court, decorated as a Mardi Gras warehouse. The lobby has French horns for light fixtures and restrooms with such great jazz coming over the speakers they could almost impose a cover charge.

In addition to compelling theming, Disney's resorts are often marked by staffs trained to bend over backward to ensure guests' happiness and well-kept,

comfortably furnished accommodations comparable in size to those found outside Walt Disney World borders. There are also many practical advantages to staying on-property. Chief among these benefits are convenience and easy access to Disney services. Other privileges enjoyed by WDW resort guests include use

The Last Word On . . .

Reservations
Book at least six months in advance by calling 407-934-7639 or visiting *www.disneyworld.com.* A deposit (one night's lodging or $200) is required within 10 to 14 days of the time a reservation is made. (Your reservationist will give you specifics.) The deposit will be refunded only if a reservation is canceled at least five days before the scheduled arrival.

Checking In
Check-in time is 3 P.M., except at BoardWalk Villas, All-Star resorts, Old Key West, Beach Club Villas, and The Villas at Wilderness Lodge, where guests register at 4 P.M., and Fort Wilderness, where it's 1 P.M. Check-out time for all these properties is 11A.M.

of WDW transportation; guaranteed admission (with ticket) to the theme parks (including the new Extra Magic Hour—see page 79); discounted golf fees; and the option to reserve tee times on Disney golf courses up to 90 days prior to their check-in date. At all WDW resorts except the Swan and Dolphin, amenities also include free package delivery and the ability to charge meals, merchandise, and recreation fees to one's room.

This resort listing is organized according to price tiers—Deluxe, Moderate, and Value—with the exception of the Home Away from Home category, used to distinguish all-suite and villa-type accommodations. These categories are consistent with Disney's rating system for its resorts (explained on page 42). But consider location as well as price, especially if you'll be spending a lot of time touring a particular theme park.

The "Vital Statistics" section of each entry will help you place the resorts on the World map. You'll notice that certain hotels are earmarked as "sister resorts"; these are adjacent properties that feature complementary designs and shared facilities. With the exception of Port Orleans Riverside and Port Orleans French Quarter, whose greater separation and distinct identities we feel merit individual attention, sister resorts' descriptions are combined.

We've packed in as much detail as possible about the offerings at each resort; to learn even more about restaurants and lounges, see our recommendations in the *Dining & Entertainment* chapter. For details about Walt Disney World transportation, consult *Planning Ahead*. For more on recreational opportunities available at the resorts, turn to the "Sports" section of the *Diversions* chapter.

Amenities Checklist

While there are significant differences in the amenities offered at Disney's Value and Deluxe properties, certain conveniences are provided at all WDW resorts. Namely: voice mail, TVs with the Disney Channel and ESPN, clock radios, in-room safes, guest laundry facilities, dry-cleaning service, an ATM, and either room service or more limited food delivery options.

Deluxe
Animal Kingdom Lodge

The zebras, ostriches, and Thomson's gazelles out back are neither mascots, nor exotic props, nor escapees from the nearby Animal Kingdom theme park. They and their hoofed and feathered comrades—about 200 animals in all, mostly African expats—live on the resort's carefully plotted pasturelands, giving round-the-clock credence to its claims as Florida's only African wildlife reserve lodge. Of course, this ambitious theme is not carried entirely by the storks and giraffes whose habitat comes within 30 feet of guests' domain. Hardly. The lodge's hut foyer opens to an immense thatched-ceiling lobby with the tantalizing depth of a lion's yawn. Here, pupils swell as the eyes dart from the suspension bridge to the huge mud fireplace, from the gushing approximation of Victoria Falls to the blur of African masks and artifacts and

Mickey Rates the Resorts

Disney's ranking system for its resorts provides a convenient framework for considering WDW lodging options. Categories reflect not only price, but the style of the accommodation and the level of service. The hotels fall into Deluxe, Moderate, and Value classifications. Home Away from Home encompasses villa-type lodgings (and the Wilderness Cabins at Fort Wilderness), while Disney's Campground category is occupied solely by the Fort Wilderness campground.

For the sake of clarity and comparison, we have used these same categories in this chapter, with a few exceptions for Fort Wilderness and other properties with two types of accommodations. In general, here's what to expect in our categories:

- Deluxe properties (rates for double rooms range from about $199 to $595 per night) are defined by their larger, practically appointed rooms, several restaurants, and such amenities as 24-hour room service.

- Home Away from Home (rates from about $36 to $1,915) applies to villas, vacation homes, all-suite hotels, wilderness cabins, and campsites.

- Moderate properties (rates from about $133 to $209) feature comfortably sized rooms, full-service restaurants as well as food courts, and bellhop luggage service.

- Value properties (rates from about $77 to $114) offer fewer frills and smaller, yet adequate, quarters. Meals are provided at food courts. Recreation options at these resorts are usually limited.

the chandeliers made of Masai shields. Oh, yes, and the four-story welcome-to-the-savanna window, which is sure to make momentary bumper cars of slack-jawed new arrivals.

Romance and adventure cling to every richly appointed inch of the semicircular lodge, which serves as a five-story animal-observation platform, from its viewing parlors to its vibrant restaurants and its expansive swimming pool. Although with 1,293 rooms, the resort is bigger than its African counterparts, it hides the fact well: Built into the landscape, its front drive leads to the third-floor lobby. (Traditionally, such buildings protect against predators.) Nine out of ten guestroom balconies overlook the savanna.

BIG DRAWS: Luxury laced with an undeniable spirit of adventure and romance. Balconies serve as box seats for animal viewing.

Animal Kingdom Lodge Tips

- Although you can view animals from many vantage points, it is not possible to touch or feed them without participating in a special program. Visit Guest Services for more information.

- Recreational activities are limited due to the presence of animals. For example, no bike rentals are available and there is no jogging path. Guests may indulge in these pursuits at neighboring Disney resorts.

- Willing to forego wildlife-watching from your balcony? Rooms *sans* animal views are significantly cheaper.

- This 33-acre tropical savanna is inhabited by 100 grazing animals and 130 birds—the safari begins as soon as you enter the resort.

WORTH NOTING: Accommodations at this resort are comparable to those at most deluxe hotels in the World; both the deluxe rooms and the smaller standard guestrooms typically include two queen-size beds. Deluxe rooms have a child's daybed. Ask and you may receive a king-size bed or the polar opposite: bunk beds. Within each room's sandy-colored walls is a unique amalgam of African art pieces, traditionally patterned textiles, and dark-wood furniture handcrafted in Zimbabwe and South Africa. All rooms have private balconies; animals and their habitats are visible from 90 percent of the rooms. Lest guests lose their sense of place while reading in bed, there are (purely decorative) mosquito nets in every room; some rooms even have a map of Africa on the wall. Amenities include hair dryers, irons (with boards), newspaper delivery, and 24-hour room service. Concierge rooms with views of the stork-to-wildebeest menagerie are available.

The primary form of recreation here is spying on the roving impalas, Thompson's gazelles, giraffes, and flamingos from every possible vantage point all day and night. In addition to the

Seasonal Rates For 2004

Rates quoted in resort entries are subject to change.

- Value rates apply January 1 to February 11, August 29 to September 29, and October 31 to December 19 for all Value and Moderate resorts, Wilderness Lodge and Villas, Animal Kingdom Lodge, and the Fort Wilderness Cabins; January 1 to February 11 and August 8 to November 18 for the Fort Wilderness Campground; and January 1 to February 11, July 5 to September 29, and October 31 to December 19 for other Disney-owned-and-operated resorts.

- Regular rates apply April 18 to August 28 and September 30 to October 30 for all Value and Moderate resorts, Wilderness Lodge and Villas, Animal Kingdom Lodge, and Fort Wilderness Cabins; April 18 to August 7 for Fort Wilderness Campground; and April 18 to July 4 and September 30 to October 30 for other WDW properties (except Swan and Dolphin).

- Peak rates apply February 12 to April 17 for all but the Swan and Dolphin.

- Pre-holiday rates apply November 19 to December 19 at Fort Wilderness Campground.

- Holiday higher-than-peak rates apply December 20 to 31 for all WDW resorts except the Swan and Dolphin.

- For details on Swan and Dolphin seasonal rates, call 800-227-1500.

floor-to-ceiling window in the lobby, a rock outcropping one story down from the lobby allows views of the animals, and indoor viewing areas line the halls of the U-shaped resort. The property's enormous pool, sun deck, and two whirlpools have great animal-viewing potential (due to a strategically placed watering hole). The pool area is surrounded by restaurants. Zahanati Health Club rounds out the resort's recreation options.

Where to eat: Boma—Flavors of Africa (buffet featuring items prepared on a wood-burning grill in an African market setting), Jiko—the Cooking Place (comfort food meets multi-cultural-influenced cuisine); and The Mara (on-the-go grazing).

Where to drink: Victoria Falls (mezzanine lounge with African drums as tables); Cape Town Lounge and Wine Bar (near Jiko); Uzima Springs Pool Bar.

VITAL STATISTICS: Animal Kingdom Lodge enjoys enviable proximity to the Animal Kingdom and Blizzard Beach; the Disney-MGM Studios is also nearby. Animal Kingdom Lodge; 2901 Osceola Parkway; Box 10000; Bay Lake, FL 32830-1000; 407-938-3000.

Rates: Standard rooms without savanna views run $199 in value season, $239 regular, and $289 peak; standard rooms with savanna views are $275 value, $315 regular, and $365 peak; concierge rooms with savanna views begin at $425 in value season, $480 regular, and $545 peak. Suites start at $635. A $25 per diem charge applies for each extra adult (beyond two) in a room.

BoardWalk Inn & Villas

This fetching resort and entertainment complex recaptures an ephemeral period in eastern-seaboard history. It has all the charm of a shore village awash in sun-bleached pastels. The name comes from the 48-foot-wide boardwalk out back, where you will find a lively piano club, a swinging dance hall, and a truly

Resort Primer

- Reservationists cannot guarantee a room location or view, so arrive early to request the best selection.
- Rooms on the upper floors afford the most privacy.
- Connecting or adjoining rooms and king-size beds can usually be requested but are not assured.
- Concierge rooms, in addition to extra service, generally include continental breakfast and afternoon snacks.

major-league sports bar, not to mention a bakery and a brewpub. When hunger calls, you can sit down to a seafood dinner or buy a slice of pizza. For dessert, try a caramel apple from the sweet-shop. Located lakefront directly opposite the Yacht and Beach Club, BoardWalk completes this seaside community in exceedingly romantic fashion.

The BoardWalk Inn (a 372-room deluxe hotel) and Board-Walk Villas (520 villas styled in the tradition of family vacation rooms) share a lobby. Filled with antique miniatures of early boardwalk amusement rides, the lobby fronts an inviting porch with rocking chairs. A sweeping staircase leads to the main recreation area as well as to the restaurants, shops, and clubs of the BoardWalk entertainment district.

Boardwalk Tips

- Take advantage of the resort's romantic assets—surrey rides and sunset cocktails on the waterfront.

- When checking in, request a room near the lobby—you'll get enough exercise walking in the parks.

- Big games attract a big crowd at the ESPN Club, so get there as early as possible.

- In the evening, catch a bus to the BoardWalk from the TTC.

BIG DRAWS: Intimate charm, an entertainment zone right out back, and a walkway to Epcot's International Gateway.

WORTH NOTING: Guestrooms at the BoardWalk Inn are comparable in size to those at Disney's other deluxe properties and offer two queen-size beds; some have a child's daybed. Decor includes curtains imprinted with images and inscriptions from old post-cards, and French doors that open to private patios or bal-conies. Two-story suites feature a master-bedroom loft (with king-size bed and adjoining bath with whirlpool tub), a living room with a wet bar, and a private gar-den enclosed in a white picket fence. Single-story concierge rooms are similarly appointed (no gardens, alas).

The BoardWalk Villas is a Disney Vacation Club resort (see page 58 for details); because its accommodations have either a kitchenette or a full kitchen, it falls into Disney's Home Away from Home category. Villas, dec-orated in the eclectic fashion of seaside cottages, feature balconies or patios and carousel-print cur-tains. Studios offer a queen-size bed and a double sleeper sofa, plus a wet bar with microwave, coffeemaker, and small refrigerator. Larger villas (with one, two, or three bedrooms) have a dining room, kitchen, laundry facilities, whirlpool tub, and VCR. They also have a king-size bed in the master bedroom, a spacious living room with a queen sleeper sofa, and two queen-size beds or a queen-size bed and double sleeper sofa in any additional bedrooms.

Both properties have room service from 6 A.M. to midnight. Room amenities include hair dryers, irons (with boards), and—at the Inn—newspaper delivery. A conference center offers business services. Guests have exclusive use of the amusement park-themed pool, two pools, and three whirlpools.

Other recreational options include fishing excursions, two clay tennis courts, a health club (massages by appointment), a jogging trail, and croquet. Bicycles, pedal-driven carts, fishing poles, and inner tubes may be rented; a poolside library rents books and videos.

Where to eat: Big River Grille & Brewing Works (microbrews, pub food); BoardWalk Bakery (baked goods, sandwiches); ESPN Club (all-American sports bar, ballpark menu); Flying Fish Cafe (creative American, steak,

and seafood); Seashore Sweets' (saltwater taffy and ice cream); and Spoodles (Mediterranean).

Where to drink: Atlantic Dance (a ballroom/nightclub with songs from the '40s and the '80s and '90s and, sometimes, a deejay); the Belle Vue Room (cocktails and cognac flights); Jellyrolls (dueling pianos); ESPN Club; and Leaping Horse Libations (poolside refreshments).

A Closer Look

Read (yes, read) the curtains, which were created using imprints of vintage postcards. During construction, a carpenter noticed one from 1933, written by his uncle to his aunt before they were married. They still live at the address on the postcard.

VITAL STATISTICS: BoardWalk guests have enviable access to Epcot, Disney-MGM Studios, and Fantasia Gardens Miniature Golf complex. BoardWalk; 2101 N. Epcot Resorts Blvd.; Box 10000; Lake Buena Vista, FL 32830-1000; 407-939-5100; fax 407-939-5150.

Rates: At the Inn, standard rooms start at $289 in value season, $329 regular, and $394 peak; concierge rooms begin at $425 value, $480 regular, and $550 peak; and suites begin at $545. A $25 per diem charge applies for each extra adult (beyond two) sharing a room.

At the Villas, studios start at $289 value, $329 regular, and $394 peak; one-bedroom villas begin at $390 value, $435 regular, and $505 peak; two-bedroom villas start at $545 value, $705 regular, and $890 peak; and three-bedroom villas start at $1,320.

Contemporary

First impressions might suggest that the enormous A-frame tower of this legendary resort is simply a 15-story concrete tent that's been pitched here, a stone's throw from Space Mountain, for the benefit of the monorail trains regularly passing through it. And the Contemporary is certainly defined by a 1970s futuristic vision. But there's more to the resort— namely, the reverie that plays out in in its bold decor and stunning views: from the sleek lobby to the quirky, clashing guestroom furnishings; three eateries, including the acclaimed California Grill; and views of the Magic Kingdom or Bay Lake, especially from rooms in the resort's tower (the higher, the better).

NOTE: Pop music often blares from the pool area, so for optimum quiet pick the Magic Kingdom side of the resort.

BIG DRAWS: Location. Monorail service. Ideally suited for serious tennis players.

WORTH NOTING: Guestrooms here are larger than at any other Walt Disney World hotel; most feature two queen-size beds plus a daybed (a king-size bed may be requested). Amenities at the 1,030-room resort include 24-hour room service. Concierge services are available to suite guests and those staying on the 12th floor.

Contemporary Tips

- The view is lovely from either side of the Contemporary, but the Bay Lake side is noisier.
- Rooms in the resort's garden buildings generally do not yield notable views, which is why the rates are lower than in the tower.
- Tennis players will do well to stay in the north wing because of its proximity to the resort's six lighted courts. Be sure to inquire about the resort's tennis clinics.
- The marina is full of choices for sailors, from Water Mouse boats and sailboats to Searaiders, which are faster than the Water Mouse boats and unavailable to the under-18 crowd.
- Tower guests have convenient access to business services at the convention center. Guests staying in the south wing are close to the pool and marina areas.

Based on its tennis facility alone, the Contemporary could be a recreational hub, but it also boasts a large pool area (with a free-form pool, an unguarded pool, and two whirlpools), a boat rental marina, a parasailing program, basketball and sand volleyball courts, a jogging trail, and a health club (massages by appointment). Waterskiing and fishing excursions may be arranged. Note that the Contemporary's theming does not exude a cozy ambience and rarely comes off as romantic.

Where to eat: California Grill (West Coast cuisine and a 15th-floor Magic Kingdom vista; in fact, the view from the observation deck is open to restaurant guests only); Chef Mickey's (breakfast and dinner character buffets); Concourse Steakhouse (casual for its genre); and Food and Fun Center (24-hour snacks).

Where to drink: California Grill Lounge (emphasis on wine); Contemporary Grounds (coffee bar); Outer Rim (comfy alcove overlooking Bay Lake); and Sand Bar (poolside refreshments).

VITAL STATISTICS: The Contemporary, which has the Magic Kingdom virtually in its front yard and Bay Lake out back, is the only hotel with a walkway—and one of three on the monorail line—to that park. Monorail links extend the resort's neighborhood to the Polynesian and the Grand Floridian, and provide conve-nient commutes to Epcot. Contemporary; 4600 N. World Dr.; Box 10000; Lake Buena Vista, FL 32830-1000; 407-824-1000; fax 407-824-3539.

Rates: Standard guestrooms start at $239 in value season, $264 regular, and $309 peak;

tower rooms begin at $335 value, $370 regular, and $435 peak; suites start at $300. A $25 daily charge applies for each extra adult (beyond two) sharing a room.

Grand Floridian Resort & Spa

This romantic slice of Victorian confectionery, near the Magic Kingdom, recalls the opulent hotels that beckoned high society at the turn of the 20th century.

The Grand Floridian's central building and five guest buildings—white structures laced with verandas and turrets and topped with gabled roofs of red shingle—sprawl over acres of Seven Seas Lagoon shorefront. Every glance embraces towering palms, stunning lake views, or rose gardens.

The resort's magnificent lobby—Victoriana in excelsis—features immense chandeliers, stained-glass skylights, and live piano and orchestra music that might inspire spontaneous dancing. Guestrooms have old-fashioned armoires, marble-topped sinks, and room service delivered atop lace cloths.

BIG DRAWS: The height of luxury with a view of Cinderella Castle. Great for honeymoons or an escape to a kinder, gentler era. And the monorail stops here, too.

WORTH NOTING: Standard accommodations at this 900-room resort are a bit larger than those at most deluxe hotels in the World and include two queen-size beds plus a daybed; many rooms have terraces. Amenities include hair dryers, toiletries,

robes, mini-bars, 24-hour room service, and nightly turndown. Concierge rooms and suites are on the upper floors of the main building and in the Sugar Loaf building.

The resort offers some of the best restaurants on property. Afternoon tea is served in the Garden View lounge. The Electrical Water Pageant (ask at the resort's front desk for information) and the Magic Kingdom fireworks can be seen from many lagoon-view rooms.

A convention center offers

access to business services (for a fee). Boats may be rented, and fishing excursions may be arranged. Two clay tennis courts and volleyball equipment are available at no charge. The Grand Floridian Spa & Health Club is among Walt Disney World's most complete fitness facilities. The two swimming pools and a whirlpool are open 24 hours, with quiet hours in effect at night.

Where to eat: Cítricos (Florida cuisine with Mediterranean flair; closed Monday and Tuesday); Gasparilla Grill & Games (24-hour snacks); Grand Floridian Cafe (breakfast and lunch); Narcoossee's (seafood served waterside); 1900 Park Fare (character buffets); and Victoria & Albert's (seven-course dinners).

Where to drink: Cítricos lounge (wines and citrus martinis); Garden View (cocktails and afternoon tea); Mizner's (classic cocktails); Narcoossee's (wines overlooking the lagoon); and the Grand Floridian Pool Bar (poolside refreshments).

VITAL STATISTICS: The Grand Floridian's prime Seven Seas Lagoon locale allows for fast access to the Magic Kingdom. Proximity to the Palm and Magnolia links pleases golfers.

Grand Floridian Tips

- For maximum quiet and a striking panorama, make sure to request a lagoon-view room.

- You can watch the fireworks over Cinderella Castle from the beach with little or no company.

- Consider a honeymoon room for your second honeymoon.

- Indulge in a treatment (or two) at the spa after a long day in the parks.

- Book a special dinner at Victoria & Albert's four months in advance.

- Note that the resort is surprisingly popular with families, despite its posh surroundings.

- For pre-dinner drinks, opt for Cítricos lounge, the lounge at Narcoossee's, or cocktail service in the lobby.

- Ask at Guest Services about sailing the Seven Seas on a private yacht (see page 176.

The monorail stretches the hotel's neighborhood beyond the adjacent Polynesian resort to include the Contemporary resort and provides for easy commutes to Epcot. Grand Floridian; 4401 Floridian Way; Box 10000; Lake Buena Vista, FL 32830-1000; 407-824-3000; fax 407-824-3186.

Rates: Standard rooms start at $339 in value season, $384 regular, and $444 peak; concierge rooms begin at $450 value, $520 regular, and $600 peak; and suites start at $900. A $25 per diem charge applies to each extra adult (beyond two) sharing a room.

Made-To-Order Surprises

Flowers, custom gift baskets, and champagne can be delivered to any WDW resort (and some off-property hotels) by calling 407-827-3505 before or during your visit.

For an additional fee, Disney personal shoppers will further scour the World to track down favorite character merchandise and other special-request items.

Polynesian

This resort echoes the romance and beauty of the South Pacific with enchanting realism. Polynesian music is piped throughout the lushly landscaped grounds, which boast white-sand beaches with hammocks, torches that burn nightly, and sufficient flowers to perfume the air.

Sprawled amid tropical gardens are 11 two- and three-story village longhouses, all named for Pacific islands, where 853 guestrooms are located. But the Polynesian's centerpiece and primary mood setter is unquestionably the Great Ceremonial House, which (in addition to the usual front desk, shops, and restaurants) contains a three-story-high garden that all but consumes the atrium lobby.

BIG DRAWS: A breathtaking, you-are-there South Seas ambience makes the Polynesian exceptionally romantic and helps to explain the resort's busy wedding calendar. And the convenience of monorail service is a definite plus.

WORTH NOTING: Standard guestrooms, comparable in size to those at the Contemporary, are roomy and feature two queen-size beds plus a daybed. Those in

The resort boasts great vantage points for Magic Kingdom fireworks and the Electrical Water Pageant. (For information, ask at the front desk.) Boats may be rented, fishing excursions may be arranged, and a 1¼-mile trail invites jogging around the tropical grounds.

Where to eat: Captain Cook's Snack Company (24-hour grazing—it's one of the better Disney snack bars); Kona Cafe (Asian-influenced casual fare and adjoining coffee bar); and 'Ohana (character breakfast and family-style Pacific Rim dinners featuring grilled meats).

Tokelau, Tahiti, and Rapa Nui are slightly larger. Room decor includes vibrant bedspreads, ti leaf-shaped mirrors, bamboo accents, and woven reed canopies draped over and behind the beds.

All third-floor rooms (and second-floor rooms in the Tonga, Tokelau, Tahiti, and Rapa Nui buildings) have balconies. Room service is offered until midnight. A concierge lounge with a choice view of the Magic Kingdom is a comfy retreat for guests in Hawaii and all-suite Tonga, the resort's most luxurious digs.

In addition to the impressive volcano-themed pool, there is a second, more removed pool. Near Tokelau, a grassy knoll known as Sunset Point offers a hammock.

Polynesian Tips

- For a taste of tropical tradition, catch the Torch Lighting Ceremony, held on weekend nights at 6 P.M. in the main lobby.

- Tahiti is a good choice for its relative seclusion and Magic Kingdom views (request a lagoonside room).

- For a better view, hit the Seven Seas Lagoon on a private specialty cruise. See page 177 for details.

- Tucked down below Sunset Point, in front of Tahiti, is a beach that many guests don't realize is there.

- Couples can celebrate a special occasion with a moonlit dinner on the beach. Call Room Service for more information.

- The Grand Floridian Spa & Health Club is a short walk away.

Where to drink: Barefoot Bar (poolside refreshments) and Tambu lounge (tropical drinks).

VITAL STATISTICS: The Polynesian is located on the shore of Seven Seas Lagoon, directly opposite the Magic Kingdom and offers fast access via monorail to the park. The monorail also links the resort with the Grand Floridian and Contemporary and provides for easy commutes to Epcot. Golfers appreciate having both the Palm and Magnolia courses nearby. Polynesian; 1600 South Seas Dr.; Box 10000; Lake Buena Vista, FL 32830-1000; 407-824-2000; fax 407-824-3174.

Rates: Standard rooms start at $299 in value season, $344 regular, and $404 peak; concierge rooms begin at $390 value, $440 regular, and $515 peak; suites start at $495. A $25 per diem charge applies to each extra adult (beyond two) sharing a room.

Special Room Requests

All WDW resorts offer rooms equipped for guests with disabilities, as well as nonsmoking rooms. For more detailed information, inquire with Central Reservations (407-934-7639). For more specifics related to travelers with disabilities, see the "Customized Tips" section of the *Planning Ahead* chapter.

Swan & Dolphin

The motto for these resorts might be "expect the unexpected." Certainly, noted architect Michael Graves designed these postmodern bookends with entertainment in mind. At the Dolphin, a 27-story triangular tower is flanked by buildings that are topped by two 56-foot-tall dolphin statues and covered in a mural of banana leaves. Guestrooms with such decorative touches as cabana-like doors do not preclude access to a first-rate fitness center or a showroom with Cartier gems. It's more of the same playful luxury next door at the Swan, which carves its own distinctive silhouette with 47-foot namesake statues perched atop its 12-story central building, and facades accented with turquoise waves. The Swan has 758 rooms, about half as many as the Dolphin, and its furnishings tend toward bird lamps and pineapple-stenciled headboards.

BIG DRAWS: Luxury in a light-hearted wrapper. Exceptional facilities. And you can walk to Epcot, BoardWalk, and, if you're feeling ambitious, the Disney-MGM Studios.

WORTH NOTING: The Swan and the Dolphin (operated by Westin and

Sheraton) are the only two WDW hotels whose value season extends through the summer months. Guests staying at either of the two hotels have access to all restaurants and lounges, recreational activities, and may charge any meals and activities enjoyed at the sister hotel to their room tab. Such charging privileges do not extend beyond the two hotels.

Guestrooms at the Swan and Dolphin are comparable to those at Disney's other deluxe resorts. Whereas standard rooms at the Dolphin feature two double beds, queen-size beds are the rule at the Swan (king-size beds are available at both). Room amenities at both hotels include stocked minibars and 24-hour room service (the best at Walt Disney World), plus nightly turndown at the Swan, and coffeemakers, hair dryers, and irons with boards at the Dolphin. Club-level rooms at the Dolphin are located in the resort's tower; at the Swan they are on the top two floors of the hotel's main building.

Both hotels boast luxurious presidential suites. In addition to a beach with a volleyball net and boat rentals, the resorts share an enviable lap pool, grotto pool with waterfalls, a small rectangular pool, and several whirlpools.

Where to eat: At the Swan: Garden Grove Cafe (greenhouse setting) and Palio (Italian bistro). At the Dolphin: Dolphin Fountain (ice cream parlor); Shula's Steakhouse (steak and seafood); and Tubbi's (cafeteria with 24-hour convenience store)

Where to drink: At the Swan: Kimonos (cocktail lounge with sushi bar); Lobby Court (coffees); and Splash Grill (poolside). At the Dolphin: Cabana Bar & Grill (poolside); and Shula's Steakhouse Lounge (cozy nook adjacent to dining area), and a lobby lounge.

Swan & Dolphin Tips

- Request a corner room with a king-size bed at the Dolphin, and if it's available, you'll get two balconies for the price of one.

- Both the Swan and Dolphin feature large convention centers. If you're visiting for pleasure, check the name-badge quotient before you book.

- Swan and Dolphin guests pay an additional $10 per day to receive a morning newspaper, in-room coffee, local calls, and use of the Dolphin's health club for the length of their stay.

- Four tennis courts at the Dolphin are kept lighted all night.

- Light sleepers should note that some rooms are steps from BoardWalk's Jellyrolls and Atlantic Dance clubs.

VITAL STATISTICS: The Swan and Dolphin resorts offer easy access to Epcot, the Disney-MGM Studios, and BoardWalk. Located side by side on the shore of Crescent Lake, a virtual stone's throw from Epcot's World Showcase, the hotels are flanked by BoardWalk on one side and the Yacht and Beach Club on the other. Walt Disney World Swan; 1200 Epcot Resorts Blvd.; Lake Buena Vista, FL 32830-1000; 407-934-3000; fax 407-934-4499. Walt Disney World Dolphin; 1500 Epcot Resorts Blvd.; Box 10000; Lake Buena Vista, FL 32830-1000; 407-934-4000; fax 407-934-4844.

Rates: At press time, rates at the Swan and Dolphin, standard rooms began at $339 in value season and $365 peak, and club-level rooms are $455 value and $519 peak. For suite prices, call 800-227-1500. A $25 per diem charge applies for each extra adult (beyond two) sharing a room. Call 800-227-1500 to make reservations or visit *www.swandolphin.com.*

Wilderness Lodge & Villas

Rustic romance infuses every detail of this resort, patterned after the grand National Park Service lodges of the early 1900s.

Hidden away on an isolated shore of Bay Lake, Wilderness Lodge is surrounded by pine forests that provide a drumroll of sorts along the winding road leading to the timbered hotel.

The soaring atrium lobby kindles the spirit of the American West with an imposing pair of totem poles, tepee chandeliers, a bubbling hot spring, and an 82-foot-tall fireplace whose layered stones actually replicate the Grand Canyon's strata. And the natural landscape is supplemented by a roaring waterfall, a swimming area surrounded by boulders, wildflowers, and even a gushing geyser. The guestrooms at the Lodge are located

Wilderness Lodge Tips

- Daily tours offer a closer look at the resort's architecture or restaurants.
- Courtyard and lakeview rooms are most romantic, with waterfalls gushing and brooks babbling. Woods views provide maximum quiet.
- The Lodge's junior suites are a good value, given their spaciousness. Honeymooners should request room 7084 for its fireworks views and whirlpool tub.
- Some rooms at the lodge come with a queen-size bed and a bunk bed instead of two queen-size beds. Be sure to make your preference known.

in two wings that extend back from the lobby to the lakefront, forming a U-shaped frame around an inner courtyard. The adjacent Villas at Wilderness Lodge are styled after the railroad hotels of the late 1800s. They extend the resort's neighborhood with 181 villas. The units are further distinguished by a red-shingled roof and a five-story central atrium. The Lodge and Villas share a lobby, and a covered walkway connects the resort buildings. There's also a concierge floor.

BIG DRAWS: Luxury. Undeniable romance. The bottom line: a truly extraordinary setting at a considerable value to guests.

WORTH NOTING: While all 728 Wilderness Lodge guestrooms have balconies or patios, quarters here are slightly more compact than those at Walt Disney World's other deluxe resorts, and feature two queen-size beds. Quilted bedspreads, buffalo lamps, and armoires etched with mountain scenes maintain the theme.

The Villas at Wilderness Lodge is a Disney Vacation Club resort (refer to page 58 for more information); accommodations are equipped with either a wet bar or a full kitchen. Studios and larger villas with one or two rooms feature balconies (or patios). Guests staying at the villas enjoy full access to the Lodge next door and vice versa.

At the Lodge and Villas, room service is available for breakfast and dinner. The four corridors ringing the lobby provide access to porches overlooking the courtyard and hold cozy nooks with sofas and tucked-away fireplaces. Fire Rock Geyser spouts off 180-foot water plumes at the top of every hour from 7 A.M. until 10 P.M. A quiet pool, whirlpool spa, and Sturdy Branches health club are located in the villa section. Both resorts share a beach that fronts the lake. Guided fishing excursions can be arranged. Boats and bicycles may be rented, and there is a three-quarter-mile path for biking, jogging, and walking that leads to Fort Wilderness.

Where to eat: Artist Point (Pacific Northwest cuisine); Roaring Fork (snacks); and Whispering Canyon Cafe (family-style dining).

Where to drink: Territory Lounge (western motif) and Trout Pass (small poolside bar).

VITAL STATISTICS: Wilderness Lodge and Villas; 801 and 901 West Timberline Dr.; Box 10000; Lake Buena Vista, FL 32830-1000; 407-824-3200; fax 407-824-3232.

Rates: At the Lodge, standard guestrooms begin at $199 in value season, $239 regular, and $289 peak; suites start at $720. Honeymoon rooms (with whirlpool tub) start at $360. A $25 per diem charge applies for each extra adult (beyond two) sharing a room (at the Lodge only). At the Villas, studios start at $279 value, $314 regular, and $379 peak; one-bedroom villas begin at $380 value, $425 regular, and $495 peak; two-bedroom villas start at $535 value, $690 regular, and $835 peak.

Join the Club?

Frequent visitors who consider WDW a home away from home might want to join the Disney Vacation Club. For a one-time price and annual dues, members may stay at Disney's Old Key West Resort, BoardWalk Villas, The Villas at Wilderness Lodge, Beach Club Villas, or at many resorts beyond WDW, including Disney's Hilton Head Island Resort, in South Carolina, and, just two hours from WDW, Disney's Vero Beach Resort (see page 62). They can also opt for the Disney Cruise Line or another Walt Disney World resort. For more details, visit *www.disneyvacationclub.com* or call 800-800-9100.

Yacht & Beach Club and Beach Club Villas

This setting conjures such a heady vision of turn-of-the-century Nantucket and Martha's Vineyard, you'd swear you smelled salt in the air. Surely, architect Robert A. M. Stern's evocation of the grand old seaside hotels has the gulls fooled. The resort stretches along a picturesque shoreline complete with a swimming lagoon, lighthouse, and marina.

As the five-story gray clapboard structure of the Yacht Club gives way to the sky-blue Beach Club (they're connected), the interior motif shifts from seriously nautical to seashore whimsical. The Yacht Club has a rich, exclusive feel to it—there's a stunning globe anchoring the lobby, and polished brass abounds. Next door at the Beach Club, beach umbrellas act as pillars, and clambakes occur nightly. The Beach Club Villas are inspired by Cape May seaside homes designed in the early 20th century.

BIG DRAWS: Compelling theming. Exceptional swimming area. Some of the World's best restaurants. Close access to Epcot and the Disney-MGM Studios.

WORTH NOTING: There are 630 guestrooms at the Yacht Club and 583 rooms at the Beach Club. Room-size is comparable to those at Disney's other deluxe resorts. As a rule, they feature two queen-size beds and a daybed (king-size beds are

Yacht & Beach Club Tips

- The stunning views belong strictly to those with lakeside rooms.
- At both resorts, it's a long walk to the lobby from the outermost reaches of guest wings.
- At the Beach Club, all rooms have patios or balconies.
- Balconies at the Yacht Club are bigger than those at the Beach Club.
- Inquire at the Yacht Club's Guest Services desk about the free weekly garden tours.
- Take a ride on a Chris-Craft speedboat. See page 176 for more.
- There are tables for two in the Yacht Club's Ale and Compass lounge.

available). At the Yacht Club, rooms maintain the nautical theme. Most rooms have good-size balconies. At the Beach Club, rooms keep the seashore motif.

Amenities at both resorts include minibars, an iron and board, a hair dryer, and 24-hour room service. Yacht and Beach Club both offer concierge rooms. The five-story Beach Club Villas is a Disney Vacation Club resort. Since accommodations have either a wet bar or a kitchen, they fall under Disney's Home Away from Home category. The 208 units, which include both studios and one- and two-bedroom villas, feature wooden porches and pastel colors.

A three-acre mini water park called Stormalong Bay earns the

Yacht and Beach Club bragging rights to the World's best resort swimming area; the sprawling, sandy-bottomed pool, open only to hotel guests, includes sections with jets, swirling currents, and a slide (traditional whirlpools also stand by). Each resort also has a smaller pool and whirlpool, so removed you must seek them out.

The Ship Shape health club is among the most extensive fitness centers at a WDW property. Boat rentals and two tennis courts are offered, fishing excursions can be arranged, and volleyball and croquet equipment is available.

Where to eat: At the Beach Club: Cape May Cafe (character breakfasts and clambake buffet dinners). At the Yacht Club: Yacht Club Galley (buffet breakfast, lunch, and dinner), Yachtsman Steakhouse (breakfast, lunch, and dinner). Shared by both hotels is the Beaches & Cream Soda Shop (a classic soda fountain).

Where to drink: At the Beach Club: Martha's Vineyard (cloud nine for wine lovers) and Rip Tide (lobby niche). At the Yacht Club: Ale and Compass (cozy lobby nook) and Crew's Cup (well-heeled beer emporium). For poolside refreshments and snacks, there's Hurricane Hanna's Grill.

VITAL STATISTICS: The Yacht and Beach Club enjoy close proximity to Epcot, Disney-MGM Studios, BoardWalk, and the Fantasia Gardens Miniature Golf complex. Located side by side on a shore of Crescent Lake that offers a footpath to Epcot's International Gateway entrance, these sister resorts are joined lakeside by the BoardWalk, Swan, and Dolphin. Yacht Club; 1700 Epcot Resorts Blvd.; Box 10000; Lake Buena Vista, FL 32830-1000; 407-934-7000; fax 407-934-3450. Beach Club; 1800 Epcot Resorts Blvd.; Box 10000; Lake Buena Vista, FL 32830-1000; 407-934-8000; fax 407-934-3850.

Rates: Standard rooms at the Yacht and Beach Club begin at $289 in value season, $329 regular, and $394 peak; concierge rooms at the Yacht Club start at $425 value, $480 regular, and $550 peak; Yacht Club suites start at $525 and Beach Club suites start at $495. A $25 per diem charge applies to each extra adult (beyond two) sharing a room. At the Villas, studios start at $289 value, $329 regular, and $394 peak; one-bedroom villas begin at $390 value, $435 regular, and $505 peak; two-bedroom villas start at $545 value, $705 regular, and $890 peak.

Home Away From Home
Disney's Old Key West Resort

Pastel-hued clapboard guesthouses with tin roofs and white picket fences set the cheerful tone of this Key Westerly retreat. Here, Disney luxury dovetails with a laid-back atmosphere to create the look and feel of a friendly resort community.

A sprawling village, it is bounded by the wooded fairways of the Lake Buena Vista golf links, and anchored at its center by a lighthouse that overlooks the main pool area, which moonlights as a sauna. A waterway called the Trumbo Canal flows from the heart of the resort, eventually uniting with Lake Buena Vista. Accommodations equipped with kitchens may set this resort apart, but what gives the place charm is its warmth.

Old Key West Tips

- For a waterfront setting that's removed from the main recreation area, book a villa near the Turtle Shack. Numbers 43 and 44 are good, given their water views and proximity to the pool, snack bar, tennis court, and bus stop.

- All accommodations but the studios feature whirlpool bathtubs.

- One-bedroom villas yield more than twice the space of a studio for a relatively small jump in cost.

BIG DRAWS: Spacious accommodations, ideal for long stays. Homey environs. Value for groups. Convenience of kitchens. Well located for golfers.

WORTH NOTING: This resort was the first Disney Vacation Club property. It features studio accommodations and one-, two-, and three-bedroom villas. The villas have a distinctly Key West feel, and are decorated in light woods with ceiling fans and color schemes of sea-foam green and mauve.

Each studio has a large bedroom with two queen-size beds; a wet bar with a microwave, coffeemaker, and small refrigerator; and a spacious bathroom. Larger villas have a dining room, and kitchen, laundry facilities, whirlpool bathtub, and VCR. They also feature a king-size bed in the master bedroom, two queen-size beds in each additional bedroom, and a living room with queen-size sofa bed. All accommodations have balconies or porches.

Boats and bicycles are available for rent. Fishing excursions can be arranged. The three tennis courts tend to be relatively quiet

and accessible. The main swimming area supplements three smaller pools. There is a small fitness center. Conch Flats Community Hall has table tennis, board games, and video rentals.

Where to eat: Good's Food to Go (meals and snacks on the go) and Olivia's Cafe (casual all-day dining with Key West flourishes). Grills and picnic tables are available. Pizza delivery from Port Orleans Riverside is offered until midnight. Conch Flats General Store stocks some grocery items.

Where to drink: Gurgling Suitcase (tiny spirited pub) and Turtle Shack (poolside refreshments).

VITAL STATISTICS: This resort is well located for golfers. It also enjoys easy access to Downtown Disney and good proximity to Epcot and Disney-MGM Studios. Disney's Old Key West Resort; 1510 N. Cove Rd.; Box 10000; Lake Buena Vista, FL 32830-1000; 407-827-7700; fax 407-827-7710.

Rates: Studios are $254 in value season, $284 regular, and $329 peak; one-bedroom villas are $340 value, $385 regular, and $445 peak; two-bedrooms are

$479 value, $560 regular, and $680 peak; and three-bedrooms start at $1,040 value, $1,160 regular, and $1,310 peak.

Fort Wilderness Resort & Campground

No fewer than 700 acres of woodland hopping with rabbits combine with WDW's largest lake to provide the foundation for Fort Wilderness, a retreat that relies on the outdoors for atmosphere.

Campsites are arranged on 28 loops, linked by thoroughfares. While some of the 784 sites are designated for tents, most are devoted to RV camping; hundreds of spots sport air-conditioned Wilderness Cabins, comfortable units that are comparable to well-equipped trailer homes.

BIG DRAWS: Natural setting. Value. And recreation galore.

WORTH NOTING: Most loops have at least one air-conditioned comfort station equipped with restrooms, phones, showers, laundry facilities, and an ice machine.

Campsite lengths range from 25 to 65 feet. All sites have a charcoal grill, picnic table, and a 30/50-amp electrical outlet. Most sites have sanitary-disposal connections; about half have cable TV hook-ups.

Wilderness Cabins are separated from other campsites and feature rustic decor and a deck with picnic table; amenities include a hair dryer and an iron and board. Each cabin is air-conditioned and offers daily housekeeping service, as well as an eat-in kitchen, living room with television and VCR, and full bathroom.

Pets are welcome at designated campsites ($3 per day). Pet loops are not wired for cable television. Recreational options include swimming, boating, tennis, and biking. Guided fishing trips may be arranged.

New this year are 45-minute horse-drawn wagon rides ($8; no reservations) and relaxing and intimate 30-minute, horse-drawn carriage rides ($30; call 407-824-2832) that take guests on a scenic trip between Fort Wilderness and Disney's Wilderness Lodge. The Hoop-Dee-Doo Musical Revue dinner show is presented nightly.

Where to eat: Most guests cook their own meals (a small selection of foodstuffs is sold at Meadow Trading Post and Settlement Trading Post), but there's also Trail's End restaurant (buffet-style dining). Grocery stores are located just minutes from Walt Disney World. Ask for directions when you check in.

Where to drink: Crockett's Tavern (cocktail service).

VITAL STATISTICS: Fort Wilderness occupies Bay Lake's southern shore. Its nearest theme park neighbor is the Magic Kingdom, and it closely borders the Osprey Ridge and Eagle Pines golf courses. The area is served by the WDW bus transportation system. Bus stops are strategically located and plentiful. Fort Wilderness; 4510 N. Fort Wilderness Trail; Box 10000; Lake Buena Vista, FL 32830-1000; 407-824-2900; fax 407-824-3508.

Rates: Preferred sites with full hookups, including water, electricity, sewage, and cable TV, are $49 in value season, $67 regular, and $76 peak; sites with full hookups minus the cable TV are $41 value, $62 regular, and $71 peak; sites with electricity hookups only are $36 value, $52 regular, and $60 peak.

There is a limit of ten persons per campsite, and a $2 per diem charge applies to each extra adult (beyond two) sharing a site. Rates for Wilderness Cabins are $229 value, $269 regular, and $299 peak. Maximum occupancy is six, and there is a $5 per diem charge that applies to each extra adult (beyond two) sharing a unit.

Fort Wilderness Tips

- Bikes and electric carts are, sudden rains aside, the preferred means for getting around.
- A car is the quickest way to get to other parts of the World from here.
- Views of Magic Kingdom fireworks and the Electrical Water Pageant are readily available.
- Tent campers should request loop 1500 or 2000 for quiet; RV campers will find greater privacy on loops 1600 through 1900 (pets welcome).

Saratoga Springs Resort & Spa

Long for the peaceful relaxation of a lakeside retreat—complete with fragrant gardens, bubbling springs, and a spectacular spa? Look no further. Disney's newest haven has all of the above, plus colorful Victorian architecture, rolling hills, and even a fireworks viewing veranda. The resort, which stands on the grounds once occupied by the Disney Institute, aims to recapture the charm and rejuvenating ambience of Saratoga Springs, New York, circa the late 1800s.

Saratoga Springs Resort & Spa is a Disney Vacation Club resort. (See page 58 for details.) The phone number is 407-827-1100.

Rates: Studios are $254 in value season, $284 regular, and $329 peak; one-bedroom villas are $340 value, $385 regular, and $445 peak; two-bedrooms are $479 value, $560 regular, and $680 peak; and three-bedrooms start at $1,040 value, $1,160 regular, and $1,310 peak.

BIG DRAWS: Relaxing environs. Great spa. Golf nearby. A stone's throw from Downtown Disney.

Saratoga Springs Tips

- While the first phase of the resort is scheduled to open by late spring of 2004, reservations may be accepted as early as January. For details, visit www.disneyworld.com or call 407-934-7639.

- A special viewing pavilion allows guests to watch nightly fireworks presentations at Pleasure Island.

- The Lake Buena Vista Golf Club is located here.

WORTH NOTING: When the resort is complete, there will be 522 guest units—studios, one- and two-bedroom villas, and grand villas—spread over 12 buildings. Each studio has a queen-size bed and full-size sofa bed, plus a kitchenette with a microwave, coffeemaker, and fridge. Larger villas sleep four to eight, and all have a dining area, kitchen, laundry room, master bath with whirlpool tub, and a DVD player. They include a king-size bed in the master bedroom, living room with queen-size sofa bed, and queen- and full-size beds in the extra room.

Guests enjoy of a smorgasbord of recreational diversions including a nearby golf course, three swimming pools, four whirlpool spas, trails for walking or jogging, tennis courts, bike rentals, and more.

Where to eat: The Artist's Palette is the one food source here (no table service), with snacks, sandwiches, and hearty entrées. There are some grocery items available, too.

Where to drink: Resort guests may imbibe at a poolside bar, or at Downtown Disney (a short water launch ride away).

Moderate
Caribbean Beach

In this colorful evocation of the Caribbean, the spirit of the islands is captured by a lake ringed by beaches and villages representing Barbados, Martinique, Trinidad, Jamaica, and Aruba.

Each village is marked by clusters of two-story guest buildings that transport you to the Caribbean with cool pastel facades, white railings, and vivid metallic roofs. Old Port Royale, which houses eateries and shops, takes cues from an island market.

BIG DRAWS: Excellent value. Cheery environs with a decidedly Caribbean feel.

Caribbean Beach Tips

- Aruba is a good choice for seclusion and for proximity to Old Port Royale (they're linked by a bridge).

- For honeymoon-style isolation, request a room in Trinidad South. Located just off the main loop, its buildings and beach are especially removed.

- Martinique tends to be the liveliest village.

- The 1.4-mile promenade circling Barefoot Bay is ideal for biking and jogging. Bikes and boats may be rented. A special length-of-stay option is available for boat renters.

- Families flock here, so plan on encountering plenty of children.

WORTH NOTING: The resort has a total of 2,112 rooms. Slightly larger than those at Disney's other moderately priced resorts, they feature two double beds (king-size beds are available) and soft-hued decor. Amenities include an in-room coffeemaker. Room service, which ventures a touch beyond pizza, is offered from 4 P.M. until midnight.

Villages are sprawled around the resort's Barefoot Bay in a way that can make travel between some guest areas cumbersome despite footbridges and "local" buses.

The resort's whirlpool is nestled into its bustling themed pool. Each village offers its own beach, pool, and courtyards.

Where to eat: Shutters at Old Port Royale (for American fare with a Caribbean influence) and a food court with six counter-service options.

Where to drink: Banana Cabana (poolside refreshments) and the above mentioned Shutters (beer, wine, and cocktails).

VITAL STATISTICS: Caribbean Beach is off on its own but well situated for pursuits other than the Magic Kingdom, with Epcot, the Disney-MGM Studios, and Blizzard Beach close at hand, on one side, and Typhoon Lagoon and Downtown Disney nearby, on the other. Caribbean Beach; 900 Cayman Way; Box 10000; Lake Buena Vista, FL 32830-1000; 407-934-3400; fax 407-934-3288.

Rates: Rooms begin at $133 in value season, $144 in regular season, and $169 during peak times. A $15 per diem charge applies for each extra adult (beyond two) sharing a room.

Coronado Springs

The architecture of this sprawling resort gives its nod to Mexico and the American Southwest, with brightly tinted buildings accented by tile roofs, soaring columns, and arched entryways. Three clusters of regionally themed guest buildings rim the 15-acre Lago Dorado lagoon. The terra-cotta Casitas occupy a citylike landscape that segues into rural surroundings. Here, pueblo-style Ranchos invite guests to dwell among cacti adjacent to a dry stream bed. In the resort's third section, the scenery shifts once

more, with rocky beaches, hammocks, and Cabanas filling the horizon. Rooms in the three areas are similarly appointed, with yellow, scarlet, or deep-blue accents.

Walkways around the lagoon lead from guestroom areas to the main recreation zone (dominated by a five-story Mayan pyramid) and the central building that holds the resort's temporal treasures: an intricately tiled rotunda lobby, two eateries, a lounge, and a gift shop.

BIG DRAWS: A standout among the moderates for its health club, suites, and business hotel facilities.

WORTH NOTING: Guestrooms at this 1,921-room resort are smaller than those at Disney's deluxe hotels. Most of the 46 suites are in the Casitas area. Decor reveals Mexican and Southwestern influences, and reflects the style of each guest

Coronado Springs Tips

- There is a ten-percent gratuity automatically added to all dine-in purchases made at the Pepper Market food court.

- January, May, September, and October are popular convention months. Most groups are housed in the Casitas area, near the convention facilities, and a separate check-in area is provided.

- The Ranchos are nearest the pool area; the Casitas are closer to the main building, convention center, and health club; and the Cabanas are convenient to both.

- There's a lot of ground to cover between the central building and some guestrooms. If you want a room near the hub, be sure to make your preference known when you make the reservation.

A convention center offers access to business services.

Where to eat: Maya Grill (steak and seafood) and the Pepper Market (food court).

Where to drink: Francisco's (lounge with Mexican snacks) and Siesta's (pool bar).

VITAL STATISTICS: Located near Animal Kingdom and Blizzard Beach. Coronado Springs; 1000 W. Buena Vista Dr.; Box 10000; Lake Buena Vista, FL 32830-1000; 407-939-1000; fax 407-939-0425.

Rates: Rooms begin at $133 in value season, $144 regular, and $169 peak; suites start at $280. A $15 per diem charge applies for each extra adult (beyond two) sharing a room.

area. Standard rooms feature two double beds (some king-size beds are available). Amenities include a coffeemaker, hair dryer, iron and board, modem port, and limited room service.

In addition to a themed pool—which has a whirlpool and a sand volleyball court on the side—there is a pool in each guest area. La Vida health club and the Casa de Belleza salon are in the Casitas area. Bike and boat rentals are available. The nearly mile-long path around the lake, known as the Esplanade, is excellent for biking and jogging.

Port Orleans Riverside

Southern hospitality takes two forms at this 2,048-room resort: pillared mansions with groomed lawns and *Gone With the Wind* elegance and, upriver, rustic homes with tin roofs and bayou charm. Rooms in the three-story Magnolia Bend mansions and the two-story Alligator Bayou lodges are similarly appointed.

The man-made Sassagoula River curls around the resort's main recreation area like a moat. Bridges link guest lodgings with this area and the steamship-style building that houses the resort's eateries, gift shop, and check-in facilities.

BIG DRAWS: Excellent value. An exceedingly lovely natural setting.

WORTH NOTING: Rooms here are smaller than those at Disney's deluxe hotels, but pleasantly inviting. Each features two double beds (some king-size beds and trundle beds are available). This is a large, sprawling resort with twice as many rooms as its French Quarter counterpart; some accommodations are a bit removed from the central building or the nearest bus stop. Room service delivers pizza and supplements from 4 P.M. to midnight. Bikes and boats may be rented. The resort's pathways are well suited for joggers, and a carriage path leads to Port Orleans French Quarter. Five additional pools (open 24 hours, provided they stay quiet) are sprinkled around the Bayou and Mansion guest areas. There is one whirlpool near the main pool.

Catch-and-release fishing excursions are offered, as is a stocked, secluded fishing hole (cane poles available). Guests may use the pool at Port Orleans

French Quarter in addition to the one here. New this year are 30-minute carriage rides ($30; call 407-WDW-PLAY for reservations) through the resort area.

Where to eat: Boatwright's Dining Hall (casual restaurant specializing in southern cuisine) and Riverside Mill (food court).

Where to drink: River Roost (fireplace and occasional entertainment) and Muddy Rivers (poolside refreshments).

VITAL STATISTICS: Port Orleans Riverside, located on a bank of the Sassagoula River, is within walking distance of Port Orleans French Quarter. Epcot and the Studios are close by, as are three of WDW's 18-hole golf courses.

Port Orleans Riverside Tips

- The Sassagoula River Cruise is a pleasant outing and a convenient means of transportation to Downtown Disney.
- For optimal atmosphere and minimal walking, request a room in Magnolia Bend's Oak Manor, or lodge number 18 or 27 in the resort's Alligator Bayou section.
- Mansion rooms exude honeymoon-style elegance and seclusion.
- Elevators are available in the resort's Magnolia Bend section only.
- Try River Roost's southern snacks (consider the spicy Cajun Hot Nuts).

Port Orleans Riverside; 1251 Riverside Dr.; Box 10000; Lake Buena Vista, FL 32830-1000; 407-934-6000; fax 407-934-5777.

Rates: Rooms begin at $133 in value season, $144 regular, and $169 peak. A $15 per diem charge applies for each extra adult (beyond two) sharing a room.

Port Orleans French Quarter

New Orleans's historic French Quarter is evoked in this resort's prim row house-style buildings, which are wrapped in ornate wrought-iron railings and set amid romantic gardens and tree-lined blocks. Old-fashioned lampposts add to the ambience, as do street signs such as *Rue D'Baga* and *Café Au Lait Way*.

The resort is entered via Port Orleans Square, an atrium with adjoining buildings that house the front desk, gift shop, and arcade on one side, and a lounge and food court on the other.

Guestrooms are located in seven three-story buildings,

Port Orleans French Quarter Tips

- A convenient water shuttle ferries resort guests to and from Port Orleans Riverside and Downtown Disney.

- This is too pretty a place to wake up to a view of the parking lot, so consider reserving a room over-looking the gardens or splurge on riverscape digs. Note that pool views can spoil the ambience.

- Of the buildings with riverfront rooms, number 1 is nicely isolated. Buildings 2 and 5 are close to the pool area.

- Experience the area's romantic atmosphere via a bike ride along the river.

- Don't miss the fresh beignets (a true taste of the Big Easy), whose aroma regularly wafts through the festive food court.

- The main whirlpool is set off in a courtyard by vine-covered arches.

which are set on either side of the central thoroughfare that begins just beyond Port Orleans Square. The whole enclave is set along-side a stand-in Mississippi known as the Sassagoula River. The Sassagoula River Cruise, which transports guests to Port Orleans French Riverside and Downtown Disney, is a pleasant and conven-ient way to travel.

BIG DRAWS: A good bang for the buck. The charming environs rank among Disney World's most memorable. It's the least sprawling of the moderate resorts.

WORTH NOTING: The pretty, homey rooms are a bit smaller than those at Disney's more expensive hotels but are perfectly comfortable. Each of the 1,008 rooms features two double beds; some king-size beds are available. A Dixieland band occasionally entertains in the main courtyard; a street artist may be available for portraits. A carriage path—ideal for jogging, strolling, and biking—wends alongside the river to Port Orleans Riverside, less than a mile upriver.

Bikes and boats may be rented. A whirlpool is centrally located. In addition to the swimming pool here, Port Orleans French Quarter guests are permitted use of Port Orleans Riverside's pool; they can also take advantage of its fishing hole (catch-and-release only). Guided fishing trips depart from the resort daily (reservations are required).

Where to eat: Boatwright's Dining Hall (at Port Orleans Riverside) and Sassagoula Floatworks & Food Factory (food court with Mardi Gras ambience and inexpensive fare).

Where to drink: Mardi Grogs (pool bar) and Scat Cat's Club (for specialty drinks).

VITAL STATISTICS: Port Orleans French Quarter enjoys special access to Downtown Disney Marketplace via water taxi, which also links it with Port Orleans Riverside. It's close to Epcot, the Disney-MGM Studios, and three 18-hole golf courses as well. Port Orleans French Quarter; 2201 Orleans Dr.; Box 10000; Lake Buena Vista, FL 32830-1000; 407-934-5000; fax 407-934-5353.

Rates: Rooms begin at $133 in value season, $144 regular, and $169 peak. A $15 per diem charge applies for each extra adult (beyond two) sharing a room.

Value
All-Star Movies,
All-Star Music &
All-Star Sports Resorts

Bright in a manner normally reserved for toy packaging, these fun-loving resorts exist at the intersection of entertainment architecture and pop art. Picture a landscape in which three-story football helmets, cowboy boots, and Dalmatians are the norm, and you have an idea of the oversize sense of whimsy that governs the All-Star Movies, All-Star Music, and All-Star Sports resorts.

Each All-Star property has its own central check-in building, complete with food court, and its own pair of signature swimming pools. Each features ten guest buildings that are divided into five distinct (movies, music, or sports) themes and 1,920 thematically correct rooms.

Sports fans enjoy All-Star Sports resort's homages to basketball, baseball, football, tennis, and surfing. The All-Star Music resort makes exaggerated overtures to calypso, jazz, Broadway, rock, and country music. All-Star Movies reprises *101 Dalmatians*, *The Mighty Ducks*, *Fantasia*, *The Love Bug*, and *Toy Story*.

BIG DRAW: All the advantages of staying on WDW turf at a fraction of the cost of its other resorts.

WORTH NOTING: Requests for specific motifs cannot be guaranteed, but are likely to be met, considering the resorts' large capacity (384 rooms per theme, five themes per resort).

The rooms, which are the smallest of those at any WDW resort, are perfectly adequate, if a tad lacking in drawer space. Rooms with king-size beds are available on request, as are amenities such as down pillows and hair dryers.

On-site recreation is limited to two whimsically designed pools at each resort. Pizza delivery is available until midnight.

Where to eat: Each hotel has a vast, themed food court: All-Star Sports (End Zone); All-Star Music (Intermission); All-Star Movies (World Premiere).

Where to drink: At All-Star Sports: Team Spirits pool bar. At All-Star Music: Singing Spirits pool bar. At All-Star Movies: Silver Screen Spirits pool bar.

VITAL STATISTICS: The All-Star resorts are close to Animal

All-Star Resorts Tips

- These resorts attract families with small children in droves. All-Star Music tends to have a higher ratio of adults to children.

- For more quiet, request a third-floor room in a building away from the food court or main pool action (at All-Star Music, it's Broadway or country; at All-Star Sports, tennis or basketball; at All-Star Movies, The Love Bug or The Mighty Ducks).

- Reservations are required for luggage assistance upon check-out; call the night before.

- All-Star guests can rent boats at any of the other WDW resorts.

- Unless you plan to drive everywhere, request a room near the lobby (i.e., bus stop).

Kingdom and Blizzard Beach; Epcot and the Studios are also nearby. All-Star Movies; 1991 W. Buena Vista Dr.; Box 10000; Lake Buena Vista, FL 32830-1000; 407-939-7000; fax 407-939-7111. All-Star Music; 1801 W. Buena Vista Dr.; Box 10000; Lake Buena Vista, FL 32830-1000; 407-939-6000; fax 407-939-7222. All-Star Sports; 1701 W. Buena Vista Dr.; Box 10000; Lake Buena Vista, FL 32830-1000; 407-939-5000; fax 407-939-7333.

Rates: Rooms begin at $77 in value season, $99 regular, and $109 peak. A $10 per diem charge applies to each extra adult (beyond two) sharing a room.

Pop Century Resort

Open up a 20th-century time capsule and throw in a yo-yo, bowling pin, Rubik's Cube, cell phone, and other icons of the century's toys, fads, dance crazes, and classic and kooky catchphrases, and then turn it into a place for travelers to stay. That's Pop Century, one of the newest additions to Disney's family of value-priced resorts. (At press time, it was scheduled to open in December, 2003.) The 177-acre property is divided into two areas, the Legendary Years and the

Pop Century Resort Tips

• Pop Century boasts a whopping 5,760 rooms (more than twice as many as Caribbean Beach, the next largest resort), which should make reserving a room at the last minute easier.

• Want to be near a pool? Request a room in the 1950s, 1960s, or 1980s lodge buildings; they're adjacent to the Bowling Pin, Hippy Dippy Pool, and Computer pools, respectively. Keep in mind that all three pools are equally bustling.

• Don't miss the catch phrases made popular over the last few decades that line the roof of each guestroom building.

Classic Years, each representing five different eras in American popular culture. Pop Century is made distinctive by an intentionally garish decorative style and larger-than-life icons found throughout the landscape.

BIG DRAW: Like the All-Star resorts, Pop Century provides a

Disney resort experience at a fraction of the cost of resorts.

WORTH NOTING: The five buildings in the 2,880-room Classic Years—each with a theme based on a different decade from the 1950s through the 1990s—began hosting guests in late 2003. (The 2,880-room Legendary Years, covering the 1900s through the 1940s, will open at a later date.) Rooms (smaller than those at other Disney resorts) are available with two double- or one king-size bed, and hair dryers and other amenities can be requested.

For amusement, there are three pools to choose from, as well as an arcade for the young at heart. Pizza delivery is available.

Where to eat: There's a food court in Classic Hall and in Legendary Hall.

Where to drink: Hippy Dippy pool bar. Each serves a wide variety of fast food.

VITAL STATISTICS: The resort is located near Disney's Wide World of Sports complex. Pop

Century; 1050 Century Dr.; Box 10000; Lake Buena Vista, FL 32830-1000; 407-938-3000; fax 407-938-3005.

Rates: Rooms begin at $77 in value season, $99 regular, and $109 peak. A $10 per diem charge applies to each extra adult (beyond two) sharing a room.

Disney Cruise Line

The Disney Cruise Line fleet features two 2,400-passenger ships, each casually elegant and designed to recapture the majesty of early ocean liners. They're equipped to satisfy even the most savvy of cruisers, with a mix of traditional seafaring diversions and classic Disney touches. Recreation areas are designed to lure families and adults *sans* kids to different parts of the ship. Each ship has a pool, restaurant, and nighttime entertainment "district" earmarked for adults only.

Lest anyone forget who owns these vessels, Disney characters crop up from stem to stern. A statue of Mickey as helmsman greets arriving guests on the *Disney Magic* and a life-size statue of Goofy hangs over the stern. Characters are also on hand to mix, mingle, and otherwise assist the captain.

By day, fun in the sun alternates with lunch, indoor distractions, and catnaps. When the sun goes down, the focus shifts to dining and party spots.

Cruise Line land-sea vacations begin with a stay at WDW and finish with a voyage on the *Disney Wonder*. At Port Canaveral, guests embark on a three- or four-night cruise to the Bahamas. (Seven-night Caribbean cruises with Eastern and Western itineraries take place aboard the *Disney Magic*.) En route to Castaway Cay, Disney's private isle, the ships make a stop at Nassau.

BIG DRAWS: The ultimate surf-and-turf experience, Disney-style. Private island rendezvous.

Disney Cruise Line Tips

- Resort IDs can be used to charge drinks, merchandise, and salon services, as well as gratuities for servers and cabin crew.
- Palo, the adults-only dining room, is the only restaurant that requires reservations. Book it as soon as you're onboard.
- Unlike a visit to World Showcase, you really do leave the country on a Disney Cruise Line vacation. Pack a passport (or birth certificate).
- Surf the 'Net (for $.75 a minute) as well as the waves, at the ships' Internet cafes.

WORTH NOTING: Each room has a safe, TV, hair dryer, small refrigerator, and telephone with "land line" (check rates before dialing). Facilities include three pools, a sports deck, and the Vista Spa & Salon. The ship boasts adult-oriented enrichment programs, deck parties, and two theaters (showing first-run films and musical stage shows).

Where to eat: On the *Disney Magic*, Animator's Palate (room undergoes a spectral metamorphosis), Parrot Cay (casual Caribbean), Lumière's (continental, casually elegant), and Palo (Italian fare, reserved for adults). Topsider Buffet is a casual daytime spot. On the *Disney Wonder*, Triton's replaces Lumière's, and Beach Blanket Buffet replaces Topsider. Should you wish to avoid the inevitable crush of wee ones, request the second dinner seating.

Where to drink: On the *Disney Magic*, The Promenade Lounge (a quiet, elegant bar), ESPN Skybox (sports bar), Offbeat (dueling pianos), Rockin' Bar D (band and deejay), and Sessions (intimate piano bar). The *Disney Wonder* has Barrel of Laughs, WaveBands, and The Cadillac Lounge. Both ships have bars poolside.

Land Ho!

Each voyage on the Disney Cruise Line includes a day-long stop at Castaway Cay, Disney's charted yet private isle. With all the perks of a tropical paradise, an afternoon at Castaway Cay is sure to cure even the most severe cases of Gilligan envy. Disney has allowed the island to retain its natural beauty while accommodating a variety of activities, including volleyball, snorkeling, biking, and boating. The 1,000-acre Bahamian island features a mile-long stretch of secluded sand reserved for adult sun worshipers, as well as those seeking private open-air massages in cabanas overlooking the ocean. There's also a lunch buffet, bar, and more for Bahama mamas and papas to explore.

VITAL STATISTICS: Shipboard accommodations are about 25 percent roomier than cabins on most other ships. Most have a queen-size bed or two twin-size beds and a convertible sofa or pull-down bed. A majority are outside staterooms with a bath and a half; almost half have verandas.

Rates: Twelve stateroom categories correspond to comparable rooms at Disney resorts. Inside and ocean-view staterooms yield Moderate resorts; veranda staterooms net Deluxe resorts. Value rates for a seven-night, land-sea vacation begin at $829 per person, based on double occupancy.

Price includes stateroom and Walt Disney World resort accommodations, park admission, and shipboard meals and recreation. (Seven-night cruise-only packages also start at $829.)

Packages including airfare and ground transfers are available. Call 800-910-3659, or visit *www.disneycruise.com* for additional information.

Resorts on Hotel Plaza Boulevard

These resorts occupy a unique position among non-Disney resorts because they, along with four other hotels (Best Western Lake Buena Vista, Courtyard by Marriott, DoubleTree Guest Suites, and Grosvenor), are within the boundaries of WDW.

Guests have easy access to Disney golf courses, priority seating at select restaurants and dinner shows, and the opportunity to buy tickets for "E-ride" nights at the Magic Kingdom.

All the hotels have Disney gift shops, as well as ESPN, and a WDW information channel. They also sell park (and other) tickets, including the "E-Ride" pass, and provide free bus service to the Magic Kingdom, Epcot, the Studios, Animal Kingdom,

Typhoon Lagoon, Blizzard Beach, and Downtown Disney (allow extra time for bus travel). Note that the Hilton is the only resort on Hotel Plaza Blvd. that participates in the "Extra Magic Hour" program. (See page 79 for details.)

Rooms can be booked through the individual hotels or through WDW Central Reservations (407-934-7639).

Hilton

Set on 23 well-groomed acres, the 814-room Hilton has an air of laid-back gentility.

BIG DRAWS: Located across the road from the Downtown Disney Marketplace. Pool areas with adult appeal. Free transportation to all Disney golf courses.

WORTH NOTING: All guestrooms have mini-bars; corner rooms have balconies. There's a health club, two swimming pools, and two whirlpools, along with 24-hour room service. This is the only property on Hotel Plaza

Hilton Tips

- Rooms with the best views overlook the pools or the fountain at the hotel's entrance.
- For easy access to the pool, request a ground-floor room.

Boulevard to offer guests the "Extra Magic Hour" perk (see page 79).

Where to eat: Finn's Grill (Key West with steak and seafood dinners); Benihana Japanese steak house and sushi bar; Covington Mill (all-day dining in a cheery, New England setting); and Mainstreet Market (deli, ice cream counter, and country store).

Where to drink: Rum Largo Pool Bar & Cafe (tropical drinks); John T's Sports Bar; and Mugs (wine and coffee).

VITAL STATISTICS: Conveniently located just across the road from the Downtown Disney Marketplace. Hilton; 1751 Hotel Plaza Blvd.; Lake Buena Vista, FL 32830; 407-827-4000 or 800-782-4414; fax 407-827-3890; *www.hilton-wdwv.com.*

Rates: Rooms are $160 to $345, and suites are $359 to $1,500, depending on the season.

Royal Plaza

As accommodating as its pineapple motif intimates, the Royal Plaza is a cozy hotel with big adult appeal (the pineapple is a symbol of hospitality). Besides an outstanding pool area, there are four lighted tennis courts on the grounds of the resort.

BIG DRAWS: Nice pool area with large outdoor whirlpool and live music; adult ambience.

WORTH NOTING: The 394 rooms, including 22 suites, are divided between a 17-story tower and two-story wings. Each room has a sitting area, bath, safe, and mini-bar. Other amenities include a hair dryer, coffee-maker, and iron.
   Where to eat: Giraffe Grill; Marketessen (for snacks).
   Where to drink: Giraffe Grill and Sips (poolside bar).

VITAL STATISTICS: Located about a half mile from the Downtown Disney Marketplace. Royal Plaza; Box 22203; 1905 Hotel Plaza Blvd.; Lake Buena Vista, FL 32830; 407-828-2828 or 800-248-7890; fax 407-827-6338; *www.royalplaza.com.*
   Rates: Guestrooms are $109 to $179 for up to five guests; suites range from $209 to $699.

Royal Plaza Tips

• There are separate gamerooms for adults and for kids, and no one under 16 is allowed in the large fitness room.

• The enormous king rooms feature baths with separate glass-enclosed showers.

• The Burt Reynolds, Barbara Mandrell, and Bermuda suites are accessorized with pertinent memorabilia.

Wyndham Palace Resort & Spa

The largest of the resorts along Hotel Plaza Boulevard, the Wyndham Palace is a cluster of towers. The grounds are lushly landscaped, with shaded walkways. Inside, the decor is elegant. The reception area offers several cozy sitting nooks that invite lingering, and the Island Suite building has secluded courtyards. Many of the 1,014 rooms and suites have a private patio or balcony with a view of Spaceship Earth.

A Great Beach Add-on

A stay at Disney's Vero Beach Resort—an oceanfront Disney Vacation Club property just two hours away by car—combines nicely with a WDW vacation. The resort's homey comforts are similar to those at Disney's Old Key West Resort (see page 61).

Among its assets are pristine beaches and proximity to manatee retreats and sunken ships fit for dive trips (this is called the Treasure Coast, after all). A tropical tangle separates the resort and beach. Packages combining a Vero Beach trip with a WDW visit are available. For more information, call 800-359-8000.

BIG DRAWS: A European-style spa (see page 180); popular nightspots; and many recreational options. Close proximity to the Downtown Disney Marketplace.

WORTH NOTING: All guestrooms have ceiling fans, two phones (one bedside, one on the desk), voice mail, and 24-hour room service. Four rooms feature whirlpool tubs. One- and two-bedroom suites are available. There's a fitness center, a luxurious spa, a sand volleyball court, three pools, three lighted tennis courts, and two lakeside gazebos.

Where to eat: Arthur's 27 (rooftop restaurant with a continental menu); the Outback restaurant (specializing in fresh seafood and Black Angus beef; not part of the chain bearing the same name); Watercress Cafe and Pastry Shop (24-hour counter service, baked goods, and deli items); and the Courtyard Mini-Market (for assorted snacks and smoothies in a quiet outdoor setting).

Where to drink: The Laughing Kookaburra Good Time Bar (spirited spot known for live music); and Top of the Palace (quiet lounge with a stunning

Wyndham Palace Tips

- The Top of the Palace lounge provides a good view of Epcot's fireworks, serves desserts and many wines by the glass, and offers a free glass of champagne at sunset.
- Arthur's 27 rooftop restaurant is popular among visitors as well as Orlando residents.
- For the allergy-prone, 65 rooms feature filtered air and water.

view and live entertainment Wednesday through Saturday).

VITAL STATISTICS: The resort is located right across the road from the Downtown Disney Marketplace. Wyndham Palace Resort & Spa; 1900 Buena Vista Dr.; Lake Buena Vista, FL 32830; 407-827-2727 or 800-327-2990; fax 407-827-6034; *www.wyndhampalace.com.*

Rates: Room rates range from $129 to $269; rates for suites are $229 to $529.

"Extra Magic Hour"

On select days, one of the theme parks opens up an hour early for some special folks: guests staying at Walt Disney World resorts. This "Extra Magic Hour" perk extends to those staying at the Hilton, but not to the rest of the resorts on Hotel Plaza Blvd. For schedules and information (including which park offers the perk on which day), check with your hotel's front desk.

Spectacular fireworks come with the territory at Walt Disney World.

Theme Parks: The Big Four

To experience Walt Disney World's quartet of major theme parks without children is tantamount to celebrating a major holiday without the complication of traffic or in-laws. It's positively liberating.

Let the Magic Kingdom runneth over with strollers and too-tired toddlers. As adults free to roam the Magic Kingdom, Epcot, Disney-MGM Studios, and Animal Kingdom on our own terms, we need not be concerned with such things. We are a minority (read: non-school-age individuals under no obligation whatsoever to facilitate the entertainment of any maturity-challenged person within 47 square miles) in one of those rare settings in which the minority holds all the advantages.

If we sometimes feel a bit conspicuous touring the parks as unaccompanied adults, it's because we're flaunting the inherent freedom. We're taking advantage of the fact that we're among friends who readily agree that a shaded bench, a nap in a hammock, or a soak in the whirlpool back at the resort would really hit the spot right now. We are free to buzz through the Magic Kingdom at a clip no character-conscious family could maintain, or meander through Epcot's World Showcase pavilions at what might be called an escargot pace. All the while we're taking advantage of time-saving techniques like Disney's Fastpass, which allows walk-on access to several popular attractions in all four theme parks.

With a dizzying array of attractions to choose from, the task of mapping out an itinerary is a critical one. Fight the urge to see and do everything and craft a manageable list of must-sees. You're on vacation. It's a time to relax and have fun.

You may want to devote day one to the Magic Kingdom to get that long-anticipated dose of classic Disney magic. Then, with Cinderella's castle a delightful memory, you'll appreciate a day at Epcot on its own merits. Follow Epcot with a day at the Disney-MGM Studios. (Enchantment is a great chaser for enlightenment.)

If you're raring to go on safari or be chased by a dinosaur, spend your fourth day exploring Animal Kingdom. (This also happens to be the order in which the parks opened: Magic Kingdom, 1971; Epcot, 1982; Disney-MGM Studios, 1989; and Animal Kingdom, 1998.)

MAGIC KINGDOM

As once-upon-a-timish and happily-ever-afteresque a place as exists, the Magic Kingdom is proof that you can judge a park by its largest icon (in this case, Cinderella Castle). While it is the most character-intensive and certainly the strongest kid magnet of all the parks, flying elephants couldn't keep us away.

What puts the Magic Kingdom on the adult map? For starters, it's manageable. Most of the essentials here are easily traversed in a day. High on the list of imperatives is Disney's own mountain range—Space Mountain, Splash Mountain, and

Big Thunder Mountain Railroad—an undeniably thrilling threesome of rides.

What it lacks in fine cuisine and opportunities to imbibe, it more than makes up for in magic. Disney has made a real art of coaxing folks into a state of wonderment that seldom occurs in adulthood, and this park represents that art taken to its highest level. It's a rare adult who doesn't fall under the spell of the Magic Kingdom's ballroom of waltzing apparitions, or its convincing den of leering pirates. For nostalgic whimsy, there are kiddie rides such as Peter Pan's Flight that don't aspire to recapture the magic of childhood so much as to momentarily revive it.

The nighttime parade is also bound to reacquaint you with your inner child. This spectacle of fiber-optic delight showcases 600,000 miniature bulbs that light in wildly changing patterns, and move in perfect concert with sound effects and a musical score. The parade is absolutely illuminating.

Of course, a gazillion children can have a way of getting on anyone's nerves after a while, so some strategies are in order. First, master the art of noticing children only when they are being cute. To keep the "magic barometer" from falling, take advantage of less crowded evening hours, and weave in and out of major traffic zones (Fantasyland and Mickey's Toontown Fair are generally the most congested areas).

Seek refuge in the quiet nooks described in the margins of this chapter and in such havens as The Hall of Presidents; for a bigger break, indulge in a leisurely lunch at one of the resorts that are easily accessible via monorail.

Save Time in Line

Disney's FASTPASS

Want to waltz onto an attraction without waiting in line? By using Disney's Fastpass system—complimentary to guests holding all valid ticket media—at selected attractions in all four theme parks, you can do just that. How does it work? Slip your admission ticket into the machine. It will spit out your ticket along with a timed voucher. Come back at any point within the voucher's time frame and you'll bypass the long wait (aka "the stand-by line"). Consult the Touring Priorities in the margins of this chapter for a roster of Fastpass attractions, and check each park's guidemap for a current list of attractions that feature this time-saving service.

GETTING ORIENTED: Go through the turnstiles, pass an area with rental lockers, and you're in Town Square, the cul-de-sac at the foot of Main Street. From here look straight out to the park's most recognizable land-mark, Cinderella Castle. It's at the opposite end of Main Street, behind an area known as the Hub, or Central Plaza. On the left before the Hub is the main **Tip Board**, an information board listing current waiting times for the park's most popular attractions. (A second Tip Board in the Magic Kingdom can be found in Tomorrowland.)

It's helpful to think of the lay-out of the Magic Kingdom as a tree. Main Street, U.S.A., is the trunk; the other six themed areas—Adventureland, Fantasy-land, Frontierland, Liberty Square, Mickey's Toontown Fair, and Tomorrowland—dangle at the ends of the tree's gnarled boughs (actually bridges). The first bridge on your left leads to Adventureland; the second bridge to Liberty Square and Frontierland; the pathway straight ahead passes through Cinderella Castle on its way to the heart of Fantasyland; another bridge passes to the right of the castle to enter Fantasyland near-est Mickey's Toontown Fair and Tomorrowland; and the bridge on your immediate right leads directly to Tomorrowland. The lands are also linked via a broad footpath that winds its way behind the castle.

A Walking Tour

Let's begin our tour in **Town Square**, which is important as the location of **City Hall**, where a person can make all manner of inquiries and arrangements (no, you can't get married here). Even if you don't need to pick up a guidemap, make priority seating arrangements, exchange foreign currency, or check the lost and found, stop by to play Q&A with the informed folks behind the counter. Note that the local ATMs are under the train station, near the lockers.

The archway we walked under to get here is the foundation of

Magic Kingdom Hours

The Magic Kingdom is usually open from 9 A.M. to 7 P.M.; park hours are extended during holiday peri-ods and summer months.

Call 407-824-4321 or log onto *www.disneyworld.com* for details. One-day park admission is $53.25 for adults. Prices are subject to change.

the **Walt Disney World Railroad** depot. A 1928 steam engine that once carted sugarcane across the Yucatán now hauls freight (largely first-time visitors, train buffs, and homesick commuters) on a 20-minute loop around the Magic Kingdom. It's a fine way to get to Frontierland and Mickey's Toontown Fair if you don't want to walk. Onward.

Main Street, U.S.A.

Main Street is notable as the tidy strip of storefronts where adults gawk at, then feel compelled to photograph, Cinderella Castle. There's no shame in it; but don't be so distracted that you over-look the street's early 1900s charm. Amusements here are decidedly low-key. For grooming as entertainment, there's the Harmony Barber Shop (tucked in between the Emporium and the Horse Barn), where the Dapper Dans sometimes accompany a haircut. Definitely check out their sweet four-part harmonies. Main Street stays open a half hour after the rest of the park has closed, although the shops (see "Shopping" in the *Diversions* chapter) tend to be less crowded in early afternoon.

Tomorrowland

Futuristic in a way that would likely go right over Buck Rogers's head, Tomorrowland is a city of the future that never was. Because it's home base for one of the park's most popular attractions—Space Mountain—Tomorrowland is best visited first thing after the gates open.

Space Mountain, a must-do for all but those who categori-cally avoid the fast stuff, is one

Along for the E-Ride

Ever dream of roaming the Magic Kingdom after hours? Guests staying at Walt Disney World resorts can do just that, and with little company. On select E-Ride Nights (guests must have multi-day tickets which they used on the day of the E-Ride Night; call 407-824-4321 for details) you can tour the park for several hours after it closes to the public. Tickets cost about $13, and must be purchased at a WDW resort. The most popular attractions are open, and on our last visit, we practically had the park to ourselves.

to head for straightaway, as Fastpasses may run out before day's end. Once the stand-by line reaches outside this white structure at the far side of Tomorrowland, it doesn't generally ease up until evening. To gauge whether Space Mountain is for you, consider how you feel about roller coasters. This one rockets through a space-age sheath of darkness, shooting stars, and flashing lights. It's a fast and furious ride with special effects—an absolute must for the adventurous, and an unforgettable adventure for the suddenly courageous. Space Mountain is also a turbulent ride, so passengers must be in good health and free from heart conditions, back and neck problems, and other physical limitations (such as pregnancy), as the posted signs warn. If you've just eaten, wait awhile. If you decide you would rather observe the rockets' red glare going only seven miles per hour, the **Tomorrowland Transit Authority** offers a preview to Space Mountain and other attractions on a track that's strictly horizontal. The train is boarded in the heart of Tomorrowland near **Astro Orbiter** (an elevated ride with rockets that's primarily for kids but good fun for adults;

it seems to go faster the lower you fly in your Buck Rogers–mobile).

The scariest thing ever to hit the Magic Kingdom, **The Extra-TERRORestrial Alien Encounter** even has scary lines. It's not a motion ride but rather an intense 20-minute experience born of an interplanetary travel demo gone awry. You are seated in a dimly lit room when unsettling events begin to occur. A restraint is lowered over your shoulders. The chairman of the corporation volunteers to come to Earth, but an alien arrives in his place. There is an explosion. Suddenly, it is completely dark and you hear screams and groans, feel panting on the nape of your neck, and are sprayed with what in this context seems to be alien slime. The verdict: Special effects are the experience; this attraction is really more suspenseful and unsettling than terrifying; if you scare easily or are simply good at playing along, you'll get some chills up your spine.

Note: This attraction may be closed or operating under another name during your visit; check a park map or guest relations, or visit *www.disneyworld.com*.

Across the street is the Day-Glo adventure-zone known as **Buzz Lightyear's Space Ranger Spin**, (yes, grown-ups love it). Here *Toy Story*'s Mr. Infinity and Beyond solicit your assistance in cuffing the universe's most insidious battery hoarder. The 4½-minute journey is part video game, part shooting gallery, thanks to your spaceship's spin-control joystick and laser guns (how else to combat the likes of Rock'em Sock'em Robot?).

Heading north toward Fantasyland, you pass Space Mountain and come upon the rather low-octane **Tomorrow-land Indy Speedway**.

Mickey's Toontown Fair

This tiny blip between Tomorrow-land and Fantasyland is the park's newest land. When you visit the area with interactive environs akin to Disneyland's Toontown, you'll find an old-fashioned county fair in progress.

The cuteness is in the details (Mickey's ear-bearing crops, Minnie as the local craft queen). Don't miss your chance to tour the homes of Mickey and Minnie. At **Mickey's Country House**, take a peek in the kitchen

Touring Priorities

DON'T MISS	DON'T OVERLOOK	DON'T KNOCK YOURSELF OUT
Splash Mountain*	Walt Disney World Railroad	Cinderella's Golden Carrousel
Space Mountain*	Liberty Bell Riverboat	Swiss Family Treehouse
Big Thunder Mountain Railroad*	Mickey's Toontown Fair	Snow White's Scary Adventures
The Haunted Mansion*	Mad Tea Party	Dumbo the Flying Elephant
Pirates of the Caribbean	Tomorrowland Transit Authority	Tom Sawyer Island
Buzz Lightyear's Space Ranger Spin*	The Hall of Presidents	The Magic Carpets of Aladdin
It's a Small World	Tomorrowland Indy Speedway	*Fastpass attraction as of press time. Consult your guide map for new additions.
Peter Pan's Flight*	Country Bear Jamboree	
The Many Adventures of Winnie the Pooh	Astro Orbiter	
	The Enchanted Tiki Room— Under New Management	

but watch out—he's in the process of remodeling. Attractions are primarily for kids, but it's still fun to wander. For a one-stop character meeting, the **Toontown Hall of Fame** can't be beat. And if you're looking to take some baby steps before venturing onto Space Mountain, **The Barnstormer at Goofy's Wiseacre Farm** may be just your speed.

Fantasyland

The optimum way to take in this cheery land is to visit just before and during the daily 3 P.M. parade or in the evening when the parks are open late. Because there is nothing adult about Fantasyland—whimsy is the name of the game.

That said, certain attractions are so artfully executed that they transcend the kiddie genre. Of these, **It's a Small World**—a ten-minute boat ride through the happiest, busiest, and most diversely populated dollhouse on the planet—is surely the most elaborate.

Much more subtle is **Peter Pan's Flight**, an alluring sprinkle of pixie dust in which you can—and do—fly for three minutes above absolutely delightful scenes of Captain Hook and nighttime London in a pirate ship built for two.

The Magic Kingdom park's newest attraction, **Mickey's PhilharMagic**, brings many of your favorite characters to in-your-face life in a 3-D musical show starring Mickey and Donald, plus such other Disney favorites as Ariel (of *Little Mermaid* fame), Jasmine (from *Aladdin*), and Simba (direct from *The Lion King*)—all coming your way from a towering 150-foot-wide screen.

Then there are the purely nostalgic attractions, worth your time only if you're hankering to relive a certain story or amusement ride from your past. Have a thing for carousels in general or **Cinderella's Golden Carrousel** in particular? Go for it. Think you'd get a huge kick out of squeezing your group into an oversize teacup and spinning yourselves silly? Get to the **Mad Tea Party**. Don't skip **Dumbo the Flying Elephant** if you'll regret it later, but at the same time, don't expect to be wowed by a straightforward kiddie attraction such as **Snow White's Scary Adventures**. Although it has more happy moments than it did in the old days, the twisting journey still feels like a trip through a witch-filled fun house. **The Many Adventures of Winnie the Pooh** is a sweetly tempting honey jar of a journey through the Hundred Acre Wood.

Whatever you do, don't miss the gorgeous mosaic murals beneath the open archway of **Cinderella Castle**. No less than a million well-placed pieces of Italian glass tell the whole tale, ugly stepsisters, glass slipper, and all.

Liberty Square

Tucked between Fantasyland and Frontierland, this comparatively small area tends to be relatively peaceful. Brick and clapboard buildings carry the theme—Colonial America— as does the Liberty Tree, a 130-something oak tree hung with 13 lanterns to recall the original Colonies.

Though Liberty Square has just a few attractions, it still takes more than an hour to see them all. **The Hall of Presidents** merits attention not just as a well-delivered 20-minute dose of patriotism in which Abraham Lincoln speaks, but as a chance to observe all chief executives of our country in action. The shifting, swaying, and nodding (and snoozing) begins the moment the curtain rises on the impeccably dressed group of Audio-Animatronic figures. The pace is slow, but just right for an air-conditioned theater with comfy seats. Don't be intimidated if there is a big line—this is one *big* theater.

The Liberty Belle Riverboat —a large, romantic, paddle wheel-driven steamboat that makes 17-minute loops around Tom Sawyer Island — is a pleasant distraction, especially on a steamy afternoon. Don't ask what **The Haunted Mansion** is doing in Liberty Square. Just note that it's a not-to-be-missed experience overrun with clever special effects and ghoulish delights (your typical ballroom of waltzing ghosts, door knockers that knock by themselves, and spirited graveyards). On your way in, be sure to stop and read the epitaphs. They're killer funny.

Frontierland

This land conjures something of the Old West, with a little country charm—and even an ATM near the Diamond Horseshoe Saloon—thrown in for good measure. Although there's more to Frontierland than mountains, it is most notable as the home to two of the Magic Kingdom's most addictive thrills—Splash Mountain and Big Thunder Mountain Railroad.

The first thing to know about **Splash Mountain** is that it's okay to feel anxious just watching the log boats plunge down this ride's big drop—you're looking at one of the steepest flumes in the world (although it appears to be a straight drop, it's actually 52 feet down at a 45-degree angle). Even so, this water-bound ride themed to Disney's *Song of the South* is tamer than it looks from the ground. Steep plunge aside, there are just three smaller dips during the 11-minute trip.

If you're like us, the first time around you'll be way too nervous about when "it" is going to happen to fully appreciate the delightful humor, enormously appealing characters, and uplifting "Zip-A-Dee-Doo-Dah" ambience. But coax yourself into riding once and you'll be hooked. If you prefer to get splashed, not drenched, sit in the back and on the left of the log. Onlookers should note that a water cannon takes aim at the observation bridge without warning. A note on timing: Both Splash Mountain and Big Thunder Mountain Railroad tend to draw big crowds all day; your best bet is to shoot for early morning or evening.

Think of **Big Thunder Mountain Railroad** as a thrilling ride on the mild side. As roller coasters go, this one's exciting as much for the surrounding scenery your runaway mine train races past—bats, goats, a flooded mining town—as for

Quiet Nooks

- Rose garden on the right as you face Cinderella Castle
- Cinderella Wishing Well, near the castle
- Walt Disney World Railroad
- Harmony Barber Shop
- Shaded tables behind the shops in Liberty Square
- *Liberty Belle* Riverboat
- Rocking chairs on the front porches of Frontierland and Liberty Square shops
- Aunt Polly's Dockside Inn on Tom Sawyer Island
- Anywhere but Fantasyland and Toontown

the ride itself. Big Thunder Mountain Railroad is not nearly so fast or turbulent as Space Mountain, and nothing in its four-minute series of reverberating swoops and jerky turns comes close to Splash Mountain's intimidating plunge. For a bigger thrill, ride it after dark, when you can't clearly see what lies ahead, even from the first car. For the wildest of rides, request a seat near the back.

But Frontierland's appeal extends beyond its two high-profile attractions. The **Country Bear Jamboree**, a 16-minute musical variety show put on by 20 or so hopelessly corny Audio-Animatronic bears, is the perfect attraction to hit when you're feeling a little punchy. **Tom Sawyer Island**, just a short raft ride away, provides a nice break from the more structured parts of the park.

Adventureland

Adventureland has been transformed into the marketplace of *Aladdin*'s Agrabah. One part is **The Magic Carpets of Aladdin**, a Dumbo-style ride on which riders pilot mystical flying carpets. Among this land's other attractions are the immensely popular Pirates of the Caribbean and Jungle Cruise, best visited during the early morning and evening.

The Enchanted Tiki Room— Under New Management is worthy of a traffic-stopping

whistle. The nine-minute affair still showcases Disney's earliest Audio-Animatronic figures but adds plucky company to the chirping, chattering birds of yore. *Aladdin's* Iago and *The Lion King's* Zazu push the limits of caged-bird choreography.

Remember **Pirates of the Caribbean** as an elaborate, engaging, not-to-be-missed boat ride in which you watch pirates raid a Caribbean village. A classic attraction, it provides plenty of leering, jeering examples of how wonderfully, almost frighteningly realistic Disney's Audio-Animatronics can be. Note that the ten-minute Pirates of the Caribbean ride includes a small dip and some loud cannon blasts.

The **Jungle Cruise** is a classic attraction that transports passengers on a steamy ten-minute boat trip through the Nile Valley and the Amazon rain forest. Although the flora is quite beautiful, the lines for this ride can be prohibitively long, so consider using Fastpass to save some time. Finally, if you feel up to climbing some serious stairs, **Swiss Family Treehouse** is a replica of the Swiss Family Robinsons' ingenious perch that's worth the effort, even though the tree itself is a product of the prop department's imagination.

Entertainment

The character-laden floats in Disney's Share a Dream Come True parade take over Main Street daily at 3 P.M. The Dapper Dans often pop onto Main Street to serenade guests with four-part harmonies.

When the park is open late, the spectacular new fireworks show is presented on selected nights. The dazzling SpectroMagic light parade, which replaced The Main Street Electrical Parade, wends its luminous way down Main Street on select nights as well.

If there are two performances of the parade, the later one is often less crowded. Note that the evening parade is subject to change.

Check a park guidemap and times guide for the parade route and show schedules.

EPCOT

Think of Epcot as an extraordinary balancing act. This park is huge—about three times the size of the Magic Kingdom—and it performs two rather ambitious feats simultaneously. While the part of Epcot known as Future World offers a multifaceted look at what lies ahead for humankind, its alter ego, World Showcase, transports guests (at least in spirit) to many different countries. This division of labor works well, and it certainly keeps things interesting here. While the more serious-minded Future World is striving to spark the

Epcot Hours

Epcot's hours are staggered: Future World opens at about 9 A.M and closes at 7 P.M.; World Showcase comes to life around 11 A.M. and closes at 9 P.M.; Hours are extended during holidays and summer.

Visit *www.disneyworld.com* or call 407-824-4321 for details. One-day park admission is $53.25 for adults. Prices may change.

imagination, illuminate the technological future, and heighten environmental awareness, lively World Showcase is serving forth Oktoberfest, traditional English pub grub, and panoramic views of France, China, and Canada.

As Future World is ushering visitors into an ultramodern hydroponic greenhouse, World Showcase is escorting others along a calm river deep in the heart of Mexico and over a stormy Norwegian sea. Together, the two entities stimulate guests to discover new things about people, places, and, indeed, their own curiosity.

If Epcot boasts a tremendous following among legal voters, it's because it has more of the things adults appreciate: live entertainment; quiet gardens; beer, wine, and frozen drinks; tasteful shops and galleries; international cuisine; sophisticated restaurants;

and specialty coffees—and that's just the supplementary stuff. Epcot also woos the older crowd by making Mickey a little more scarce and by splicing enrichment of one form or another into the greater part of its amusements. It appeals to adults on a purely aesthetic level as well: World Showcase, wrapped around a vast lagoon, has a commanding natural and architectural beauty that changes with each border crossing. And Future World more than holds its own with the massive, gleaming silver geosphere of Spaceship Earth. Not surprisingly, we've met a number of Walt Disney World regulars who spend their entire vacations here at Epcot.

Epcot has its die-hard Future World fans and its World Showcase fanatics, but most visitors list favorite pavilions on both sides of the lagoon. Ongoing renovations and additions to Epcot make this especially true today. Disney imagineers have made smart changes

Entertainment

Epcot's entertainment slate is ever-changing. So pick up a times guide at Guest Relations (or elsewhere in the park) and check it often.

In Future World, acrobats and a trash-can percussive unit dressed in custodial wear are popular head-turners.

The Innoventions Fountain erupts into a computer-choreographed water ballet every 15 minutes.

In addition, each World Showcase pavilion has performers, any of whom could be appearing at some point during your visit. Among the possibilities: a rock 'n' roll band in Canada, a mop-top band paying tribute to the British Invasion in the United Kingdom, belly dancers in Morocco, drummers in Japan, oompah musicians in Germany, acrobats in China, and a mariachi band in Mexico. The American Adventure features the Voices of Liberty and American Vybe a cappella groups and stage shows at America Gardens Theatre.

Epcot's IllumiNations: Reflections of Earth all but sets fire to the senses in its dramatic, hypnotic simulation of our planet's evolution. This nightly finale starts off with a bang and ends on an even more explosive note. Stand anywhere along the promenade and prepare to be moved.

Keep in mind that the lineup of entertainment is ever-changing and may be altogether different when you visit Epcot.

in Epcot's entertainment mix that have lightened up Future World, livened up World Showcase, and in the process, earned the theme park a fresh crop of admirers—both young and old.

We'll describe the attractions later so that we can first present "The Official Six Things We Bet You Didn't Know You Could Do at Epcot" list:

(1) You can get some terrific gardening tips. (2) You can simultaneously break a sweat and split the 100th annual Rose Bowl Parade right down the middle. (Pedaling against the tide, and seemingly catching floats, bands, horses, and majorettes quite by surprise, we got a Wonder Cycle up to 15½ miles per hour.) (3) You can experience the British Invasion. Or at least think you did, when you hear this band playing Beatles tunes. (4) You can watch a butterfly open its wings for the first time. If you want, you can nibble on a freshly picked spearmint sprig while that beautiful orange-barred sulphur butterfly decides when to flee the hatching box. (5) You can send a picture postcard of yourself anywhere in the world via e-mail. (6) You can get an impromptu lesson in belly dancing from an obliging Moroccan dancer.

Hot Tips

- Not a morning person? Head to crowd-free World Showcase (opening around 11 A.M.) while everyone else is in Future World.
- Fight the urge to start at Spaceship Earth. The line thins out as the day wears on.
- Epcot is bigger than it seems, so allow yourself plenty of time to get from place to place—especially if you've already got priority seating arrangements at a World Showcase restaurant.

The most important thing to know about Epcot is that it is no small undertaking. Even the choosiest visitor will need two full days to cover the park effectively at a comfortable pace. Since Future World and World Showcase keep different hours, strategically minded guests will do well to follow our lead. In the name of efficiency, here's what we say: Take in a few key Future World pavilions during the hours before World Showcase opens. Explore World Showcase during the early afternoon, when Future World is most congested. Return to Future World to explore a few more pavilions during the relatively uncongested hours of late afternoon and early evening. Finally, revisit World Showcase during pleasant evening hours to experience the beauty of the park at twilight, as well as IllumiNations.

GETTING ORIENTED: It's helpful to think of Epcot as the park with the hourglass figure. In this conception, the gleaming silver ball of Spaceship Earth is the head and northernmost point; the other Future World pavilions, arranged on either side of Spaceship Earth in southward arches, form the outline of Epcot's "upper body"; and the promenade of World Showcase pavilions connects to Future World at Epcot's "waist" and, tracing the lines of a long, full skirt, wraps around World Showcase Lagoon. The American Adventure pavilion, located due south of Spaceship Earth along the bottom hem of the World Showcase skirt, effectively serves as the foot of Epcot.

Visitors should come prepared to do a great deal of walking, as the World Showcase Promenade itself is 1.2 miles around. Avid walkers and the health-conscious will be interested to know that a person typically covers more than two miles in one full day of touring Epcot. Don't be dismayed, though; Epcot is equipped with plenty of resting spots (see the margins of this section for tips to the whereabouts of said nooks), as well as a key foot-saving alternative. Water taxis link Showcase Plaza at the foot of Future World with Germany and Morocco, located at the farthest corners of World Showcase. Many seniors who choose to tour the smaller theme parks on foot rent a wheelchair or a self-driven Electric Convenience Vehicle (ECV) here at Epcot.

A Walking Tour

Our tour begins at the main entrance. This is where you take care of logistics while the gleaming ball of Spaceship Earth offers a 16-million-pound hint as to the precise direction of Future World. Epcot's monorail station is right outside the gates here, as is an ATM (located on the far left just before you enter the park). On the far right side of the entranceway, also outside the gates, you can exchange currency, make a phone call, and pick up any cumbersome purchases you arranged to have forwarded here during your visit.

Note: If you need to use any of these services mid-visit, have your hand stamped upon exiting the turnstiles so that you may re-enter the park. Lost and Found is in the Guest Relations lobby at Innoventions East. As you close in on the big ball, remember that there are still more services in its shadows. If you need a storage locker, pass around Spaceship Earth's right side. Otherwise, keep left. This course will lead you past the stroller and wheelchair rentals.

If you haven't made dining plans, stop by Guest Relations next to Spaceship Earth to make priority seating arrangements or hold your horses until you get to the eatery of your choice. Otherwise, focus on Innoventions Plaza, where you'll find the **Tip Board**, listing current waiting times for popular attractions.

Future World

You know you're in Future World when you see a thunderous fountain that acts like it owns the place, something resembling a remarkably oversize golf ball that would require a club bigger than the Empire State Building, kaleidoscopic fiber-optic patterns in the walkway, gardens that could pass for modern art, and freewheeling water fountains that do swan dives and geyser imitations.

This land is awash in the sort of grand music that might trumpet the credits of an Academy Award–winning film. And it wears its sleek architecture and futuristic landscaping like a power suit.

The nine themed pavilions that make up Future World document humanity's progress in this world and offer visions of our technological fate. Such major concerns as communications, health, and

Touring Priorities

DON'T MISS	DON'T OVERLOOK	DON'T KNOCK YOURSELF OUT
Living with the Land*	Innoventions	Food Rocks in The Land
Wonders of Life	Spaceship Earth	El Rio del Tiempo boat ride in Mexico
Test Track*	Journey Into Imagination with Figment	
Universe of Energy	China**	
The Living Seas	Mexico	* Fastpass attraction as of press time.
Honey, I Shrunk the Audience*	Italy	** Pay close attention to performance schedules.
France**	Morocco	
The American Adventure**	Germany	
Canada**	United Kingdom	
Maelstrom (in Norway)*	Circle of Life in The Land	
	Norway	

the environment serve as springboards for the attractions, which make stimulating experiences of topics that commonly make boring conversation.

If you haven't paid a visit here in the past few years, you'll notice that an ongoing tweaking spree has invigorated Future World. In fact, Test Track and the new Mission: SPACE pavilions put Epcot in a novel spot—atop the thrill seeker's list.

A reminder: This park tour is designed to provide a sense of place, not a recommended plan of attack. Future World pavilions are described here as you would encounter them geographically, beginning with Spaceship Earth.

Spaceship Earth

This 180-foot-tall "geosphere" sticks out like a wayward planet come to roost. You may be interested to learn that the silver exterior comes from layers of anodized aluminum and polyethylene, and is composed of 11,324 triangular panels, not all of equal size or shape (although it takes a keen eye to discern any differences). Or maybe you would rather hear the story of how the gleaming exterior funnels every raindrop that hits it into World Showcase Lagoon.

The **Spaceship Earth** ride inside the geosphere winds past exquisitely detailed three-dimensional scenes, tracing the evolution of human communication using Audio-Animatronic figures that here, in their element, seem more natural than many sitcom actors. In about 14 minutes you've gone from Cro-Magnon grunts all the way to the fabled information superhighway. Narration by Jeremy Irons adds an element of drama.

The finale provides a forward-looking finish for Spaceship Earth. Take away the lasers and it would still be the ride's biggest head-turner. This popular attraction—your worst bet first thing in the morning—is least crowded during the hours just prior to park closing.

Innoventions

Think of the latest incarnation of Innoventions as a trip down future lane. Disney recast this showcase of technological goodies as entertaining rest stops and scenery along a very important piece of pavement: The Road to Tomorrow. When it comes to this

traffic on this engaging excuse for a freeway, pedestrians—and the occasional electric car—rule the road.

If The Road to Tomorrow is frequently congested, it's because Innoventions is a bright labyrinth of activity that hot rods and Sunday drivers alike find difficult to pass through quickly. Well-marked exits ensure that you won't miss a single turnoff (hands-on exhibit), even if you're looking at your handy, dandy road map upside down. That's right, there's a road map.

The Living Seas

The Caribbean is not as far away as you think. If you want to catch a wave, some mammoth lettuce-munching manatees, and a richly stocked coral reef environment (pop.: 2,000) that even a scuba diver would find extraordinary, look no further. This pavilion, dedicated to the study of oceanography and ocean ecology, ranks among Epcot's most inspired areas. During the toasty summer months, it's particularly refreshing to ogle The Living Seas' *pièce de résistance*, a 5.7-million-gallon tank in which a simulated Caribbean Sea and man-made reef support a glorious array of life, including sharks, dolphins, sea turtles, rays, and crustaceans.

There are two paths to this not-to-be-missed underwater vista, where in addition to colorful sea life you can observe one-person submarines and divers conducting marine experiments. If you're certified in scuba diving or want a little Dolphin 101, take the behind-the-scenes route. To immerse yourself thoroughly without getting wet, take a make-believe voyage to the bottom of the sea at the **Caribbean Coral Reef**. This journey features a waterlogged film that takes you

on a simulated descent to the ocean floor, and, finally, to the **Sea Base Alpha**. Here, you can linger all you like in front of enormous eight-inch-thick windows to the undersea world (be on the lookout for moray eels, sea turtles, sharks, and puffers). Exhibits offer insight into marine research methods, additional display tanks, and—unless you encounter those endangered, impossibly animated sea barges known as manatees frequently in your travels—compelling reasons to stick around awhile.

Of course, no seafaring adventure is complete without the opportunity to shout "Land ho!" so it's only right that The Land is the next pavilion.

The Land

This popular six-acre plot explores themes related to food and farming while planting seeds of environmental consciousness.

Underneath this pavilion's dramatic skylighted roof, you'll find a well-balanced slate of attractions, a bountiful food court, and a lazy Susan of a restaurant, the Garden Grill, which rotates very slowly past several of the ecosystems featured in the pavilion's boat ride. All things considered, The Land merits two green thumbs up as the purveyor of one of Future World's strongest lineups.

The **Living with the Land** boat ride is an informative 13½-minute journey that escorts you through a stormy prairie, a windswept desert, and a South American rain forest en route to experimental greenhouses and an

area given over to fish farming. The dripping, squawking rain forest is so realistic, you'd need to chomp on a faux fern to convince yourself it's all plastic. The narration is an interesting commentary on the history and future of agriculture. The greenhouses show futuristic technology at work on real crops (many of which are served right here at Epcot), with NASA experiments and cucumbers in desert training among the high-lights. This popular attraction is best visited in the morning or during the hours just prior to park closing. If you're an avid gardener or Living with the Land has you intrigued, we recommend **Behind The Seeds** (for details on this behind-the-scenes tour, see page 102).

The Circle of Life is an eco-logical fable featuring Timon and Pumbaa, the wisenheimer meerkat-warthog duo from *The Lion King*, as developers, and Simba as the environmentally sensitive lion. The 20-minute film includes stunning nature footage.

If you have time, you might want to take in **Food Rocks**, a silly musical tribute to good nutrition. This 15-minute concert performed by Audio-Animatronic

---

A Healthy Crop

If you're eating your vegetables (and fruits) at the Garden Grill, Coral Reef, or Sunshine Season Food Fair, odds are good that you're sharing in The Land pavil-ion's bounty. Some 30 tons of pro-duce are harvested each year from The Land's greenhouses. Talk about fresh local ingredients!

---

lip-synchers is Disney showing its sense of humor. Among the reasons you'll be a groupie: Pita Gabriel singing, "I wanna be your high fiber," and The Refrigerator Police's arresting refrain, "Every bite you take, every egg you break" (guess who is a milk carton with dark sun-glasses?). It's usually possible to get into the next show.

Imagination!

While you'd think that glass buildings would leave very little to the imagination, the glass pyramids that house the Imagi-nation! pavilion have quite the opposite effect. If necessity is truly the mother of invention, then this is where she resides, playing with minds as if they were Play-Doh. Fronted by foun-tains that seem to have agendas of their own, this pavilion is one of Epcot's more whimsical.

Ever-curious about what it feels like to be an inventor with those little lightbulbs always appearing above your head, you enter the **Journey Into Imagination with Figment** attraction and discover that you have stumbled upon an open house hosted by the Imagination Institute.

This attraction features the antics of a character named Figment. The little purple dragon is here to teach you a few secrets about capturing the imagination.

Before you can fasten your thinking cap, you've become a test subject for a project called the Imagination Scanner. During your visit, you're put through a series of illusory experiments

Future World Unplugged

For a close-up look at Future World, check out:

- **Behind The Seeds:** One-hour greenhouse tours at The Land ($6; Epcot admission required) cover much the same terrain as the Living with the Land boat ride, but more intimately. Tours are offered throughout the day. For information or to book in advance, call 407-WDW-TOUR (939-8687).

- **Epcot Seas Aqua Tour:** Non-scuba divers can use snorkel equipment at The Living Seas in this 2½-hour tour ($100) of the Disney version of the deep.

- **DiveQuest:** This 2½-hour program ($140) invites certified scuba divers to a dive in The Living Seas aquarium. For information call 407-WDW-TOUR (939-8687).

- **Dolphins in Depth:** A bit more ($150) buys you a 3-hour introduction to dolphin research and conservation, 30 minutes in the water with the dolphins at The Living Seas, and a videotape to prove it. Call 407-WDW-TOUR (939-8687) for details.

designed to spark your imagination. Afterward, stop by **Image-Works**, an interactive area meant to stimulate sensory skills.

But the attraction at the Imagination! pavilion that earns the most exuberant high five is **Honey, I Shrunk the Audience**. If you have time to visit only a few attractions at Epcot, this spectacle of a 3-D movie should be high on your list. The 25-minute film is so riddled with effects that the audience is consistently reduced to a squirming, giggling mass. The experience is not rough, but the effects are heightened with a bit of suspense, so we'll say no more. Crowds are smallest early in the morning and late in the evening.

Test Track

Behind this pavilion's steely doors lies the fastest ride at Walt Disney World. In this supercharged introduction to the world of automobile testing, the ride's computer-controlled vehicles barrel up steep hills, zip down straightaways, squeak around heavily banked hairpin turns, and slam on the brakes. Test Track is much more than a thrilling ride: It's a realistic runthrough of tests performed on real cars at real facilities, known as proving grounds.

As you walk through the plant you see everything from the all-important seat-squirming test to the crucial trials endured by air bags, tires, and the human interface clan (our courageous crash-prone counterparts) to ensure our safety. Then you hop into a six-person vehicle, fasten your seat belt, and—making note that you've got a video display, but no steering wheel or brake pedal—prepare for an exciting five-minute road trip. As the sporty open-top cars traverse the nearly one-mile track, you experience a rough-and-tumble suspension workout, become seriously indebted to antilock brakes, narrowly avoid a crash, and whiz outside and around the pavilion at speeds up to 65 miles per hour. Incredible insight into cars is a given; you'll also gain respect for the complex systems contained therein. On the way out, be sure to stop and check out the smarty-pants car demo and the "Inside Track," which features gear for car buffs.

Test Track is an altogether different experience by day and by night (you can guess which is more intense). If it's raining, we suggest you turn your face to the sky and ask yourself this question: Would I enjoy zooming down a highway in a convertible with the top down right about now?

For the least intimidating crowds, grab a Fastpass or try to visit in the evening while everyone else is viewing IllumiNations. **Note:** Since this is something of a rough attraction, riders must be free from heart conditions, back and neck problems, and other physical limitations.

Mission: SPACE

Three . . . two . . . one . . . lift-off! Words you only expect to hear from flight control at Cape Canaveral are now part of the ever-expanding magical lexicon at Walt Disney World. Mission: SPACE is Epcot's newest attraction. Its mission? To train guests—provided they be free of motion sickness and/or claustrophobic tendencies—to be astronauts.

In lieu of an actual blastoff, guests are shot into orbit via a motion simulator—not unlike the ones real astronauts use. Former NASA advisers and astronauts worked with Disney Imagineers to lend more than a bit of authenticity to this thrill ride.

Wonders of Life

While the 72-foot-tall-steel DNA molecule certainly marks the territory of this mostly whimsical pavilion devoted to health and fitness concerns, the sculpture also provides a visual reminder of the uniqueness of Future World.

First, the pavilion's main attraction: **Body Wars**, a frenetic five-minute trip through the human body in a flight simulator. This ride could be the fraternal twin of Star Tours, the rocky ride through space located at the Disney-MGM Studios, but for a couple of things. It is a few months older

and a few notches rougher than its Studios counterpart. The premise of Body Wars is that you are along for the ride on a routine medical probe to remove

Hidden Mickey

If you look very, very closely, you can spot Mickey in the mural above the entrance to Body Wars at the Wonders of Life pavilion.

a splinter (from the inside) when things get out of hand. Before you know it, you're barreling through regions such as the human lungs, heart, and brain. Body Wars is a tremendously exciting journey, both visually and physically, that rates among Epcot's biggest thrills, but it is also a turbulent ride with a lot of very herky-jerky movements.

Note that if you're especially squeamish, you may find the visual content to be too much in this context. In addition, you should not venture onto this ride if you are pregnant. You should also bypass Body Wars if you've eaten recently, have a back problem or heart condition, are susceptible to motion sickness, or have any other physical limitations. Note that this is a popular attraction. It tends to be the least

congested early in the morning, and in the hours just prior to Future World's closing.

Another Wonders of Life attraction that merits not-to-be-missed status is **Cranium Command**, an utterly tame, utterly delightful 17-minute journey into the mind of a 12-year-old boy. This is an attraction so good, Billy Crystal would have a tough time making it funnier. Here's the setup: The commander of a specialized corps of brain pilots is issuing assignments, and our pal Buzzy must pilot an adolescent boy. The show follows a day in this boy's life, with Buzzy calling the shots. Celebrity cameos include George Wendt (Norm from *Cheers*) manning the stomach, Dana Carvey and Kevin Nealon (playing Hans and Franz of *Saturday Night Live* fame) as the heart, and comedian Bobcat Goldthwait as the adrenal gland.

For some more mind-bending fun, explore the challenges of the Sensory Funhouse, located just outside Cranium Command. And don't neglect the Wonder Cycles, computerized stationary bicycles that let you pedal (headlong into traffic) through the Rose Bowl Parade and Disneyland. Hey, when will that opportunity present itself again?

Universe of Energy

Behind this mirrored facade lies a pavilion on a serious power trip (it draws some of its electricity from photovoltaic cells mounted on the roof). Universe of Energy has always been notable for its lifelike dinosaurs, some of Walt Disney World's largest Audio-Animatronic animals. But the show here also boasts some familiar faces and fetches a few nominations for Best Comedy in an Epcot Pavilion.

The pavilion is given over entirely to a 45-minute presentation that explores the origins of fossil fuels and muses about alternative energy sources. **Ellen's Energy Adventure** is powered by Ellen's sudden yen for knowledge about such things—largely so that she can beat her know-it-all former college roommate Judy (a face you'll likely recognize) when they land on a game show together.

Bill Nye, the Science Guy, offers to educate a befuddled Ellen, and just happens to have some rather extensive visual aids handy. As Bill lectures Ellen, arresting visuals are shown on a series of huge screens. (Keep your eyes peeled for a cameo by a caveman you'd swear was a famous sitcom actor.)

When Bill insists they travel back 220 million years to seek greater knowledge, the seating area rotates and splits into six vehicles that then move into the clammy air of the primeval world. Here, you encounter erupting volcanoes, an eerie fog, and prehistoric creatures locked in combat, rearing up suddenly from a tide pool, and gazing down at you like vultures. You also come upon an Audio-Animatronic Ellen, desperately attempting to reason with a creepy, snakelike dinosaur. She makes it out of the forest in one piece, and happily hits the big time on her game show, if only in her dreams.

This pavilion is best visited in the late afternoon. A large group is let into the theater every 17 minutes, so don't let a crowd scare you. If the line extends beyond the marquee, try again later.

Leave Future World by walking through Innoventions Plaza. As you head to World Showcase, be sure to look to each side. On the right, you'll pass an ATM near a spontaneously erupting fountain delivering a merciless soaking (mostly to children). Down on the left, you'll spot what appears to be an ancient pyramid. Welcome to the flip side of Future World!

World Showcase

Think of World Showcase as a handful of gourmet jelly beans, the sort so flavorful, they make your taste buds believe you're actually putting away strawberry cheesecake, champagne punch, and chocolate pudding. You know they're just jelly beans, of course, but you pretend, fully savoring the essence of that piña colada.

In the same way, World Showcase cajoles your senses into accepting its international pavilions at face value, enveloping you in such delectable representations of Germany, Japan, Mexico, and more, that you are content to play along.

This parade of nations, a cultural thoroughfare wrapped around a lagoon the size of 85 football fields, is marked by dramatic mood swings. The atmosphere changes markedly with each border crossing, going from positively romantic to utterly serene, toe-tappingly upbeat, patriotic, festive, wistfully Old World, or cheerfully relaxed in a matter of yards.

Of course, the World Showcase pavilions are not simply outstanding mood pieces but occasions to get uniquely acquainted with the people, history, and beauty of the world's nations. Each pavilion has a strong, unmistakable sense of place that announces itself with painstakingly re-created landmarks and faithful landscaping that ensures bougainvillea in Mexico and lotus blossoms in China. Each contributes culinary specialties from the apple-tart-to-ice-cream smorgasbord that makes World Showcase one of the hottest meal tickets in Walt Disney World.

To transport yourself totally, try to supplement the smattering of attractions—panoramic films,

Quiet Nooks

Parts of Epcot boast an energy that interrupt the calm you might crave; here are some of our favorite quiet spots.

- Fountain View Espresso and Bakery in Future World
- Plaza de los Amigos inside Mexico's pyramid
- Stave Church Gallery in Norway
- Benches near the reflecting pools in China
- Lagoonside benches near the gondola in Italy
- Garden alongside The American Adventure
- Bijutsu-kan Gallery, hillside gardens, and Matsu No Ma in Japan
- Tucked-away garden with benches in France
- Gardens at rear of United Kingdom pavilion and Rose & Crown Pub
- Waterfall and mountain setting in Canada

theater and dinner shows, boat rides, and the nightly not-to-be-missed fireworks extravaganza—with the legions of less structured pursuits.

Start by trying to catch at least one street performance per country. So frequent it's practically ongoing (check your guidemap for exact times), this feast of live entertainment encompasses everything from mariachi bands to acrobats and belly dancing, and it makes a great accompaniment to a mobile wine tasting. Take time, too, to chitchat with the "locals" in each village (nearly all of whom claim the represented country as their homeland).

To personalize your journey even more, make a mission of snacking, drinking, shopping, gallery-hopping, or even bench-warming your way around the World. For adults, these relaxing activities are the very essence of a visit to World Showcase.

Structurally, World Showcase is perhaps the most user-friendly area of Walt Disney World's theme parks. You may get tired walking along the 1.2-mile promenade that leads past all pavilions as it encircles the lagoon, but you won't lose your sense of direction. While locations of countries here don't correspond at all to their placement on the planet, the landscape offers a wealth of Eiffel Tower-like clues that *almost* preclude the use of a map. Because World Showcase focuses less on attractions (6 of the 11 pavilions have no attractions, per se), it requires less strategic maneuvering.

If World Showcase came with instructions, the handy booklet might say:

- Touring is a clockwise or counterclockwise proposition best begun on an empty stomach.
- Shops are optimally saved for the afternoon, when the throngs from Future World have descended, lengthening lines for movies, rides, and shows.
- The movies at Canada, France, and China are often better appreciated when spaced out over two days.
- IllumiNations is the biggest entertainment draw in all of Epcot. The nightly spectacle of fireworks, lasers, and music is visible from most any point around World Showcase.

Moving along, this Epcot tour describes pavilions in the order they're encountered when entering World Showcase from Future World and walking counterclockwise around the lagoon.

Canada

In a marked departure from the real world, a refreshment stand poised a good 50 yards before the border makes it possible to arrive in Canada with a cup of Moosehead in hand. This pavilion is the site of an outstanding panoramic film, an "underground" steak house, interesting shops, and the coolest spot in World Showcase. It covers an impressive amount of territory in its bid to capture the distinctive beauty and cultural diversity of

International Gateway

Think of this second entrance as Epcot's back door. The turnstiles here provide a direct "in" to World Showcase, depositing guests between the France and United Kingdom pavilions. Because the International Gateway is connected via walkway to the Yacht and Beach Club, BoardWalk, Swan, and Dolphin resorts, guests at these lodgings have exceptional access to Epcot. (Water launches also make the trip.) Note that:

- Wheelchairs are available for rent at this entrance.

- Nothing in World Showcase opens until about 11 A.M., so guests arriving earlier must walk to Future World at the far end of the park.

- You can make a quick exit from here after IllumiNations.

the Western Hemisphere's largest nation. An artful ode to the Indians of Canada's Northwest (towering totem poles and a trading post) leads to an architectural tribute to French Canada (the Hôtel du Canada here is a hybrid of Ottawa's Château Laurier and Quebec's Château Frontenac).

From here, follow the sounds of rushing water to find the cooling sprays of a miniaturized Niagara Falls that's tucked neatly into the face of a Canadian Rocky and usually blessed with a rainbow. A feature film, a visual anthem of sorts appropriately called **O Canada!**, is shown in all its Circle-Vision 360 glory within the mountain itself.

The 17-minute standing-room-only movie places you in the middle of most things Canadian, including a hockey game, enormous reindeer herds, and the Royal Canadian Mounted Police.

As you leave, check out the bountiful greenery inspired by the famous Butchart Gardens, in Victoria, British Columbia—while not as cool as the falls, they're still a great place to claim a bench, especially when the Pipes of Nova Scotia or the Off Kilter troupe of Celtic rock musicians is performing.

United Kingdom

This cheery neighborhood, which reveals its cultural identity via the bright-red phone booths dotting its cobblestoned streets, is a fine place for a bit of shopping or a pint of ale. What's less obvious: the herb garden tucked behind the thatched-roof cottage (note the spearmint plants); the butterfly hatchery on the hill; and the courtyard at the rear of the pavilion, where you'll find a traditional English hedge maze. You may even catch a decidedly Beatlesque rock group that

Tired of Walking?

The *FriendShip* water taxis link Showcase Plaza at the foot of Future World with Germany and Morocco, across the lagoon at the farthest corners of World Showcase. It's convenient—but keep in mind that it may be quicker to walk.

performs in the garden. A table at the Rose & Crown Pub is the best perspective from which to view this pavilion, because the Tudor, Georgian, and Victorian struc-tures seem all the more real from the window of a friendly pub.

Architectural enlightenment is a great excuse to dally in the fine shops. You can cover 300 years of building styles just by walking from the slate floor of The Tea Caddy straight through to the carpeted room with the Waterford crystal chandelier, which signals your arrival at the Neoclassical period and the shop known as The Queen's Table.

France

A footbridge from the United Kingdom leads across a pictur-esque canal to one of the most romantic areas of World Showcase. Petite streets and Eiffel Tower aside, you're look-ing at Paris during the Belle Epoque ("beautiful age") of the late 19th century.

The one-time Parisian institu-tion Les Halles is re-created here, as is a one-tenth-scale Eiffel Tower that would be infi-nitely more evocative were it not so obviously perched atop a building. Luxurious boutiques, sidewalk cafes, and, of course,

---

For the Lovebirds. . .

Epcot's World Showcase has some great romantic spots, namely:

- El Río del Tiempo boat ride and the San Angel Inn in Mexico
- The lovely courtyard at the rear of the United Kingdom
- Italy's piazza and gondola landing
- Every inch of France

---

pastries that announce their pres-ence *par avion* are among the big draws here, as is the wine-tasting counter at the nicely stocked La Maison du Vin. Beckoning, too, is one of the most peaceful spots in all of Epcot—a quiet park on the canal side of the pavilion that might have leapt off the canvas of Georges Seurat's *Sunday Afternoon on the Island of La Grande Jatte.*

But the biggest lure here is the 18-minute film **Impressions de France,** which puts its five 21-by 27-foot screens to terrific use in a *tour de France* that ranges from Alpine skiing to foothills of buttery pastries. If you know France, you'll love it; if you aren't familiar with the country, you'll want to be. The superb score, featuring French classical composers, could stand on its own. *Impressions de France* is least congested during the morn-ing and early-evening hours.

Morocco

This enchanting area—arguably the most meticulously crafted of all the represented nations—also happens to be the loudest World Showcase pavilion. The authenticity has something to do with the fact that nine tons of tile were handmade, hand-cut, and hand-laid by Moroccan artisans into the mosaics seen here. The prayer tower at the entrance takes after the famous Koutoubia Minaret, in Marrakesh. The Bab Boujouloud gate, patterned after one in the city of Fez, leads to the Medina (old part of the city), a tangled array of narrow passageways where baskets, leather goods, and brass items are among the wares for sale.

The Medina also brings you to the entrance of the Marrakesh restaurant, notable for its North African menu, its belly dancers, and the fact that it's one of the only full-service restaurants in World Showcase where you can often get a table without priority seating. You can also savor Mediterranean-style chicken, beef, and lamb sandwiches, salads, and desserts at the more casual Tangierine Cafe.

Stop at Mo' Rockin' for Arabic rhythms with a contemporary flair. Make a point of checking out the extraordinary tile work and costumes displayed at the Gallery of Arts and History, and be on the lookout for visiting artisans demonstrating their crafts.

It's interesting to note that the gardens are irrigated by an ancient working waterwheel located on the promenade. Morocco is easily toured any time of day. If you'd like a more structured look at the pavilion, sign up for a guided tour at the Morocco National Tourist Office inside. The complimentary tours last from 20 to 40 minutes and are available at 1, 3, and 5 P.M.

Where the Art Is

Exhibits change periodically, but here's an indication of what you can expect to see:

- Mexico's "Reign of Glory" exhibit features pre-Columbian pieces (some are on loan from the Smithsonian).

- Norway's tiny Stave Church Gallery holds exhibits documenting the once-common churches.

- Japan's Bijutsu-kan Gallery becomes a baseball museum with "Diamond Warriors: Traditions and Japanese Baseball."

- Morocco's Gallery of Arts and History showcases intricate tile work and costumes.

- China's House of Whispering Willows displays ancient Chinese art and artifacts.

Japan

As quietly inviting as Morocco is vibrantly enticing, Japan is a pavilion of considerable beauty and serenity. Its most prominent landmarks are the red torii gate (a good-luck symbol), which stands close to the lagoon, and the five-tiered pagoda, created in the mold of an eighth-century shrine located in Nara. Each level of the pagoda represents one of the elements that, according to Buddhist teachings, produced everything in the universe (from bottom to top: earth, water, fire, wind, and sky).

The most compelling features of this pavilion are the entertainment (Matsuriza drummers), the elaborate detail of its manicured gardens, and the art exhibit "Diamond Warriors: Traditions and Japanese Baseball" at the Bijutsu-kan Gallery.

Japan also claims one of the largest shops in Epcot. Housed

inside a structure reminiscent of a section of the Gosho Imperial Palace, which was originally constructed in Kyoto in 794 A.D., the Mitsukoshi Department Store counts bonsai trees, kimonos, dolls, tea sets, incense, jewelry, and decorative ceremonial swords among its offerings.

All that shopping may spark your appetite. At Teppanyaki Dining Rooms, a feast consisting of vegetables, steak, chicken, and seafood is prepared tableside by authentic Japanese chefs. This pavilion is easily toured any time of day.

The American Adventure

The centerpiece pavilion of World Showcase is so devoted to Americana, it can bring out the Norman Rockwell in you even when you're cranky. Housed in a Colonial-style manse that combines elements of Independence Hall, the Old State House in Boston, Monticello, and various structures in Colonial Williamsburg, it's dressed for the part.

The 26-minute show inside—an evocative multimedia presentation about American history—is among Disney's best, both for its astonishingly detailed sets and sophisticated Audio-Animatronic figures and for its ability to rouse goose bumps from unsuspecting patriots. Ben Franklin and Mark Twain lead what's been called "a hundred-yard dash capturing the spirit of the country at specific moments in time."

Two superb a cappella vocal groups, the Voices of Liberty and American Vybe, sometimes entertain in the lobby before the show begins.

The wait for The American Adventure attraction can be long because the show itself is lengthy, so check a times guide or stop by for curtain times and plan accordingly. It's definitely worth the effort.

This patriotic pavilion also features an All-American fast-food restaurant and the lagoonside **America Gardens Theatre**, where you just may find some rousing entertainment. An interesting aside: The garden alongside The American Adventure pavilion acknowledges the days before red, white, and blue by showcasing different plants used traditionally by Native Americans for food and medicinal purposes.

Italy

This little Italy is defined by an abiding you-are-there ambience and meticulous authenticity that extends from the gondolas tied to striped moorings at the pavilion's very own Venetian island to the homemade (before your very eyes) fettuccine and spaghetti at its popular L'Originale Alfredo di Roma Ristorante.

Look to the very top of the scaled-down Venetian campanile dominating the romantic piazza here, and you'll see an angel covered in gold leaf that was molded into a spitting image of the one atop the bell tower in the real St. Mark's Square, in Venice.

The Doge's Palace here is so faithfully rendered that its facade resembles the marbled pattern of the original. Adding to the effect are tall, slender stands of Italian cypress, replicas of Venetian statues, an abundance of potted flowers, and fragrant olive and citrus trees.

This Italy pavilion has no major attractions per se, but between its memorable street performers and the strolling musicians who play during dinner at Alfredo's, it has all the entertainment it needs.

Among the various shopping options is a gem of a gourmet food purveyor, called La Bottega Italiana, that also stocks fine Italian wines.

Germany

In a word: *oompah*. Arguably the most festive country in all of World Showcase, Germany is immediately recognizable by its fairy-tale architecture. To the rear of the central cobblestoned square (which is named for Saint George), you'll see an enormous cuckoo clock, complete with Hummel figurines that emerge on the hour. Immediately past this clock lies the Biergarten, the vast restaurant and entertainment hall that—thanks to spirited dinner shows primed with German beer, sausages, and yodelers— serves as the pinnacle of this festive pavilion's entertainment.

Germany also scores with tempting shops, and the Weinkeller, which offers wine-

tasting opportunities. In Glas und Porzellan, it's usually possible to watch a Goebel artist demonstrating the elaborate process by which Hummel figurines are created. Outside, note the miniature 1930s German village, complete with castle, farmhouse, monastery, and even a wee commuter railroad. Germany is easily toured at any time of day.

China

This pavilion is marked by a dramatic half-scale replica of Beijing's Temple of Heaven set behind stands of whistling bamboo and quiet reflecting pools. Traditional Chinese music wafts over the sound system. In addition to its gardens, the pavilion features the House of Whispering Willows, an exhibit of ancient art and artifacts from well-known collections that's always worth a look. Live entertainment here is invariably stirring, especially when it's a demonstration by the local acrobats.

But the main reason to visit China is the new Circle-Vision 360 film shown in the Temple of Heaven. Basically, you stand, and *Reflections of China* whisks you on a 19-minute, blink-and-you've-missed-the-Great Wall journey that reflects the ways in which China has changed over the past 20 years—with the addition of Hong Kong and Macau. From ancient Mongolia and Beijing's Forbidden City to ultramodern Shanghai, the film provides the most fascinating glimpses of China and its people. Pay special attention to the fleeting mist-enshrouded Huangshan Mountain, if you can; the filming of this amazing view of China was no small endeavor: the film crew and 40 laborers had to haul the 600-pound camera nearly a

World Showcase Unplugged

These walking tours offer great insight into one of Disney's more enlightened creations.

- **Hidden Treasures of World Showcase:** The instructor stops short of turning pavilions inside out to display their scrupulous detailing and eye-fooling design.

- **Gardens of the World:** A horticulturist leads guests through the distinctive gardens. Discover the lengths to which Disney goes to create authentic-looking landscapes, and find out how to apply clever techniques at home.

Tours last three hours and cost $59 (and require Epcot admission). Schedules vary; reservations are necessary but may be made the morning of the tour. Call 407-WDW-TOUR (939-8687).

mile uphill for those three seconds of footage.

Norway

This 11th addition to the World Showcase landscape is immediately intriguing. A curious array of buildings rings the pavilion's cobblestoned square, including a reproduction of a wooden stave church (an endangered species of sorts, with just 28 remaining in Norway) and a replica of the 14th-century Akershus Castle that still stands in Oslo's harbor. Beside a grassy-roofed, thick-logged structure, there's a statue of a Norwegian running champion, living legend Grete Waitz. This Land of the Midnight Sun has added some twists to the World Showcase lineup—among them, the promise of troll encounters and Norwegian handicrafts of the hand-knit-sweater variety.

The stave church houses a gallery of artifacts recalling the history of these charming benchmarks of Norwegian culture (don't skip it, if only to see the inside of this teensy church)s. But Norway scores with **Maelstrom**, a trip in dragon-headed boats through Viking territory that is good fun, if not thrilling. An inspired voyage that surprises you with a troll here, a backward plunge there, a sudden waterfall here, a storm there, Maelstrom doesn't throw many big punches; it just keeps you guessing.

The five-minute trip lets you out at a Norwegian village, then finishes up with a brief film on the essence of Norway. This attraction is least crowded in the evening. If you'd like to take a more in-depth look at this pavilion or learn more about the architecture of Norway, stop at the Tourism information desk at the end of the ride. Free tours are given twice daily.

Mexico

There's no mistaking this pavilion's identity. A wild thicket of tropical foliage leads to a great pyramid. Inside, you wend your way through a brief but consistently engaging cultural exhibit to the main event. What you see next—a thoroughly romantic vision of a quaint Mexican village at dusk—is among the most wondrously escapist visions in World Showcase. True to form, there are stands selling colorful sombreros, baskets, pottery, and piñatas (the shop off to the left sells higher-quality Mexican handicrafts). In the rear of the plaza, note the dimly lit San Angel Inn and, behind it, the river and smoking volcano.

Here, too, you'll find the embarkation point for El Río del Tiempo, a pleasant six-minute boat trip through Mexican history that might be described as a subdued, south-of-the-border It's a Small World. If you encounter long lines early in the day, skip it, and check back later. Note, too, that the mariachi band that performs inside and outside this imposing pavilion is quite good.

Drinks Around the World

There's Samuel Adams lager at The American Adventure and at least one good imported excuse to bend the ol' elbow in each World Showcase country. Namely: Moosehead and more from carts in Canada; shandies, Guinness, black and tans, Tennent's, and beyond from the Rose & Crown Pub in the United Kingdom; a bottle of Kronenbourg from the Boulangerie Pâtisserie or a glass of wine from La Maison du Vin in France; Kirin beer or sake specialty drinks at Matsu No Ma, in Japan; vino from Italy can be sampled (with a pastry, of course) at La Bottega Italiana in Italy; Beck's beer and H. Schmitt Söhne wine at Germany's Sommerfest; Chinese wine and beer at the Lotus Blossom Cafe; Ringnes drafts from Kringla Bakeri og Kafe, in Norway; and what else but margaritas in Mexico's Cantina de San Angel.

DISNEY-MGM STUDIOS

Like an actress just right for the part, the Disney-MGM Studios is perfectly cast as the vivacious, showbiz-obsessed theme park that is seemingly incapable of keeping a secret. Since its debut, this park has worked to make the transition from sidekick to leading lady, and it has succeeded.

Think of the Studios as the adults' Magic Kingdom: magical, but in a more sophisticated way; marked by a whimsicality far

more ageless than that which pervades the Magic Kingdom. Sure, it has a Beauty and the Beast stage show, and

there's a funny 3-D Muppet movie, but these hardly constitute a satellite Fantasyland. At times the Studios even seems to have been scripted for a mature crowd, crafted with a wink of the eye by (and for) grown-ups to elicit knowing laughs and no-holds-barred nostalgia.

GETTING ORIENTED: The Disney-MGM Studios is smaller than Epcot, but somewhat difficult to navigate since it has no distinctive shape or main artery. You enter the park—and 1940s Tinseltown—via Hollywood Boulevard, a bustling shopping venue. The first major intersection you come to is Sunset Boulevard, an equally starry-eyed venue that branches off to the right of Hollywood Boulevard; this shopping and entertainment strip ends in a cul-de-sac right at the foot of the park's tallest (and spookiest) landmark, the 199-foot Tower of Terror.

Hollywood Boulevard ends where The Great Movie Ride begins—at a replica of Mann's (formerly Grauman's) Chinese Theatre. This ornate building is tucked behind the 12-story Sorcerer Mickey hat, the most centrally located landmark at the Studios; the plaza fronting it is

Disney-MGM Studios Hours

The park is usually open from 9 A.M. to an hour after sunset; hours are extended during holiday weekends and summer months. Some shows may not open until late morning, depending on the season. Call 407-824-4321 for schedules. One-day admission is $53.25 for adults (see *Planning Ahead* for ticket options). Prices are subject to change.

called Hollywood Plaza. If you stand in Hollywood Plaza facing Disney's Chinese Theater, you'll see an archway off to your right; this leads to Mickey Avenue, an area with more of a backstage feel, where tours of working animation and movie studios are among the attractions. If you make a left off Hollywood Boulevard and proceed past Echo Lake, you are on course for such attractions as Sounds Dangerous starring Drew Carey, Indiana Jones Epic Stunt Spectacular, and Star Tours. Just past Star Tours lies one more entertainment pocket. Jim Henson's Muppet*-Vision 3-D theater is the main draw here, together with New York Street, a realistic reproduction of a Manhattan block (complete with skyline facade). Walk left past the skyscraper end of New York Street and you're on a track back to Hollywood Plaza and the Chinese Theater.

A Walking Tour

Just inside the gates, you may be too distracted by the bright Art Deco looks of Hollywood Boulevard to notice a building on your left. This is Guest Relations, where you can go for information as well as first aid. Stop here or at Crossroads of the World (the gift stand in the center of the entrance plaza) to pick up a guidemap if you need one. To your immediate right, check out Oscar's Super Service, which has a 1949 Chevrolet tow truck parked out front. This is one of several striking and utterly unscratched classic autos you'll notice along the streets. (We're not sure how they got through the turnstiles.) Oscar's is the spot for lockers and wheelchair rentals; the lost and found, along with package pickup, is right next door. There is an ATM just outside the turnstiles here.

Hollywood Boulevard

One look at this main drag and you have a hunch you're not in Central Florida anymore. The strip oozes star quality with a Mae West sort of subtlety. Movie tunes from Hollywood's Golden

Hot Tips

- Don't miss Fantasmic!, a look into the dream world of Mickey Mouse, highlighted by fireworks, lasers, and special effects. This lavish musical is very popular, so plan ahead: if there are two shows, opt for the second, and allow 90 minutes before showtime for good seating (we recommend sitting toward the back for the best view—and the easiest exit).

- There is a path that leads you from the BoardWalk resort area on to Epcot. (It takes about 20 minutes.)

Age waft through the air. Palm trees make like Fred and Ginger in the tropical breeze. Streamlined storefronts with neon and chrome Art Deco flourishes line the boulevard like would-be movie sets hoping to get noticed.

Note that the shops along Hollywood Boulevard typically stay open about a half hour after the rest of the park has closed. (Consult the "Shopping" section in the *Diversions* chapter for specifics on our favorite shops; wares generally include a sampling of movie memorabilia and plenty of Disney character merchandise.

However you get there, it's important to stop at the corner of Hollywood and Sunset boulevards to check the **Tip Board** (it lists current waiting times for popular studios' attractions). Until 1 P.M., this is also the place

to make priority seating arrangements for full-service restaurants.

Sunset Boulevard

This Studios block is a broad, colorful avenue every bit as glamorous as Hollywood Boulevard. It has the same high-cheekbone style and its own stock of towering palms, evocative facades, and tempting shops. It also has stage presence, in the form of the 1,500-seat Theater of the Stars amphitheater, where you can see live performances of *Beauty and the Beast*. Sunset Boulevard begins innocently enough, with a friendly farmers' market, and a shop called Once Upon A Time that's housed in a replica of the Carthay Circle Theatre where *Snow White and the Seven Dwarfs* premiered. But don't let your guard down: none other than the white-knuckle Tower of Terror looms at the end of the road.

Somehow, **Beauty and the Beast—Live on Stage**, a production that was the *raison d'être* behind the Broadway musical, manages to remain oblivious to its eerie neighbor. The show is 30 minutes of rich musicality, costuming and choreography, and uplifting entertainment. While a canopy keeps the sun's heat at bay, we still aim for an evening performance during the summer. For early birds, note that this show generally opens soon after the park does.

Then there's **The Twilight Zone Tower of Terror**, a hair-raising experience. Because few of us have a natural yen to drop several stories (more than once, we might add) down a dark elevator shaft, this one requires some bravery. It helps to know what to expect.

Basically, "guests" enter the mysteriously abandoned Hollywood Tower Hotel and are invited into a library, where even the cobwebs seem to be circa 1939. Here, Rod Serling appears on a black-and-white television set to brief you (dark, stormy night, Halloween 1939, lightning strikes, guests disappear from hotel elevator) and welcome you to tonight's episode of *The Twilight Zone*: "If you'll just step this way into the boiler room, this is where you'll board our service elevators." You reach a boarding area—last call for chickening out—and file into an elevator (look at the diagram above the doors to avoid, say, the front row). Once you are seated and restraints are secured, the doors shut and the elevator ascends. You're soon so entranced by astonishing special effects—apparitions that appear in a corridor that vaporizes into a dark, star-filled sky and a gigantic eye straight from the fifth dimension that dread becomes (almost) secondary. When the elevator moves over into a second, pitch-black shaft, anything can happen, since Disney's Imagineers deviously transformed this ride from a two-screamer into a five-screamer. The bottom falls out more than once, and not subtly: Multiple plummets are scripted. One thing's for sure: Your cue to strike a great casual pose—perhaps a scream resembling a yawn—is when you're at

the top of the shaft. You want to look good in the group picture, which is taken as a panorama of the park suddenly gives way to a drop. The plunges are incredibly fast downward pulls with surprisingly smooth landings. It may be a small comfort, perhaps, but the really hairy part is over faster than many vocal cords are able to respond.

A few notes: The jitters tend to stay with you a bit after the 12-minute drama has ended. If you have back or neck problems, a heart condition, or are pregnant, we suggest you pass on this one. Finally, we urge you *not* to try it on a full stomach. (We made that mistake once. It wasn't pretty.)

If you're willing (and able) to continue the thrill-fest after your tumultuous stay in The Hollywood Tower Hotel, get ready to shake, rattle, and roll on the **Rock 'n' Roller Coaster starring Aerosmith**. As the first WDW roller coaster to flip you upside down, this dark, indoor, steel construction goes from zero to 60 miles per hour in just under three seconds.

The premise: You've just scored backstage passes and VIP transport to a sold-out Aerosmith concert at the Hollywood Bowl. During your drive through Southern California, you twist and turn to a rockin' sound track—and feel like you may

Touring Priorities

DON'T MISS

Tower of Terror*

Star Tours*

Jim Henson's Muppet*Vision 3-D*

The Great Movie Ride

Beauty and the Beast —Live on Stage**

Rock 'n' Roller Coaster*

The Magic of Disney Animation

Sounds Dangerous starring Drew Carey

Who Wants to Be a Millionaire—Play It!*

DON'T OVERLOOK

Voyage of The Little Mermaid*

Indiana Jones Epic Stunt Spectacular*/**

Disney-MGM Studios Backlot Tour

Walt Disney: One Man's Dream

Fantasmic!

DON'T KNOCK YOURSELF OUT

Honey, I Shrunk the Kids Movie Set Adventure

Playhouse Disney—Live on Stage

* Fastpass attraction as of press time. Consult a guidemap for new additions.

**Pay close attention to performance schedules.

have stepped inside a runaway music video.

Pay attention to the warning signs posted as you enter the

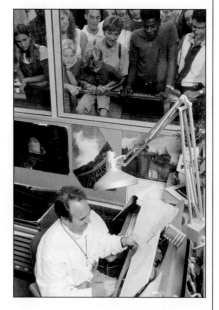

ride. If you have back or neck problems, a heart condition, or if you're pregnant, sit this one out.

Animation Courtyard & Mickey Avenue

Adjacent to Sunset Boulevard and Hollywood Boulevard is the section of the park that takes you under the sea with a diminutive mermaid and into working animation and television production studios. Passing under an archway located off Hollywood Plaza, you see Animation Courtyard immediately in front of you, with Mickey Avenue to your left.

A word about timing: The tours here—The Magic of Disney Animation and the Disney-MGM Studios Backlot Tour—are most exciting on weekdays before 5 P.M., because glimpses of Disney's magic makers at work stop when they call it a day.

Consider **The Magic of Disney Animation** a non-negotiable must. A guided walking tour through working animation studios, it's a chance to learn the facts of life as they relate to Mickey Mouse. Although big changes were made here in recent years, the tour still includes the very entertaining

Quiet Nooks

- Starring Rolls Bakery
- Tune-In Lounge
- Sunset Ranch Market
- Benches on Sunset Boulevard near Theater of the Stars
- Shaded benches around Echo Lake
- Brownstone stoops on New York Street
- Washington Square, at the far end of New York Street

commentary of Robin Williams and Walter Cronkite. The expansion of the animation facility brings Disney animation to life before your very eyes. You don't spend the whole 35 minutes peering over shoulders, however. First, you watch a film that transforms Williams into one of the lost boys from *Peter Pan*. Next, you gather round an actual artist, who reveals still more secrets of animation. Then, you see the animation studio and view snippets from a future movie release. Finally, you are led into a theater and treated to a finale of great moments from Disney classics, from *Snow White and the Seven Dwarfs* to *Tarzan*.

The **Disney-MGM Studios Backlot Tour** is a two-pronged gig that begins with an entertaining six-minute demo of how a realistic sea storm or naval battle might be filmed. The second segment, a 29-minute tram ride, starts calmly enough, but sit on the right side to stay dry. You visit the wardrobe area; the lights, camera, and props departments; and the backlot neighborhood of facades where you can see *The Golden Girls* house, or at least its exterior. Then, all of a sudden, there you are smack-dab in the middle of a special-effects zone

called Catastrophe Canyon, which specializes in nature's wrath: violent downpours, fiery explosions, flash floods, and the like. Things calm down with a visit to a realistic-looking Manhattan block. (It's a neighborhood of facades made mostly of fiberglass and Styrofoam.) Lines here tend to be shorter in the late afternoon (ask the attendant for an E.T.A., and if it's more than 30 minutes, check back later). The tour exits through the **American Film Institute Showcase**, a revolving display of costumes, props, and partial sets that features interactive elements related to film lore and legends.

Whether or not you're lucky enough to glimpse a hot set, you'll want to park yourself in TV's most famous "hot seat" at **Who Wants to Be a Millionaire— Play It!** Although Meredith Viera doesn't actually make an appearance, the attraction is otherwise a surprisingly faithful re-creation of the classic game show, right down to the high-tech set and lighting, distinctive music, and 50/50, Ask the Audience, and Phone-a-Friend (or in this case, a randomly chosen park guest) lifelines. Players are chosen from the 600-member audience based on scores from a fastest-finger round, and answer trivia questions to win points that can be redeemed for fabulous prizes. The half-hour presentation runs continuously.

At the Lights! Camera! Action! theater, you won't want to miss **Walt Disney: One Man's Dream**, a tribute to the man who really did start it all. A combination artifact-filled walk-through exhibit and retrospective film, the attraction looks at the life and times of Walter Elias Disney as both imagineer and innovator.

If you can get near **Voyage of The Little Mermaid**—and at this 15-minute musical adapted from the movie, that's no easy task—give it a go. What makes the show so compelling is the upbeat music, amusing puppetry, the occasion to watch children ogle this real, live mermaid *whose tail is moving*, and the mist-infused feeling that you are underwater. Check the times guide for schedule. Seats in the middle to back rows afford the best views.

Only if you're eager to return to your *Romper Room* roots, follow the trail of giddy toddlers to **Playhouse Disney—Live On Stage** (keeping in mind that there are no seats in the theater, though you are welcome to sit on the floor). If this isn't your speed, it's time to move on to bigger and better things.

Echo Lake Area

Heading back through the archway into Hollywood Plaza, you come upon **The Great Movie Ride**. This drive-through theater, of sorts is a classic in its own right and the best ticket we know to a quick video rental decision your next time out. Housed in an artful replica of Mann's Chinese Theatre, this not-to-be-missed

22-minute attraction is bursting with Audio-Animatronic figures that bring motion-picture legends and moments from almost every genre to life. It's "Chim Chim Cher-ee" meets "Here's looking at you, kid," cigarette-puffing Clint Eastwood meets broom-brandishing Wicked Witch of the West, *Alien* meets *Singin' in the Rain,* and then some—be prepared for surprises.

The ride has meticulous detailing and astounding realism. However, with queues that wind past some *Wizard of Oz* props and a screening of famous movie scenes, it provides one of the most entertaining waits in Walt Disney World (or anywhere for that matter).

Note: The Great Movie Ride may not be operating—or be different than the above description—during your visit to the park.

Heading through Hollywood Plaza toward Echo Lake, the next major landmark you encounter is the ABC Sound Studio, home of **Sounds Dangerous starring Drew Carey**. But you'd better arrive all

ears. Expect 12 of the most interesting minutes you have ever spent wearing headphones (in the dark!). Easy-listening this is not.

Here's the deal: You're attending a sneak preview of a live-action TV show that stars Drew Carey as an undercover detective. Thanks to a camera discreetly tucked into Carey's tie tack, you see everything his tie tack wishes it could see. And, of course, no one whispers, crashes, or so much as whimpers during the determined detective's madcap pursuit of diamond smugglers without word—or major vibrations—getting back to your headphones.

When a bad move by a panic-stricken Carey (open mouth, insert camera) zaps the television

Did You Know . . .

Although Disney Feature Animation Florida has contributed to hits such as *Beauty and the Beast, Aladdin,* and *The Lion King* since 1989, 1998's *Mulan* was actually the first feature film produced primarily in the Florida studios. Disney's *Lilo and Stitch* was also largely created in Florida. Thousands of guests watched the films' creation at The Magic of Disney Animation. Who knows? During your visit, you might meet one of the animators who brings new Disney characters to life.

A Striking Resemblance

- Chinese Theater—Mann's Chinese Theatre in Hollywood
- Once Upon A Time storefront—Carthay Circle Theatre in Hollywood, where Disney's *Snow White* premiered
- Mickey's of Hollywood storefront—Frederick's of Hollywood
- Jim Henson's Muppet*Vision 3-D theater—the theater from *The Muppet Show*
- Hollywood Brown Derby—Brown Derby of Hollywood's heyday

picture, you have no choice but to follow the action in the dark. Those clean ears you toted into the theater strain and contort with every twist in the furious plot. Fully enveloped in the audacious realism of 3-D audio, you attempt to sit calmly while your ears carry you into a swarm of 5,000 restless bees.

Listen carefully and you'll doubtless marvel at the palpable snip, snip, snip of the barber's scissors. Your head will spin with the wildly screeching tires of Carey's speeding car. And as attuned as you become, you'll likely still be unprepared for the finale (think close encounters with a circus elephant).

If you are a fan of the action-movie genre, it's worth risking life and limb to catch a performance of the **Indiana Jones Epic Stunt Spectacular**. Arrive a good 45 minutes before showtime to snare a seat toward the front of the 2,000-seat amphitheater. The half-hour performance steals its thunder from *Raiders of the Lost Ark* and begins with the selection of a few fearless "extras" (they're put to use during a scene involving a sword fight in Cairo).

Nimble stuntpeople perform one death-defying caper after another, leaping between buildings, dodging snipers and boulders, and eluding fiery explosions. You feel the heat of the flames, you fear for the Harrison Ford look-alike. Tricks of the trade are revealed and you're *still* impressed. The Indiana Jones Epic Stunt Spectacular nearly always plays to capacity audiences, so your best bet for getting a great seat is the first or last show of the day. Seating begins 30 minutes prior to each performance.

As exciting as the Indiana Jones Epic Stunt Spectacular is, the attraction just around the corner packs even more punch. At **Star Tours**, you don't sit in an amphitheater; you strap yourself into a flight simulator.

You don't live vicariously through professional stuntpeople;

you experience the sensation of barreling through space at the speed of light for yourself. The premise: Enterprising droids R2-D2 and C-3PO are working for an intergalactic travel agency whose fleet of spacecraft makes regular trips to the Moon of Endor. As luck would have it, you draw a rookie pilot who gives new meaning to reckless abandon. Soon you're spiraling through space, dodging lasers and giant ice crystals. Be prepared for an intense five-minute ride that encompasses a lot of bucking, tilting, and a few disorienting movements.

VIP Tour Allure

You may have seen them in the theme parks—those perky people in the plaid vests. They are VIP guides, happily leading guests on customized trips through Walt Disney World.

The VIP program minimizes the hassle factor while maximizing the overall magic component. In addition to the aforementioned guide, tours entitle guests to special seating for many stage shows and parades. VIP transportation is also an option. For pricing information or to make a reservation, call 407-560-4033.

Star Tours is one of those don't-miss-unless-you-have-a-very-good-reason attractions. (Among the very good reasons: just ate, heart condition, pregnancy, susceptible to motion sickness.) The lines are generally shortest in the morning, with waits of about 30 minutes the rest of the day.

New York Street

Moving along, you arrive at the Studios' back corner. This is a glimpse of Manhattan as it used to look, with a few alterations having to do with the Empire State Building's dimensions and the size of the puppet population (correction: *muppet* population).

You're here for *one* thing: the fabulously entertaining, special effects-laden presentation of **Jim Henson's Muppet*Vision 3-D**. Miss it and you've deprived your sense of humor. So head straight for the Muppet theater and fill up on a 25-minute stream of amusing Muppet antics that push the creative envelope of 3-D movies with such effects as a cannon blast through the screen, some bubble magic, and a floating banana cream pie. (Yes, all you Muppet

fans, the curmudgeons from *The Muppet Show* are in attendance, in their familiar balcony spot, cynical and crotchety as ever.)

After bonding with the Muppets, walk straight toward New York Street, where you can take in the skyline or sit down on a stoop. A sign in the window of our favorite brownstone cautions NO SOLICITING, but it says nothing about stoop trespassing. So we take a seat, do some people-watching and simply gaze at the

The Mouse Is Spoken For

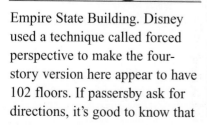

Walt Disney himself supplied the voice for Mickey Mouse from 1928 to 1946.

Empire State Building. Disney used a technique called forced perspective to make the four-story version here appear to have 102 floors. If passersby ask for directions, it's good to know that

the **Honey, I Shrunk the Kids Movie Set Adventure** playground is behind one of the facades here. It's worth a peek if you've got time to kill. And if they want to know where to find the Toy Story Pizza Planet Arcade (and its resident ATM), tell them it's across from the Muppet theater.

Entertainment

Disney's Tinseltown sticks close to its Hollywood heritage in its live entertainment. Because the marquee is ever changing, it's essential to check a times guide. You might run into budding starlets and gossip columnists along Hollywood Boulevard, or there may be a visiting celebrity about.

Disney Stars and Motor Cars Parade is an honest-to-goodness "stars in cars" Hollywood motorcade—only this lineup includes Ariel, Mary Poppins, Mulan, and other stars of Disney-MGM Studios, all riding in classic cars that have been customized to fit their unique personalities.

Last, but hardly least: Fantasmic!— a 26-minute pyrotechnic dazzler— cranes necks nightly in a lagoon-endowed amphitheater behind Tower of Terror. Shown just after dusk, this expression of Mickey's dreams (and nightmares) is filled with dancing fountains, characters galore, and special effects synchronized to classic Disney tunes. Note that the best seats are actually toward the back of the theater.

DISNEY'S ANIMAL KINGDOM

So strong is this park's sense of purpose that it's as if the animals of the world put their antlers and antennae together and created it themselves—to celebrate their aardvark-to-zebra diversity, remind us of their prehistoric heritage, and rally support for wildlife conservation efforts. Not that Disney's creative hand isn't greatly evident in this park.

Endangered-species breeding programs coexist with blockbuster attractions. Sophisticated Audio-Animatronic dinosaurs share the marquee with more than 1,700 animals (some 250 species), whose habitat needs dictate much of the landscape. Dinosaur fossils are abundant; plastic straws and Styrofoam cups, conspicuously absent. (One glimpse at the park and it's no surprise that Animal

Animal Kingdom Hours

Disney's Animal Kingdom is usually open from about 9 A.M. and closes at about 5 P.M. Park hours may be extended during holiday weekends and summer months. Call 407-824-4321 for up-to-the-minute details. One-day park admission is $53.25 for adults (see *Planning Ahead* for ticket options). Prices are subject to change.

Kingdom is accredited by the American Zoo and Aquarium Association, an organization that supports conservation, education, science, and recreation.)

GETTING ORIENTED: Although greenery reigns in these parts, relegating concrete, and indeed most architecture, to garnish status, successful penetration of this particular jungle requires no compasses, scythes, or snakebite kits. The park is set up as a set of themed lands decidedly unlike any you've encountered in your neighborhood.

To see the forest through the trees, look up: Like the icons of its Worldly siblings, Animal Kingdom's Tree of Life serves as an instant beacon for the momentarily disoriented. This massive spectacle also anchors the park's most central land, Discovery Island.

The layout of this park might be compared to the silhouette of

a simple daisy. Acting as the stem is the lush expanse of the Oasis. Discovery Island (the land that serves as the park's hub), encircled by a river, is the flower's center. And extending from the center like petals are bridges leading sharply southeast to the primeval area known as DinoLand U.S.A.; northeast to Asia; northwest to Africa, the park's largest land; and southwest to Camp Minnie-Mickey, a character vacationland.

It's true that Disney's Animal Kingdom is more than double Epcot's size, but thanks to the considerable roaming room designated for animal residents only, it takes no more legwork to circumnavigate this park than to explore Epcot. As anyone who's been to Epcot can attest, this is still a good amount of walking—so follow our efficient touring plan and take advantage of the park's many pleasant resting spots. Seniors who opt to tour the smaller parks on foot may choose to rent a wheelchair at Animal Kingdom—or better yet, given the steep inclines throughout the park, a self-driven Electric Convenience Vehicle (ECV).

A Walking Tour

Our tour begins much like any other intrepid adventure, assuming that intrepid adventurers have inexplicably omitted mention of turnstiles that must be traversed en route from urbane Central Florida to the Great Unknown. No matter. You're about to be enveloped by **The Oasis**, a canopy of nature that serves as

Touring Priorities		
DON'T MISS	**DON'T OVERLOOK**	**DON'T KNOCK YOURSELF OUT**
Kilimanjaro Safaris*	Rafiki's Planet Watch	
Dinosaur*	Discovery Island Trails	The Boneyard
Maharajah Jungle Trek	Tarzan Rocks!**	TriceraTop Spin
It's Tough to be a Bug!*	The Oasis	Primeval Whirl
Festival of the Lion King**		
Kali River Rapids*		* Fastpass attraction as of press time. Consult a guidemap for new additions.
Pangani Forest Exploration Trail		** Pay close attention to performance schedules.

Animal Kingdom's inviting foyer. Two paths lead north to Discovery Island and the looming Tree of Life. Before you proceed farther into the fragrant tangle of tropical trees and flowers, where you're bound to be distracted by waterfall-laden streams and glimpses of macaws, iguanas, and giant anteaters, *stop!* Tell yourself it's all a mirage and pause to pick up a map and a times guide near the front gate. You don't have to cool your jets for any other practicalities, unless you're picking up some wheels for the day, using the ATM, renting a locker, or visiting package pickup.

Emerging from the northern reaches of the Oasis entry-zone, you arrive at a bridge to Discovery Island and receive your cue to gasp—a panoramic view of Animal Kingdom's central land, the moat-like river, the soaring Tree of Life, and the balance of the park before you.

Discovery Island

Exotic in a neither-here-nor-there-but-certainly-not-North America sense, Discovery Island is awash in the sort of vivid color paintbrushes dream about imparting. Meticulously carved and painted building facades and

Hot Tips

- This park's layout can be confusing, especially for first-time visitors. Pick up a guidemap as soon as you enter the park. Use it to help plan your day, allowing enough time to travel from one area to the next for a show with a set start time.
- The animals are out and about all day—so any time's a good time to experience the safari ride.
- Weekends tend to be the most crowded days at Disney's Animal Kingdom.

smatterings of African and Caribbean folk art add to the eye-catching allure of environs intended to replicate a village in the Tropics. Notable as the land that serves as the gateway to all other Animal Kingdom lands, it's also the park's core dining and shopping zone.

Take a minute to glance at the **Tip Board**, listing showtimes and current waiting times for popular attractions. This board is on the right as you enter Discovery Island. Checking the board to align your schedule with certain showtimes (listed in a park times guide) will help you structure your day.

The big draw here is **The Tree of Life**. The man-made tree looms 145 feet over the park as its main icon. Even dung beetles

have their place on this arboreal masterpiece, whose 50-foot-wide trunk and windblown limbs contain nose-to-nose carvings of every animal Disney artists could fit. Certainly, Mickey's lineage is represented. The carvings are a tribute to the richness and diversity of animal life on our planet.

Don't neglect to check out the cockatoos, flamingos, deer, and other wildlife living among the tree's roots along **Discovery Island Trails**.

Before you leave The Tree of Life vicinity, consider the possible advantages of starting small. If you can bear eight minutes of animated insects creeping and crawling into your personal space, see **It's Tough to be a Bug!**, a 3-D special-effects show shown—where else?—inside the tree. It's a decidedly Off-Broadway show, starring Flik (from the film *A Bug's Life*) and a cast of a million bugs whose previous credits include such shows as *Beauty and the Bees* and *My Fair Ladybug*.

You become an honorary bug in an effort to understand their world, but things go awry when several of Flik's buddies don't appreciate a visit from you.

After a demonstration of their talents, you may suddenly cease to be fazed by any creature with fewer than six legs.

Note: Anyone leery of spiders, roaches, and the like is advised to skip the performance, or risk being seriously bugged.

DinoLand U.S.A.

Once you stroll beneath the big brachiosaurus skeleton, you'll enter what appears to be a kitschy park created around a remote paleontological dig site.

This zone features intimate rendezvous with winners (crocodiles) as well as sore losers of the Cretaceous period's Survival of the Meteorproof. The big attraction here is **Dinosaur**, a time-travel trip fraught with asteroids and frightening run-ins with Disney's largest and most realistic Audio-Animatronic figures yet.

A 3½-minute thrill attraction that has earned raves, Dinosaur is inside the Dino Institute, a museum-like building that reveals nothing of the fast, jarring, and heart-pounding ride ahead. Of course, there's a larger mission that has nothing to do with the desire for an adrenaline rush and everything to do with selfless intentions to save an iguanodon. (Don't worry, we'll explain.) Basically, you have it on good authority that if you shoot 65 million years back in time, there's a chance you can bring back an iguanodon for paleontologists to study. The catch: You must do this seconds before the meteor blast thought to have sealed the dinosaurs' fate

and ended the Cretaceous period. So you strap yourself into the vehicle and contemplate what to say to the 16-foot-tall creatures.

And so it is that you find yourself in a race against time, ducking meteors and attempting to blink away encroaching non-vegetarian dinosaurs as your vehicle rages out of control. Just when you think you've spied some friendly faces in the crowd, you notice the nostril-flaring carnotaurus hot on your tail. What happens next is for us to know and for you to find out. Dinosaur is not to be missed (unless, of course, you have dinophobia, are pregnant, suffer from back or neck problems, or have a heart condition).

There's the potential for one last stop in these parts: a detour to the Theater in the Wild to take in **Tarzan Rocks!** In-line skaters and singers rock out as a live band plays tunes from Disney's animated feature.

Asia

A footbridge that wouldn't look out of place in the Himalayas, were it not filled with strolling theme park guests, leads from Discovery Island to this chip off Earth's largest continent. Your gateway to Asia is the village of

Anandapur, where a musical welcome is provided by tiny brass bells that dangle from the eaves of pagodas, dancing in the wind. Speckling the landscape are temples overtaken by gibbons, ruins frequented by tigers, a pavilion leased to fruit bats, and the like.

If you're up for some adventure (and a quick shower) head to **Kali River Rapids**. You'll know you're in the right queue if you see a steady stream of soggy, happy people filing by.

Did You Know . . .

- The carvings on The Tree of Life represent about 325 of the 1.4 million existing species.

- Many of the plastic benches in Animal Kingdom were made from recycled material.

- The Disney Wildlife Conservation Fund helps nonprofit organizations protect endangered animals. You can donate by adding a dollar for conservation projects to your shop purchase.

- Most of the animals here were born in other zoological parks. Many are registered in special management and breeding programs called SSPs (Species Survival Plans).

- WDW has eliminated most of its insecticide use, replacing chemicals with millions of predatory insects—many of which are bred at The Land in Epcot.

Once your raft shoves off from the boathouse, it parts the waters beneath a fog-shrouded steeple of greenery. Don't be lulled into security, no matter how sweetly the birds chirp. Soon you'll be trading this calm for a smoldering obstacle course lined with freshly shish-kebobbed forest. Yes, just ahead lies a precarious game of limbo under an abandoned logging truck and a burning tree. The sum total is a jostling five-minute ride that is best left to nonpregnant people sans heart conditions and neck or back problems.

Note that cameras and other non-waterproof valuables should not be taken on Kali River Rapids. While there is a storage space in the middle of the raft, we suggest entrusting them to a nice, dry locker or non-riding member of your party.

Continue your Far East itinerary with the **Maharajah Jungle Trek**, a tour through the nearest Southeast Asian rain forest in the

The Better to See Them With

Have a pair of binoculars? The 14-story Tree of Life is reason to tote them along. There are more than 325 animals carved into the tree, and you'll want to be able to see the ones at the top.

Quiet Nooks

Who says you can't find peace in a jungle? Consider these relatively relaxing spots and seek out others.

- The Oasis in the afternoon
- Discovery Island Trails (especially near the back of The Tree of Life)
- Pangani Forest Exploration Trail
- Tables along the river at Flame Tree Barbecue in Discovery Island (except at lunchtime)
- Cretaceous Trail
- Rafiki's Planet Watch
- Anywhere but Camp Minnie-Mickey

most primitive of tour vehicles (your own two feet). Led by an unobtrusive, insightful guide (yourself), you do what great explorers in the wilds can't: parade unharmed past roving tigers and Komodo dragons.

Don't be afraid to linger. Even Olympians of these species can't breach Disney's security systems. Chicken out on passing through the darkened bat chamber, and you may never see a *Pteropus vampirus*—the closest thing to a Chihuahua with a six-foot wingspan—eating pineapple chunks. But you'll still spot Malaysian tapir, birds, and acrobatic gibbons galore.

Speaking of chickens, here's another feather for your explorer's cap. The Caravan Stage, which

struts out performances of **Flights of Wonder** several times daily, can accommodate 1,000 people and all manner of flappers. Check a guidemap for times.

Note: This show is scheduled to undergo some changes in the not-too-distant future; check your park map or with Guest Relations for updates.

Africa

If imitation is the sincerest form of flattery, then Africa has got to be blushing. In creating this largest section of the park, Disney seems to have stopped just shy of moving mountains (Kilimanjaro is conspicuously missing). The artfully reconstructed African savanna and woodland aren't merely stunning to behold. They're designed to satisfy the habitat specifications of each meerkat, zebra, and elephant. Countless trips to the continent, exhaustive planning, and some slick adaptations have enabled Disney to mesh the intimacy of a zoo with the aura of a safari.

Disney's Africa is truly a land of opportunities, among them: treading just yards from cavorting gorillas; observing rhinos, gazelles, and hippos en masse; exchanging glances with a passing giraffe; getting up to speed on wildlife protection and conservation efforts; and chasing renegade ivory poachers.

Of course, you wander over and find yourself suddenly surrounded by hippos and elephants. You acclimate to the continent in the atmospheric village of Harambe, patterned after modern coastal communities in East Africa. Harambe is important as the spot for food, drink, and shopping during your stay in Africa. It is also the gateway to some exceptional attractions.

Kilimanjaro Safaris, Disney's variation on the classic African travel adventure is one to beat a path to. The 20-minute guided trip through a simulated savanna escorts you within boasting distance of many of the world's most beloved animals—so close you'll begin to wonder which of the 32 people in your open-air gawkmobile (as we've loosely dubbed the roofed, rugged transportation of choice) has irrepressible animal magnetism. As the vehicle bumps along the dust-caked road, you'll observe animals on the move; watch for elephants, gazelles, rhinos, baboons, and lions. Such animals as giraffes and zebras may draw quite near.

Your guide will fill you in on less familiar species; for a preview, steal quick glances at the species identification cheat sheet above the seat in front of you. These animals have room to roam and thus better things to do than stare back at you. Of

course, as on a real safari, you might not see certain animals on a given trip; they could be sleeping, hiding, or otherwise engaged. So consider riding more than once during your visit to Animal Kingdom.

A good follow-up to the safari is a walking tour that invites lingering and offers a closer look at gorillas and other animals. Also accessible from Harambe, **Pangani Forest Exploration Trail** segues from a research lab to the enchanting environs of a free-flight aviary and an aquarium. Beyond that, you'll come upon a stream dammed with glass—the site of a synchronized swimming demonstration by hippos. Okay, so maybe it's not synchronized.

Animal Kingdom Snacks

For a healthy treat, try the juice blends at the outdoor Safari Bar next to Rainforest Cafe or fruit from a stand in Africa. If you need a sweet break, brave the crowds for the fresh-baked cookies or ice cream in Camp Minnie-Mickey, or the pastries at Kusafari Coffee Shop & Bakery, in Africa. For a cool pick-me-up, try chocolate-covered frozen bananas or Simba's Paw Print ice cream bars from a vendor, or the ice cream or fresh fruit smoothies from Tamu Tamu Refreshments, in Africa. Or try chicken-fried rice and other Asian specialties at Chakrandi Chicken Shop or the smoked turkey legs on Discovery Island.

Entertainment

Entertaining distractions include African musicians and super-knowledgeable wildlife experts who wander the park with interesting animals. And don't miss Mickey's Jammin' Jungle Parade, featuring off-road-style floats like Rafiki's Adventure Rover and Goofy's Safari Jeep. Check a park times guide for current entertainment schedules.

But the buoyant beasts don't have to wear nose plugs to be amusing in their underwater glory. Even so, we know what you're thinking: "Are we there yet? Where are the gorillas?" Rest assured, the chest thumpers are close at hand.

There's a bit more to see before you reach the gorilla sanctuary, however, namely, a scenic savanna overlook and an ensemble of Timon's meerkat cousins (FYI: Don't expect to see any Pumbaas. Meerkats and warthogs don't pal around in the real world).

After you peer into their habitat at close range through floor-to-ceiling glass, walk over a suspension bridge to the gorilla valley, and begin turning your head U.S. Open–style to take in the antics of the family brood and the bachelor brood now flanking you (provided, of course, that they're in the mood to see and be seen). What does it feel like to walk alongside these expressive creatures with little between you and their *Planet of the Apes* physiques? Privileged.

Back in Harambe, you'll find the train depot for the **Wildlife Express to Rafiki's Planet Watch**, a narrated 5½-minute train trip that chugs quietly behind the scenes of Africa, providing a reverse perspective of Kilimanjaro Safaris along with insights into the park's inner workings. For those wanting a rest, it offers a leisurely lift (and the only mode of transportation) to and from **Rafiki's Planet Watch**, the attraction that serves as Animal Kingdom's ideological cornerstone. As the park's center for wildlife preservation efforts and veterinary care, Rafiki's Planet Watch acts as a sweeper

of sorts, crystallizing the environmental themes presented in the other areas of the park and encouraging active support of wildlife programs while the safari's still fresh.

Camp Minnie-Mickey

If you want to commune with animals more accustomed to standing still for pictures, take a trip to Camp Minnie-Mickey.

The not-to-be-missed attraction here is **Festival of the Lion King**, an entertaining 30-minute spectacle of dance, song, and acrobatics by a troupe of talented tribal performers.

Animal Kingdom Unplugged

If Rafiki's Planet Watch doesn't sate your curiosity, there are two three-hour behind-the-scenes tours that will. Backstage Safari, basically Animal Care 101, takes you through such creature facilities as the elephant barn and the veterinary hospital. The tour is offered on Monday, Wednesday, Thursday, and Friday, and costs $65, plus park admission.

Another tour, Wild by Design, shows how Disney's Animal Kingdom came to be—from architecture to artifacts and a whole lot more. It's offered on Tuesday, Thursday, and Friday. The cost is $58, plus park admission. Call 407-WDW-TOUR (939-8687) for reservations.

The sky's the limit for recreational activities beyond the theme parks.

Diversions: Sports, Shopping, and Other Pursuits

You've flown with Peter Pan in the Magic Kingdom, blasted into outer space at Epcot, got a backstage peek at Tinseltown at the Disney-MGM Studios, and bonded with bugs and dinosaurs at Animal Kingdom. Now what?

The World beyond the major theme parks offers a slew of terrific diversions that, interspersed between park visits, help establish perfect symmetry in a well-rounded Walt Disney World vacation. Once you get over the shock of finding such activities here in the first place, you're still pinching yourself because the quality of the experiences is so good. You'll find that even more world-class adventures for adults (thoroughly described on the following pages) exist within the playground that is Walt Disney World.

We're just hinting at the possibilities when we mention golf courses, widely considered among the country's best; tennis facilities, health clubs, and the Disney's Wide World of Sports complex—all perfect examples of Disney's ability to dazzle in the most unexpected arenas. On the shopping front, tantalizing stores (including a collection of character-defying options at Downtown Disney) are popping up property-wide. Add the last word in water parks, including a sky-scraping water slide and a humongous wave pool, and the list is still incomplete. For a full inventory of distractions (the categories: sports, shopping, and other pursuits) so compelling you might wonder why anyone bothers with those theme parks, read on.

Sports

Golf

Disney's 99-hole "Magic Linksdom"—second only to the Mouse in drawing power—is renowned for the challenge, variety, and fairness of its courses. Disney World has become a familiar name on *Golf* magazine's biennial list of the best golf resorts in the country. *Golf Digest* has tabbed four of the World's five par-72 courses as outstanding ("plan your next vacation around it") or very good ("worth getting off the interstate to play"). And noted golf writer Glen Waggoner is hardly alone in giving Mickey Mouse's backyard the nod as America's greatest golfing haven. In Waggoner's own words, "Some other places have an individual course that is superior to any in Walt Disney World's lineup, but no other resort in the entire country has five courses this good." Solidifying this reputation is the Funai Classic at Walt Disney World Resort (October), a PGA tour event with over a quarter century of prestige behind it.

KNOW BEFORE YOU GO: WDW's peak golfing season extends from January through April. During this period it is especially important to secure reservations well in advance for play in the morning and early afternoon (though starting times after 2 P.M. are usually available at the last minute). Tee times are particularly difficult to get during the third and fourth weeks of January, when some 30,000 truly serious golfers descend on the area for the PGA of America's Merchandise Show, and during the Funai Classic at Walt Disney Resort (October). The Citrus Bowl (January) and Daytona 500 (February) have also proven capable of filling the courses quickly. During such busy periods, the advance reservations and guaranteed tee times afforded by golf packages can be absolutely indispensable. Call 407-WDW-GOLF (939-4653) for information about packages.

Rates: Greens fees for the 18-hole courses vary according to when you visit (peak versus nonpeak seasons), which course you play (Osprey Ridge and Eagle Pines are more expensive), and your guest status (WDW resort guests get a break). Basically, though, you can count on paying $60 to $175 per round (depending on your tee time), including the required cart. Throughout the year, golfers can save some money by teeing off in the late afternoon, when twilight rates may afford savings of more than 50 percent. The biggest savings can be had from late April through late September, when rates for all courses drop to about $60 after 10 A.M. At Oak Trail, a 9-hole walking course, play starts at about $38 (half price on the second round), depending on the time of day. Annual Golf Memberships ($53), available to Florida residents only, can provide big savings (depending on the season) for play after 10 A.M., and also include complimentary use of a cart and a 20 percent discount on golf lessons given by the PGA teaching staff.

Reservations: Anyone buying a golf package may reserve tee times up to 90 days ahead. Golfers who book lodging at any on-property resort may also secure tee times up to 90 days in advance. For everyone else, the window of opportunity is 30 days out. (In other words, it's difficult for guests staying outside Walt Disney World to obtain prime tee times during busy weeks.) Note that four golfers are assigned to each starting time, so parties may be matched up. To book tee times, call 407-WDW-GOLF (939-4653).

Golf Rates

The following greens fees were in effect at press time for the WDW golf courses. Prices do not include tax and are subject to change. Prices fluctuate between Peak and Nonpeak seasons. Walt Disney World resort guests get $5 off the Day Visitor Rate.

Day Visitor Rates
(subject to change)

- Osprey Ridge: from $80* to $185.

- Eagle Pines: from $70* to $154.

- Magnolia: from $65* to $144.

- Palm and Lake Buena Vista: from $60* to $129.

- Oak Trail: starts at about $38.

* Summer discounts (late April through late September) lower rates for all courses to about $60 as of 10 A.M.

* Twilight rates begin at 3 P.M. during much of the year, starting an hour earlier in certain seasons. Rates range from $50 to $80, depending on tee time and course chosen.

Reservations must be made with a credit card. Cancellations must be made 48 hours in advance or you'll be charged in full.

Transportation: Complimentary taxi service to the Palm, Magnolia, Osprey Ridge, Eagle Pines, and Lake Buena Vista courses is available for all WDW resort guests. Call Guest Services; the taxis work on a voucher system.

Dress: Proper golf attire is required on all courses. Shirts must have collars, and if shorts are worn, they must be Bermuda length.

Equipment rental: Gear, including Footjoy shoes ($7) and range balls ($6 a bucket), is available for rent at all WDW pro shops. Golf-club rentals run $45 to $55 per set for men, $45 for women, depending on the style, plus a refundable $500 credit card deposit; photo ID required. Prices are subject to change.

INSTRUCTION: Players looking to improve their games have several options: one-on-one instruction, swing analysis sessions, and playing lessons. At the Walt Disney World Golf Studio, based at the Palm and Magnolia, PGA professionals offer 45-minute sessions that concentrate on improving players' swings through video analysis; cost is $79.50 including tax.

Playing lessons, in which a PGA pro provides on-course instruction, delving into strategy, club selection, and short game skills, as well as the psychological side of golf, are $159. Private lessons are available for $63.60 per half hour. Reservations are required for all lessons; call 407-WDW-GOLF (939-4653) up to one year ahead.

TOURNAMENTS: The Funai Classic at Walt Disney World Resort, which draws top PGA Tour players every fall, is among the most celebrated events on Disney's sports calendar. Because the Classic is one of the last regular PGA Tour stops of the year (usually in October), exciting competition is a given; pros are looking to vault themselves into the Tour Championship or secure spots on the top 125 money list.

Venues for the tournament are the Palm and Magnolia courses. During the first two days of the competition, the pros play each course once with an amateur player. After 36 holes, the field narrows to the low 70 pros, who compete for a percentage of the tourney's multimillion-dollar purse in the final two rounds, played on the Magnolia. Tickets are available on-site each day of the tournament, with one-day admission ranging from $15 for the first two rounds to $20 for the third round and $25 for the final round. A badge good for all of the rounds costs $50. Practice rounds (held several days before the tournament) are open to spectators at no cost. For more information, call 407-824-2250. Prices are subject to change.

Those who are willing to pay big dues may play the Classic alongside the pros. Card-carrying members of the Classic Club play with a different competing pro each day for the first two

Mickey and Mini Golf

Leave it to Disney to create 18-hole miniature-golf courses that eschew the typical tackiness for clever designs, both fanciful and devious. The first round is about $10; it's half price for the second. Hours are 10 A.M. to 11 P.M. Call 407-WDW-PLAY (939-7529) for more on these locations.

- Disney's Fairways, one of the two courses at the Fantasia Gardens Miniature Golf complex near the BoardWalk, is ruled by daunting doglegs, sand traps, water traps, par 3s, and par 4s. Astute players may notice shrunken signature holes from famous links. (Play time: about 1½ hours.)

- At Fantasia Gardens, the second course near the BoardWalk, whimsical tees offer odes to *Fantasia*. En route, balls hit chimes and xylophone stairs, and spur water spouts and fife playing. (Play time: about an hour.)

- Disney's Winter Summerland, vacation spot to Santa and Christmas elves, offers the best of both seasons. Near Blizzard Beach, surfboards and sand castles speckle the summer-themed course, while igloos and ice sculptures give the wintry course the freeze. (Play time: about an hour per course.)

rounds of the tournament. Some memberships include lodging, reduced greens fees on Disney courses for a year, and admission to the theme parks for a week. For details, call 407-824-2250.

The Courses

PALM: This prickly yet picturesque course (located just west of the Polynesian resort) is marked by tight wooded fairways, a wealth of water hazards, and elevated greens and tees, which bear Joe Lee's unmistakable signature and make for challenging club selections. The par-72 Palm plays shorter and tighter than its mate, the Magnolia, and measures 5,311 yards from the front tees, 6,461 from the middle, and 6,957 from the back. The palm-dotted venue hosts the Funai Classic at Walt Disney World Resort, along with a fellow Lee design, the Magnolia course. Of the holes garnering the most locker-room curses (numbers 6, 10, and 18), the sixth, a 412-yard par 4, is the most notorious. There's a lake on the left, woods and swamp on the right, and more water between you and the two-tier green. Although Palm number 6 is the number one handicap hole, number 18 (the number 2 handicap hole) has consistently baffled the pros more than any other Disney hole. The course—whose greens were rebuilt in 1993 from the drainage basin up—opened in 1971 with the Magnolia and the Magic Kingdom itself. Facilities shared by the Palm and the Magnolia include two driving ranges, two putting greens, and a pro shop. The Walt Disney World Golf Studio is also based here. Course record: 61 (Mark Lye, 1984).

Slope Scope

The slope ratings for the five par-72 Disney courses from the back tees are: Osprey Ridge, 135; Magnolia, 133; Palm, 133; Eagle Pines, 131; Lake Buena Vista, 128. By way of comparison, an average slope rating is around 115. The famously challenging links at Pebble Beach check in at 139; the formidable TPC Stadium course at Ponte Vedra, at 135.

MAGNOLIA: Like the Palm, the Magnolia opened with the Magic Kingdom in 1971. It received a major face-lift in 1992. Course designer Joe Lee realigned teeing areas, recontoured greens, and replaced the original playing surface with a "faster" grass, among other things. The Magnolia features abundant water and sand, but what sets it apart—aside from the 1,500 magnolia trees and a mouse-eared bunker beside the sixth green—is exceptional length, vast greens, and a flaw-exposing layout that requires precision and careful course management. Meandering over 175 acres of wetlands and rolling terrain, the par-72 course measures 5,232 yards from the front tees, 6,642 from the middle set, and 7,190 from the back markers. Among the signature holes is number 17, a long par-4 dogleg left that dares long hitters to bite off the edge of a lake, then avoid water to the right of the green.

It is the Magnolia that has final say in the outcome of the Funai Classic at Walt Disney World Resort, and it takes full advantage with a final hole that rates among the tournament's testiest. Facilities shared by the Magnolia and the Palm are two driving ranges, two putting greens, and a pro shop. The WDW Golf Studio is based here. Course record: 61 (Payne Stewart, 1990).

OAK TRAIL: This nine-hole par-36 walking course in a 45-acre corner of the Magnolia is a good venue for beginners, yet it's no cream puff for better players. The 2,913-yard layout unleashes plenty of challenges—including two fine par 5s—and boasts well-maintained greens.

OSPREY RIDGE: Tom Fazio has taken his signature mounding along fairways and around greens to monumental heights here—most dramatically with a namesake ridge that meanders through the property and elevates some greens as high as 25 feet above the basic grade. The designer counts Osprey

Tee Time

Want to increase your chances of getting a WDW course tee time? Heed this advice:

- Play on Monday or Tuesday.
- Tee off in late afternoon.
- Come in the summer (when special rates are available).

In the Rough

"There's a lot of wildlife around the Palm course's property," says a former Disney pro. "People have seen deer, otters, turkeys, bobcats, and even panthers. One day, someone said he saw a couple of bald eagles."

Ridge among his best efforts, and the sentiment is echoed in the course's considerable popularity among experienced golfers. The long par-72 layout winds through a beautifully remote and thickly forested part of the property near Fort Wilderness; it has a deceptively gentle start, then raises the stakes en route to its three great finishing holes. Along the way, players will confront the signature par-3 third hole, with its elevated tee, and the fierce 14th, a long par 4 with a carry over water. Osprey Ridge plays to 5,402 yards from the front tees, 6,680 from the middle, and 7,101 from the back. Facilities shared by Osprey Ridge and Eagle Pines include a driving range, a putting green, pro shop, restaurant, and lounge. Course record: 65 (Daniel Young, 1992).

EAGLE PINES: The subtle contours of this low-lying link provide a decided contrast to the dramatic landscaping of its companion course, Osprey Ridge, which also plays from the Bonnet Creek Golf Club. Designed by Pete Dye on a (successful) mission to create a unique challenge for players of all levels, Eagle Pines features target fairways, expansive waste areas, and roughs lined with pine needles. True to its rustic environs (it's located on the outskirts of Fort Wilderness), the course is sufficiently nestled in foliage and marshlands to summon comparisons to a nature preserve. Although water comes into play on 16 holes, the overall impression is one of great variety, from short par 4s to far sterner challenges—this is one course that lives up to the cliché of making you use every club in the bag. The course measures 4,838 yards from the front tees, 6,309 from the middle, and 6,772 yards from the back

Course for Celebration

Disney's town of Celebration, Florida, is home to the Celebration Golf Club, a joint venture of father-and-son designers Robert Trent Jones, Sr., and Robert Trent Jones, Jr. Fees for the par-72 course range from about $55 to $115, depending on the time of day and season; call 407-566-4653.

The Ten Most Humbling Holes

Cumulative toughest-playing
Classic holes since 1983:

1. Palm No. 18
2. Palm No. 6
3. Palm No. 10
4. Palm No. 4
5. Magnolia No. 5
6. Magnolia No. 18
7. Magnolia No. 17
8. Magnolia No. 15
9. Magnolia No. 1
10. Palm No. 12

markers. Facilities shared by Eagle Pines and Osprey Ridge include a driving range, a putting green, a pro shop, a restaurant, and a lounge. Course record: 60 (Bart Bryant, 1993).

LAKE BUENA VISTA: This Joe Lee design is a Rodney Dangerfield of sorts. One of the shortest of the five 18-hole courses, it features a good amount of water, and its fairways, hemmed in by stands of pine and oak, are Disney golf's tightest. Lake Buena Vista honors its reputation as a friendly course for less experienced golfers. But it is also well equipped to challenge more-skilled players. As golf writer Glen Waggoner once put it, Lake Buena Vista may be the weakest link in the Disney chain, but it's still head and shoulders above the number two venue at most other golf resorts in the United States.

The course's toughest holes—the 11th and the 18th—were at one time counted among the ten most humbling tests in the history of the Funai Classic at Walt Disney World Resort. But perhaps no one has greater respect for the course than Calvin Peete, who, in the 1982 Classic, blitzed the Palm in a record-breaking 66 strokes, only to give it all back—and more—on little ol' Lake Buena Vista.

The course plays to 5,194 yards from the front tees, 6,268 from the middle, and 6,819 from the rearmost markers. Facilities at Lake Buena Vista include a driving range and a practice green. Course record: 61 (Bob Tway, 1989).

Tennis

Even if you can't quite picture Mickey with a midsize racquet in his hand, Walt Disney World can still serve up plenty of tennis action for players of any caliber. There is a total of 25 courts scattered around the World, including four located at the Dolphin hotel and shared with the Swan. You'll find a pair of hard courts at the

Yacht and Beach Club, two at
BoardWalk, two more at Fort
Wilderness (watch out for swinging toddlers), and a
nice, quiet trio (the
courts, not the players)
at Old Key West.

The Grand Floridian
resort's duo of courts
boasts clay surfaces.
Tennis courts lighted for
night play are available at
many Disney resorts; this is a
big deal, given the daytime heat
during much of the year. For
quality court time, the most
important three words that
serious tennis buffs need to
remember when planning a trip
to Walt Disney World are:
Disney's Racquet Club.

150

Disney's Racquet Club

Disney's Racquet Club should
please even the pickiest players.
The six courts, lighted for night
play, are state-of-the-art hydro-
grid clay, with a subterranean
irrigation system that keeps
them evenly watered without
sprinklers. They're not quite in
the shadow of Cinderella castle,
but they are in close proximity to
the Magic Kingdom.

KNOW BEFORE YOU GO: Disney's
Racquet Club is just beside the
Contemporary resort. Courts are
busiest during June and July,
when leagues may take over
from 10 A.M. to 4 P.M. Two
courts are open to guests
at these times, but they
are first come, first
served (so to speak).
February, March, and
April also tend to be busy,
especially around holidays
and spring break. January,
October, and November should
be considered prime time to play.
The courts are generally open
from 8 A.M. to 6 P.M., but hours
vary seasonally. Court time is
without charge. Equipment
rentals are not available. Courts
are available on a first-come
basis. Locker room facilities are
available at no charge.

All Walt Disney World tennis courts are available to guests on a first-come basis. Call 407-824-3578 and ask for the player match-up sheets.

Dress: It's hot down here, so we recommend cool, loose-fitting tennis whites. As for showing up in footwear other than flat-bottomed tennis shoes, note that cross-trainers and running shoes tear up clay courts.

TOURNAMENTS: Private tennis tournaments may be arranged. For information and pricing, call 407-827-4433.

Fishing

Drop a line, it's promptly answered. That's typical fishing at Walt Disney World. Bay Lake, which adjoins man-made Seven Seas Lagoon, was stocked with 70,000 largemouth bass in the mid-1960s. A restrictive fishing policy allowed the fish to swell in both numbers and size.

On these waters you're not just likely to catch fish—you're apt to catch largemouth bass weighing eight pounds or more. And it's not uncommon for a group to catch 15 to 20 fish over a couple of hours, or for a first-timer to reel in half a dozen good-size bass.

The official policy is catch-and-release, and no license is required for fishing on Walt Disney World waterways. Fishing guides know their territory well, keep close track of where the fish are biting, and serve in whatever capacity guests prefer—from straight chauffeurs to casting coaches and even all-out facilitators.

Reservations for all Disney fishing excursions must be made at least 24 hours in advance and may be made up to 90 days ahead. Call 407-939-7529 for reservations and pricing.

Guided Fishing Trips

BAY LAKE & SEVEN SEAS LAGOON: Guided expeditions offering first-rate largemouth bass fishing depart from the Fort Wilderness marina at 7 A.M., 10 A.M., and 1:30 P.M. (hours vary seasonally) for two-hour trips on Bay Lake and Seven Seas Lagoon. Trips are made on pontoon-style boats and can accommodate up to five people.

The fee per boatload runs from $180 to $210 (tack on about $80 more for an extra hour) and includes guide, gear, and beverages. Guides will pick up guests at the Contemporary, Fort Wilderness, Grand Floridian, Polynesian, and Wilderness Lodge marinas. Call 407-WDW-PLAY (939-7529).

LAKE BUENA VISTA: Guided two-hour excursions plying Lake Buena Vista and adjacent waterways depart at 6 A.M. and 9 A.M. from the Downtown Disney Marketplace marina. On 6 A.M. trips, anglers have the lake and the largemouth bass therein all to themselves (later, rental boats may infringe on prime fishing territory).

The cost for up to five people, including guide, gear, and beverages, is $180 to $210 for two hours. Guides will also pick up guests at Port Orleans French Quarter, Port Orleans Riverside, and Old Key West. Call 407-WDW-PLAY (939-7529).

CRESCENT LAKE: Daily fishing excursions depart at 7 A.M. from the BoardWalk dock and 7 A.M. and 10 A.M. from the Yacht and Beach Club marina. Cost is $180 to $210 for two hours (about $85

more for an extra hour) for up to five people, including guide, fishing gear, bait, and refreshments. Call 407-WDW-PLAY (939-7529).

Fishing on Your Own

Individuals who prefer to fish solo may do so on the canals of Fort Wilderness, BoardWalk, and off the dock at the Downtown Disney Marketplace—catch-and-release only. Poles may be rented for about $4 per hour at the Marketplace, BoardWalk, and at the Fort Wilderness Bike Barn (the latter also rents rods and reels for $6 per hour or $9 per day; bait costs $3.50).

Port Orleans Riverside has a pond

Fishing Tips

Although the fishing is good here year-round, it's most pleasant from November through May, when temperatures are cooler. As for strategy, one local recommends going with plastic worms. To stack your odds, he suggests shiners (about $12 for a dozen; ask for them when you make reservations). Also, top-water baits work well in spring and fall.

called the Ol' Fishin' Hole that's stocked with catfish, bass, and bluegill. Catch-and-release only, the quiet spot features a small dock among tall reeds where, from 7 A.M. to 3 P.M. every day (hours may vary seasonally), fishing is returned to its cane-pole-and-worm roots. Pole rental is $4 per half hour, including worms. Call 407-934-6000, extension 6278.

Biking

While Fort Wilderness is certainly prime territory for some leisurely cycling, the World is filled with picturesque roads that wind within some of its most sprawling and scenic resorts.

Bikes are available for rental (about $8 per half hour or $22 per day, with some variation among locations) in precisely the spots where guests will want to ride them: Fort Wilderness, Wilderness Lodge, Old Key West, Port Orleans Riverside, Port Orleans French Quarter, Caribbean Beach, BoardWalk, and Coronado Springs.

Boating

Guests looking to cruise, paddle, or even create a small wake on the pristine lakes and waterways of Disney World have nothing short of the largest fleet of pleasure boats in the country at their disposal. Resort marinas stand by with sailboats, pontoon boats, canopy boats, canoes, pedal boats, and mini-speedboats, all of which are available for rent on a first-come, first-served basis.

On the World's most expansive boating forum, the 650-acre body of water comprising Bay Lake and the adjoining Seven Seas Lagoon, watercraft from the Contemporary, Wilderness Lodge, and Fort Wilderness marinas converge with boats lighting out from the Polynesian

and Grand Floridian. Other areas are more contained. Craft rented at the Caribbean Beach cruise around 45-acre Barefoot Bay. As boats on brief loan from the Downtown Disney Marketplace roam 35-acre Lake Buena Vista, small flotillas of rental craft drift in from the upriver marinas of Old Key West and Port Orleans French Quarter and Riverside. Meanwhile, watercraft from the Yacht and Beach Club and the Swan and Dolphin make ripples on Crescent Lake, while pedal boaters ply the 15-acre Lago Dorado at Coronado Springs.

Resort marinas are usually open from 10 A.M. until early evening (hours vary seasonally). No privately owned boats are permitted on WDW waterways. Renters must present a WDW resort ID card, a driver's license, or a passport. Some boat rentals carry other restrictions.

CANOEING: Paddling among the narrow channels of Fort Wilderness during the peaceful morning hours, canoers pass through forest and meadows, encountering solitary anglers and quacking contingents along the way. Fishing and canoeing are an irresistible combination for many, with fishing gear available

for rent right alongside the canoes (which run about $7 per half hour or $11 per hour) at the Fort Wilderness Bike Barn. Canoes may also be rented at Caribbean Beach, and Port Orleans Riverside and French Quarter. Use of these watercraft is restricted to WDW canals.

CRUISING: For groups interested in taking a leisurely sunning, sightseeing, or party excursion on the water, motorized canopy boats and pontoon boats are the only way to go. Sixteen-foot canopy boats accommodating up to eight adults (about $26.50 per half hour) and 21-foot pontoon boats holding ten adults (about $32 per half hour) are available for rent at most marinas. Guests must be 19 years old to rent a pontoon boat and 16 years old to rent a canopy boat. For information on special-occasion cruises, see page 176.

PEDAL BOATING: For those who prefer pedal-pushing to paddling, pedal boats (accommodating two pedaling passengers and two freeloaders) are available for about $6.50 per half hour or $11 per hour at most marinas. WDW resort guests can rent the boats at the Caribbean Beach, Port Orleans Riverside, Swan and Dolphin, Coronado Springs, and Yacht and Beach Club marinas, and Fort Wilderness. The Swan, Dolphin, and Old Key West also rent Hydro Bikes (singles, $8 per half hour; doubles, about $16 per half hour), which resemble upright bicycles affixed to pontoons. Guests of Animal Kingdom Lodge, the All-Star resorts, and Pop Century can rent boats at any of the above-mentioned locations.

SAILING: Bay Lake and Seven Seas Lagoon offer pretty reliable winds and unparalleled running room. Sailing conditions are generally best in March and April. Sailboats may be rented at the Grand Floridian, Polynesian, Contemporary, Wilderness

Lodge, and Caribbean Beach marinas. Rental fees range from $20 to $25 per hour. Among the options are SunFish (two passengers max), Monohulls (good beginner boats holding up to six), and catamarans for two or three people (experience is required).

SPEEDBOATING: Among the most enjoyable ways to cool off at Walt Disney World is the legion of mini-speedboats called Water Mouse boats (which replaced Water Sprites). The boats' small hulls ride a choppy surface as though they were galloping steeds, maxing out at 22 miles per hour. (A bonus: Drivers must be 12 to pilot the boats.) Fort Wilderness Marina offers one of the more uncrowded arenas at WDW. While the boats ostensibly seat two, adult boaters will reach greater speeds going solo (and

creating tiny wakes for one another). Water Mouse boats are restricted to lakes only and are available for about $22 per half hour at the Grand Floridian, Polynesian, Contemporary, Wilderness Lodge, Fort Wilderness, Yacht and Beach Club, Caribbean Beach, Port Orleans French Quarter, Port Orleans Riverside, and Coronado Springs marinas.

WATERSKIING AND WAKEBOARDING:
Enthusiasts interested in hitching a ride around Bay Lake and Seven Seas Lagoon will pay about $75 single, $125 tandem per hour for a boat and instructor. Cost is by the boatload, and up to five people can be accommodated at a time.

Trips depart from the Contemporary. Reservations must be made at least 24 hours in advance and can be made up to 90 days ahead. Call 407-WDW-PLAY (939-7529).

Jogging

Despite pleasant terrain that looks like it's been spread with a rolling pin, Walt Disney World can be a

rough place to pursue the world's most mobile form of exercise. From late spring through early fall, comfortable running conditions are fleeting, with early birds getting the best shot at an enjoyable run. In the cooler seasons, joggers have greater freedom to explore the many compelling choices here. Inquire about maps of the jogging trails and footpaths accessible from most WDW resorts at the hotel's Guest Services desk. Courses range from one mile to just over three. Port Orleans Riverside, Old Key West, and Fort Wilderness offer some of the most extensive and scenic venues.

Parasailing

If the notion of flying like a kite above Bay Lake with a panorama of the Magic Kingdom appeals to you, factor in a harness that allows you to sit in a reclined position and you have an idea of the parasailing experience as it exists at Walt Disney World.

The flight lasts seven to ten minutes, and the landing is quite soft, thanks to the parachute and the two-person crew's skillful handling (as one reels in the cord,

the other slows the boat just so).
You won't even get wet!

Parasailing excursions are
offered at the Contemporary marina, with none other than four-
time World Overall
Champion Sammy Duvall
and his world-class
instructors.

The cost is about
$75 for single riders
and $115 for tandem
riders. Make reserva-
tions up to 90 days in
advance by calling
407-939-0754. Guests
must check in 20 minutes
before departure. (If you're
afraid of heights, this adventure
will scare you silly.)

Swimming

As if it weren't enough to have an
inside track to two massive water
parks (see "Other Pursuits" in the
latter part of this chapter), Walt
Disney World resorts are
themselves bursting at
the seams with watery
playgrounds. With no
fewer than 60 pools
spread throughout
Disney's hotel grounds,
guests at each resort can
be assured of easy
access to at least one
pool. However, it is important to note that due to a policy
initiated to prevent overcrowding,
Walt Disney World hotel pools are
open only to guests staying at that

resort; pool-hopping is permitted between sister resorts (the Yacht and Beach Club; Pop Century resorts; Port Orleans Riverside and Port Orleans French Quarter; All-Star Movies, All-Star Music, and All-Star Sports; and the Swan and Dolphin).

Stock Car Driving

The drone of stock cars burning up a one-mile oval sets most anyone's mind to racing. Ergo a pumped-up driver's ed has been introduced at the Walt Disney World Speedway, near the Magic Kingdom parking lot.

The Richard Petty Driving Experience even welcomes backseat drivers. (Or passenger-seat drivers, as the case happens to be.)

Prefer to keep your sweaty palms off the wheel? Try the Riding Experience, about $90 for three laps; no reservations necessary.

Want your foot on that gas pedal? If you can drive a stick shift (and can prove it), consider reserving the three-hour Rookie Experience (about $370). It includes instruction and eight high-speed laps. If that doesn't sound like enough of a challenge, perhaps the 18-Lap King's Experience (about $740) is more your speed. Or, finally, ponder the Experience of a Lifetime (about $1,270). It delivers three rounds of Petty practice.

To get in the driver's seat, call 800-237-3889.

Disney's Wide World of Sports Complex

Should your definition of paradise include slam dunks, screeching fastballs, and the intoxicating aroma of steamed weenies, welcome to nirvana. Disney's Wide World of Sports complex, which sprawls over 200 acres, is one agile place. Capable of hosting a dozen events at once, the facility has an archery-to-wrestling lineup that can can make for some compelling competition.

The complex serves as the spring-training ground for Major League Baseball's Atlanta Braves and the summer training camp of the National Football League's 2003 Super Bowl champion Tampa Buccaneers. It also hosts the Amateur Athletic Union (AAU) and a veritable turntable of tournaments.

Despite its large size, the complex somehow comes off as almost quaint. Its old-time Floridian architecture harks back to a simpler time and place. It recaptures the essence of a neighborhood ballpark, beckoning friends and families to spend a lazy afternoon together.

The complex, near the junction of I-4 and U.S. 192, has an armory of box and bleacher seats to accommodate all manner of spectators. There's a 7,500-seat baseball stadium; a field house that hosts basketball, wrestling, and volleyball; a track-and-field complex; 11 clay tennis courts; and five multipurpose fields for football, soccer, lacrosse, and more.

The $10 general admission ticket (good only on days when events are scheduled) allows you the freedom to take in a number of nonpremium events—that is, competitions that are worth watching, but not quite major league. Tickets for all premium

Sports Complex Tips

- For a complete, updated sporting event calendar, call 407-828-FANS (3267) or pay a visit to *www.disneyworldsports.com.*

- WDW resort guests may take buses from the Disney-MGM Studios during park hours or from Downtown Disney. Note that transfers can take quite a bit of time.

- Tailgating in the parking lot is not permitted. (Parking is free.)

- Take an umbrella to outdoor contests (the area's prone to afternoon showers), and know that games may be canceled due to inclement weather.

- Want to be a part of the action? Volunteer to work at a Wide World of Sports event. Call 407-828-3267.

Which Way to the Beach?

WDW resort guests need not set out for the coast to find pretty strands to sunbathe on and get sand between their toes. Between the resorts fronting Bay Lake (the Contemporary, Wilderness Lodge, and Fort Wilderness) and those alongside Seven Seas Lagoon (the Grand Floridian and Polynesian), there are over five miles of white-sand beaches. And that does not include the powdery white stretches at the Caribbean Beach, Yacht and Beach Club, Swan and Dolphin, and Coronado Springs resorts. The beach fronting the Polynesian's Tahiti guest building is among the more secluded shores. All beaches are reserved exclusively for guests staying at those properties. Note that swimming is not permitted.

events, such as Atlanta Braves games, are available through TicketMaster (407-839-3900; www.ticketmaster.com) and include license to roam the complex. Premium tickets can also be purchased at the complex's ticket office on the day of the event, if available.

For the whole sports lineup, a visit to the complex's website: www.disneyworldsports.com.

If an afternoon of cheering (pom-poms

160

optional) and rooting for the next-best-thing-to-the-home-team leaves you with a line-backer-style appetite, head straight for the All Star Cafe. The burgers are good, the atmosphere's festive, and as far as restaurants go, it's the only game in town. Vendors offer stadium snacks for those dining in their seats or on the run.

Health Clubs

Not all fitness centers at the Disney resorts are reserved just for guests staying at that resort. Olympiad Health Club at the Contemporary (407-824-3410), Grand Floridian Spa & Health Club (407-824-2332), Muscles & Bustles at BoardWalk (407-939-2370), La Vida at Coronado Springs (407-939-3030), R.E.S.T. at Old Key West (407-827-7700), Ship Shape at the Yacht and Beach Club (407-934-3256), Sturdy Branches Health Club at The Villas at Wilderness Lodge (407-938-4222), the Spa at Disney's Saratoga Springs Resort (407-827-4455), and Zahanati Health Club at Animal

Kingdom Lodge (407-938-4715) are accessible to all WDW resort guests; Body By Jake at the Dolphin (407-934-4264) is open to all.

The bare-bones facility at the Swan (free for all Swan and Dolphin guests) is fine for on-the-road maintenance. Better equipped—more cardiovascular machines and saunas—are the Contemporary Fitness Center, Muscles & Bustles at BoardWalk, La Vida at Coronado Springs, Sturdy Branches at The Villas at Wilderness Lodge, Ship Shape at the Yacht and Beach Club (which has a whirlpool, steam room, and

sauna), and Zahanati Health Club at Animal Kingdom Lodge (which boasts a steam room plus spa services including massages, manicures, and pedicures); cost is about $15 per day, $30 for length of stay, or $40 for length of stay per family of up to five to use any of the six clubs. R.E.S.T. at Old Key West is free for WDW resort guests.

The best of the lot distinguish themselves by offering exceptionally pleasant environs and the likes of personal trainers and Cybex machines. Body By Jake at the Dolphin ($10 per day; free for Swan and Dolphin guests) offers aerobics and Polaris equipment, and the Grand Floridian Spa & Health Club ($12 per day, about $30 for length of stay) comes with frills; for details, see this chapter's "Spas" section.

The well-appointed Spa at Disney's Saratoga Springs Resort ($15 per day, $35 for length of stay, or $50 for length of stay per family of four) could be a Cybex warehouse if not for its airy setting.

WDW's Most Striking Feature

Walt Disney World lies squarely within a band of Central Florida known as the Lightning Capital of the World. Prime striking season runs from May through September, peaking during July and August, when Mother Nature unleashes about 40 thunderstorms over just 62 days, according to National Weather Service figures. Most of these storms come and go rather quickly.

To protect yourself, seek shelter (the type with four walls and a roof) the moment you see a storm developing, and wait a good 15 minutes after the last rumble before resuming outdoor activity. Trees and umbrellas do not provide safe refuge. For a weather report, call 407-824-4104.

SHOPPING
In Downtown Disney Marketplace

THE ART OF DISNEY: If you skip this showroom filled with limited-edition art pieces, collectibles, and animation cels, you've missed out on some of the most spectacular ogling to be had in all of Walt Disney World. A Disney artist is on hand daily to draw personalized sketches of favorite characters, as well as answer questions about the animation process.

Downtown Disney, Defined

In addition to the World's best shopping, the Downtown Disney Marketplace offers restaurants, lounges, a marina, special events, and interactive fountains. Walkways link the Marketplace to its spirited neighbors: Pleasure Island and Downtown Disney West Side. The three locales (and the stockpile of clubs, shops, and restaurants therein) are collectively known as Downtown Disney—a district zoned exclusively for entertainment. Buses and boats service the area. Marketplace shops are described in this section (starting above), while Pleasure Island and West Side shops are summed up in the margin on the next page. See our "Restaurant Guide" and "Nightlife Guide" in the *Dining & Entertainment* chapter for further details on the restaurants and clubs located here.

BASIN: Scents make sense at this shop, which soothes body and soul with bath crystals, soaps, and custom candles. Time seems to stand still here, too—the decor is reminiscent of a 19th-century shop.

DISNEY'S DAYS OF CHRISTMAS: It even smells like Christmas here in the World's largest excuse to say "Ho, ho, ho." Rather than tick off the many delightful trimmings—both traditional and Disney-style—proffered at this trove of decorative items, ornaments, and collectibles, we'll cut to the chase: Just add eggnog.

DISNEY AT HOME: One look around this shop might inspire you to re-accessorize the house with subtle (and not-so-subtle) Mickey-revering dishware, blankets, clocks, and (dare we suggest) furniture. Or to find a good home for a signature piece of embossed pottery or a wrought-iron candleholder.

GOURMET PANTRY: This Marketplace institution is positively crammed with delectables (soup, sandwiches, and beverages are also available); while many sweets and savories are meant for instant gratification, others (Mickey-shaped pasta and Mickey Shorts Bread) make good souvenirs.

TEAM MICKEY'S ATHLETIC CLUB: This expansive shop specializes in sport-specific Disney character apparel, gear, and souvenirs that run the gamut from Goofy golf club covers to Minnie Mouse tennis whites.

DISNEY'S WONDERFUL WORLD OF MEMORIES: In this nook, you'll find Disney World-branded scrapbook supplies (including kits, glue sticks, scissors, and Disney stickers), plus a host of Disney books, stationery, and postcards—a wealth of materials to leave you with lasting memories of your Walt Disney World vacation.

Beyond the Marketplace

The shops at Pleasure Island and Downtown Disney West Side are light on Mouse goods and heavy on offbeat items with adult appeal.

At Pleasure Island, Reel Finds yields stars' collectibles; Suspended Animation offers cels; and Island Depot delivers novelty T-shirts.

On the West Side, Starabilias peddles Hollywood memorabilia; Magic Masters offers crystal balls, linking handcuffs, and other magician's wish list items; and Magnetron is the place for umpteen magnets. The Guitar Gallery is the vintage guitar source; Virgin Megastore is CD central; and Sosa Family Cigars offers premium smokes.

WORLD OF DISNEY: The most comprehensive collection of Disney character merchandise available anywhere and a shopper's concierge desk equipped to locate any item in stock make this vast retail emporium an unbeatable venue for one-stop souvenir sprees.

As you make your way through the maze of displays, ranging from limited-edition watches to stuffed animals, from intimate apparel to office accessories, and from frames to photo albums, notice how each room has a different theme, replete with colorful murals and whimsical character sculptures. The villains room is one of our favorites.

EUROSPAIN: Presented by Arribas Brothers, this shop offers crystal keepsakes (engraved on-site by cutters who demonstrate the age-old art of glass sculpting), porcelain figurines, glass slippers, and more.

In the Parks
Magic Kingdom
AGRABAH BAZAAR
(Adventureland): This open-air marketplace was designed to resemble a Moroccan port, where merchants from around the world come to sell their vases, brass, and other exotic wares.

BRIAR PATCH (Frontierland): The specialty of the house is merchandise that sweetly portrays Winnie the Pooh and cohorts.

CRYSTAL ARTS (Main Street): This shop offers cut-glass bowls, vases, plates and clear-glass mugs and steins similar to those found at Eurospain in the Downtown Disney Marketplace. Items can be engraved on-site, and guests have the opportunity to observe an engraver or glassblower at work.

DISNEY & CO. (Main Street): Victorian wallpaper, elaborate woodwork, and old-fashioned ceiling fans are a fitting back

164

Did You Know?
Orlando Earport, a new shop in Orlando International Airport, lets you browse Disney goodies up until your flight time.

drop for the intimate apparel at this lovely shop.

DISNEY CLOTHIERS (Main Street): Souvenir clothing earns big style points here, as various Disney characters appear on silk scarves, ties, and leather goods, and are appliquéd on collared shirts, denim shirts, sweaters, jackets, and nightshirts. Selection is small but choice.

EMPORIUM (Main Street): The Magic Kingdom's largest gift shop offers an array of WDW logo and character merchandise (including lots of stuffed animals, T-shirts, sweatshirts, and hats) whose variety is eclipsed only by that found at the Marketplace. Be sure to get a glimpse of the display windows out front.

THE KING'S GALLERY (Cinderella Castle): You'll pay a king's ransom to walk off with some of the treasures at this richly appointed shop with suits of armor and Spanish-made swords. But don't overlook the Cinderella keepsakes.

MAIN STREET ATHLETIC CLUB

(Main Street): A nifty stash of sports-related character apparel can be found here. If you want to score some great gear sporting classic Disney characters in action, don't pass.

MAIN STREET CONFECTIONERY

(Main Street): The sweet-toothed fall in line for peanut brittle, fudge, and marshmallow crispy treats made on the premises. For Pooh's Hunny Pots (chocolate filled with gooey caramel), chocolate-covered Mickey-shaped pretzels, and creatively candy-coated marshmallows, this is the source. Who knows? You may even get to watch the candy-makers in action.

MAIN STREET GALLERY (Main

Street): This is one of five WDW showrooms featuring limited-edition art pieces, collectibles, and animation cels (an extraordinary eyeful that should not be missed). Displays are different at each gallery.

MAIN STREET MARKET HOUSE

(Main Street): Brass lanterns and oak floors provide the background for a selection of old-fashioned snacks and dishware. There's a small selection of candy, too.

UPTOWN JEWELERS (Main Street):

If you're shopping for a character watch, 14-karat gold or sterling silver jewelry, or souvenir charms, this elegant catchall is the place.

THE YANKEE TRADER (Liberty

Square): A front porch with a rocking chair sets the tone for this cozy niche chock-full of Disney country kitchenware.

YE OLDE CHRISTMAS SHOPPE

(Liberty Square): Although smaller than Disney's Days of Christmas at the Downtown Disney Marketplace, this locale is a fine resource for traditional and character holiday decorations. Ho, ho, ho.

Epcot Standouts

THE AMERICAN ADVENTURE (World Showcase): Heritage Manor Gifts waxes patriotic with Americana. Highlights include decorative throws, history books, and colonial memorabilia.

THE ART OF DISNEY (Future World): The Art of Disney serves as the park's repository for Disney animation cels and limited-edition art pieces and collectibles. It is one of five such showrooms at Walt Disney World.

CANADA (World Showcase): A vast array of Canadian handicrafts and Indian artifacts puts the Northwest Mercantile on the essential-shopping circuit. But don't neglect the refined pottery and pewter candlesticks at La Boutique des Provinces.

CHINA (World Showcase): Yong Feng Shangdian is so huge, it's almost a province. The montage of paper fans, Chinese prints, silk robes, antiques, vases, and tea sets is truly something to behold.

FRANCE (World Showcase): Boutiques offering all things beautiful and French. Our favorites are Plume et Palette (collectibles), Les Vins de France (fine French wines, cookbooks, and some hand-painted dishes), and La Signature (Guerlain cosmetics and fragrances).

GERMANY (World Showcase): The little shops here are simply irresistible. Die Weihnachts Ecke is bursting with cuckoo clocks, nutcrackers, and wood carvings. Volkskunst features beer steins in all sizes, while Der Teddybär is simply a delightful toy shop. Weinkeller boasts about 50 vintage varieties and holds daily wine tastings. Kunstarbeit in Kristall offers steins, crystal, and assorted Christmas goodies. Finally, Glas und Porzellan is a boutique stocked with Goebel's M. I. Hummel figurines.

GREEN THUMB EMPORIUM (The Land, Future World): Don't be misled. While this great shop is flush with seeds, kits, and garden-themed knickknacks, gardening prowess is not sold here. Trust us: No green thumbs change hands.

ITALY (World Showcase): When in this multishop pavilion, we gravitate toward Enoteca Castello for Italian wines, plus some chocolates, La Bottega Italiana for decorative ceramics and glassware, plus masks from Venice, and Il Bel Cristallo for Armani figurines, silk scarves, and leather purses and bags.

JAPAN (World Showcase): In the vast emporium known as the Mitsukoshi Department Store, kimono-clad dolls (priced from $20 to $500) merit special attention, as do colorful kimonos, origami kits, bonsai, candy, and children's toys. You will also find a variety of items with which to set the table and decorate the home.

MOUSE GEAR (Innoventions, Future World): Epcot's best address for character merchandise also stocks a selection of souvenirs relating to surrounding pavilions (most notably, Spaceship Earth). This shop stays open about a half hour after the rest of the park. It's a great place to wait out the big exit crush.

MEXICO (World Showcase): At the Plaza de los Amigos you can find all things South of the Border, including Mexican liquor, salsa and other hot sauces, sombreros, and a fine selection of ceramics and other handicrafts.

MOROCCO (World Showcase): At least half the fun of shopping in this pavilion's maze of Berber bangles, basketry, and clothing is never knowing just what awaits around the bend (we found a lovely little bottle filled with rosewater, known as *cortas*).

NORWAY (World Showcase): The Puffin's Roost is undoubtedly Central Florida's best source for trolls and gorgeous, often hand-knit, Norwegian ski sweaters (bargains when compared to the cost of flights to Oslo). Wood

167

carvings and handcrafted jewelry add to the purchase panorama.

UNITED KINGDOM (World Showcase): Some of Epcot's finest shops lie within this pavilion's borders. There's The Toy Soldier (where Winnie the Pooh and Thomas the Tank Engine star); The Crown & Crest (a British free-for-all complete with intricately designed chess sets and pub glasses); Sportsman Shoppe (a bounty of cashmeres and sports apparel); The Queen's Table (with fragrances, soaps, and other collectibles); and The Magic of Wales (tartans). And there's a prime spot for fans of fine bone china and English teas—The Tea Caddy.

Disney-MGM Studios

ANIMATION GALLERY: One of six Walt Disney World venues showcasing limited-edition art pieces, collectibles, and animation cels from a variety of Disney movies. The difference here: the chance to watch an artist creating and to buy the resulting artwork right on the spot.

KEYSTONE CLOTHIERS: Characters turn up on smartly styled men's and women's casual wear, luggage, and shoes, not to mention accessories of the silk character tie and boxer short sort.

MOUSE ABOUT TOWN: A well-heeled wardrobe of subtly mouse-infused jackets, sweatshirts, and sports apparel in colors a human-about-town would also appreciate. Golf-related accessories and apparel abound.

Pin Trading

In the mood for some Olympic-Village-style pin trading? You're in luck. A veritable bartering brouhaha has erupted at Walt Disney World. Here's how it works:

Simply purchase—or pack—some starter pins (available throughout WDW). Put the pins in a highly visible place (say, on your hat). Then keep your eyes peeled for pin-bearing park-goers or Disney cast members.

If your pin-trading etiquette is not up to snuff, ask a cast member for advice. Remember: If you're displaying a pin, it's assumed you are willing to trade it—so don't flaunt family heirlooms or other pins you can't part with. And when it comes to swapping with cast members, it's strictly Disney pin for Disney pin.

Talk About an Eclectic Mix . . .

The unique array of merchandise found in shops at the Studios is best quantified by example. Recently, you could have filled the following unlikely shopping list:

- An end table once owned by Cecil B. DeMille
- Limited-edition Disney animation cel
- Frank Sinatra's electric piano
- *I Love Lucy* silk tie
- *Austin Powers* movie lot crew ID badge
- A cocktail dress from Susan Lucci's closet

ONCE UPON A TIME: . . . there was a little shop that offered one of the classiest souvenir collections the World over—musical snow globes featuring artfully rendered Disney characters and lovely character-infused housewares.

SID CAHUENGA'S ONE-OF-A-KIND: Celebrity encounters abound in this den of movie and television memorabilia. There's lots of autographed photos and original movie posters, and if you time it right, belated premiere invitations to Disney animated films.

There's also ample opportunity to snap up hand-me-downs direct from the stars, so when someone compliments your handbag, you can say, "Yeah,

Mae West liked it, too." Closet contents turn over too frequently to allow for specifics, but past fashion statements have come courtesy of Clark Gable and Elizabeth Taylor. Cher's closet tends to be disproportionately represented. The merchandise changes often and the offerings may be different when you visit.

SUNSET CLUB COUTURE: This purveyor of jewelry and limited-edition timepieces has the sort of incomparable selection that makes collectors' eyes widen. Consider gold pocket watches with conspicuous ears, marcasite pieces with stylized Mickey

Conservation Initiative

As anyone who has ever given a gorilla a dollar could tell you, animals aren't great money managers. Which is why initiatives like the Disney Wildlife Conservation Fund come in handy.

This fund was established to support conservation efforts worldwide. You can help by tacking on a dollar for the Wildlife Conservation Fund when you make a purchase at any Animal Kingdom shop. If you're interested, pick up a brochure from a shop display for a list of nonprofit organizations assisted to date.

Expect a gentle solicitation at the cash register. Don't expect a gorilla looking for a handout.

designs, and custom-made watches with tremendous face value (namely, your choice of characters, drawn and then sealed onto the watch's face).

THE WRITER'S STOP: A cozy commissary of cookies, cappuccino, stationery (and scrapbooking accessories), and Hollywood-themed page-turners that provides a comfy pit stop (and shop).

Animal Kingdom

DISNEY OUTFITTERS (Discovery Island): Nature-themed apparel and descriptive gifts can be found here. Selections vary from everything you need to start your own backyard habitat to tinkling chimes, aromatic candles, and soothing fountains, as well as many other unique treasures.

ISLAND MERCANTILE (Discovery Island): The park's largest shopping oasis in a nutshell: stuffed animals on safari. Certainly, this is the last word in safari hat style, as interpreted by every Disney character that ever saw the embroidered front of a sweatshirt.

MOMBASA MARKETPLACE/ZIWANI TRADERS (Africa): Take one of the striking Kenyan-made walking sticks for an in-store test

170

The Mouse Delivers

- Prowling the property but can't find the object of your obsession? Ask a park employee, and if that must-have Donald Duck screen saver or Tinker Bell tea set exists, he or she should be able to find out where it's sold.

- Have a sudden, not-to-be-denied yearning for a certain music box, watch, or tie that you saw in a shop during your visit? Call WDW Mail Order at 407-363-6200.

- If your Disney cravings are still unfulfilled, call 800-237-5751 for the Disney Catalog or 818-265-4660 to find the Disney Store nearest you. Or browse through the Disney Store's offerings online at www.disneystore.com.

- Theme park shoppers may arrange to send purchases to a location near the gates for later pickup. In the past, Walt Disney World resort guests could have purchases delivered to their hotel free of charge, but this service had been suspended at press time. For an extra charge, shoppers may arrange to have packages shipped home.

stroll, and you may well receive raves on your carving skills while perusing the soapstone elephants, hand-painted boxes, raku animal figurines, straw hats, colorful apparel, and other traditional African wares—as well as a selection of Disney character inspired items.

OTHER PURSUITS

You're at Walt Disney World, but you're not in the mood for a theme park, don't feel much like swatting a little yellow ball or sitting by the pool, and have already shopped (and dropped). You're up for something, but lack inspiration. What do you do? Don't despair. Disney's got this one covered.

Water Parks

Typhoon Lagoon

The centerpiece of this 34-acre water park—ostensibly a small resort town transformed by nature's wrath—is a surf lagoon larger than two football fields that incites happy pandemonium with every five-foot wave it

> **Did You Know?**
> Pontoon boats may be chartered for a party cruise at any time of day. The cost for a one-hour excursion—including snacks, soda, and champagne or cake—is $175 for up to five guests, $230 for as many as ten. Call 407-WDW-PLAY (939-7529) for details.

unleashes. But there are also three speed-slides (which drop 51 feet at 30 miles per hour), three quick and curvy body slides, and a trio of raft rides that send tubers rollicking through caverns and waterfalls. It's all encircled by a lazy river in which swimmers—or more accurately, inner-tube innards—leisurely beat the heat.

KNOW BEFORE YOU GO: Typhoon Lagoon is near Downtown Disney. Pools are heated during winter, and the park is typically closed for refurbishment for about two months each year (usually around November and December; call 407-WDW-PLAY [939-7529] for exact dates). During warmer months, the masses arrive early, often filling the parking lot before noon. When capacity is reached, no one is admitted until crowds subside, often around 3 P.M. (Typhoon Lagoon is usually the second water park to reach capacity. Blizzard Beach is first.)

HOW TO GET THERE: Direct buses from the TTC and all Disney resorts except the Grand Floridian, Contemporary, Polynesian, Wilderness Lodge, and Fort Wilderness (which require transfers at the TTC until 4 P.M.).

WHERE TO EAT: Of the two main snack stands, Leaning Palms offers a larger selection than Typhoon Tilly's. Picnic areas are close at hand. Outside food is welcome, but alcoholic beverages are not.

Typhoon Lagoon Tips

- Tidal conditions in the lagoon change every hour, alternating (with warning) between gentle waves and surf city. Call 407-WDW-PLAY (939-7529) for current conditions or to ask about early-morning surf lessons.

- For time checks, look to the shrimp boat marooned atop Typhoon Lagoon's makeshift mountain; it sounds its horn and shoots a 50-foot flume of water into the air every 30 minutes.

- Bad weather or capacity crowds can prompt the park to close.

- Women will find that one-piece suits fare better on the slides here.

VITAL STATISTICS: Hours vary, but are generally 10 A.M. to 5 P.M., with extended hours in effect during summer months (call 407-939-7529 for current times). Adult admission is $31.75, including tax. Entry to the Typhoon Lagoon water park is included in an Ultimate Park Hopper Ticket and is an option on a Park Hopper Plus Ticket.

Dressing rooms are available, and lockers and towels may be rented. Singapore Sal's stocks beach basics.

Blizzard Beach

Disney legend has it that this 66-acre water park—Walt Disney World's newest and largest—is the melted remains of a failed Disney ski resort. Call it a not-so-little white lie. The bottom line on this place built around a "snow-covered" man-made peak called Mount Gushmore: It has some amazing runs. Chief among them is a ski-jump-turned-speed slide that sends giddy riders down the watery equivalent of a double-black-diamond run (a 120-foot drop at a 66-degree angle, in which speeds reach 60 miles per hour). A second slide plunges from 90 feet. Less intimidating highlights include a raft ride accommodating five people per raft, side-by-side "racing" slides, and flumes that slalom. For cool yet calm, there's a lazy floatable creek that encircles the park (though it does at one point run through a cave dripping with ice-cold water) and a free-form pool with gently bobbing waves.

KNOW BEFORE YOU GO: Blizzard Beach is located near Animal Kingdom, adjacent to Disney's Winter Summerland miniature-golf course. All pools are heated during the winter; the park is

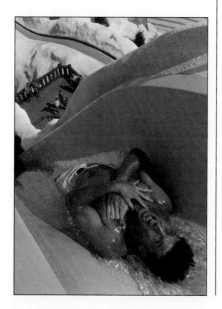

Blizzard Beach Tips

- The chairlift that transports guests to the summit of Mount Gushmore affords a wonderful view, as does an observatory located at the summit itself.
- Women will find that one-piece suits fare better on the speed slides here.
- Inclement weather or maxed-out crowds can cause the park to close.
- The concrete pathways can get hot, making water shoes a coveted commodity.

typically closed for refurbishment for at least one month each year (usually January and part of February; call 407-WDW-PLAY [939-7529] for the exact dates). During the warmer months, the masses descend upon Blizzard Beach early in the day, and the parking lot frequently closes before noon. When peak capacity is reached, no one is admitted until crowds ease up, usually around 3 P.M. The park may also close due to inclement weather.

HOW TO GET THERE: Buses are available from Disney-MGM Studios and all WDW resorts.

WHERE TO EAT Of the four snack stands, Lottawatta Lodge is the largest and most centrally located. Picnic areas are nearby.

VITAL STATISTICS: Hours vary, but are generally from 10 A.M. to 5 P.M., with extended hours in effect throughout the summer months (call 407-939-7529 for current times). Adult admission is $31.75, including tax. A Blizzard Beach/Disney's Winter Summerland pass, including Blizzard Beach admission and a round of mini golf, costs $39.17. Entry to Blizzard Beach is included with an Ultimate Park Hopper Ticket and is an option on a Park Hopper Plus Ticket. Dressing rooms are available, and lockers and towels may be rented. The Beach Haus stocks essentials.

Natural Distraction
Fort Wilderness

Simply put, no place on Walt Disney World property is better equipped to satisfy yens related to the great outdoors than this campground and recreation area, set on 700 forested, canal-crossed acres on the shore of the World's largest lake. Between its

174

wonderfully canoe-worthy canals and its guided fishing excursions, Fort Wilderness gives anglers unparalleled access to Bay Lake's largemouth bass. Since the lake was stocked with over 70,000 bass in the sixties, this waterway is teeming with fish that are ready to tangle with your line.

A marina invites guests to strap on water skis and rent all manner of boats for explorations of the lake. (See "Sports" earlier in this chapter for more details on fishing and boating excursions.) Escorted trail rides and a three-quarter-mile hiking path deliver nature lovers into peaceful areas where it's not uncommon to see deer, armadillos, and birds. Myriad pathways provide inspiring venues for joggers and cyclists (bikes are available for rent), and tennis, volleyball, and basketball courts are scattered about the property. There's also a goat-heavy petting farm (hey, grown-ups like animals, too), a blacksmith shop (where you can meet the man who shoes the horses that pull the trolleys on Main Street,

U.S.A.), and a funky tree that has mysteriously grown around a lawn mower. The two swimming pools are open only to camp-ground guests. In the evenings, carriage rides and wagon rides (see pages 64 and 176 for more information), Mickey's Backyard Barbecue, and the popular dinner show, the Hoop-Dee-Doo Musical Revue keep things humming.

HOW TO GET THERE: This isn't the easiest place to get to—but there are several travel options. The quickest way is generally by car. But know that guests staying at any Walt Disney World-owned property may take boat launches from the Magic Kingdom park, Wilderness Lodge, or the Contemporary resort. Buses also transport guests with a Disney resort ID or a multi-day admission ticket.

Fort Wilderness Tips

• You can survey the beauty of Fort Wilderness via bicycles rented from the Bike Barn for about $8 per half hour or $22 per day.

• Getting to and from this area can take a lot of time—inquire at WDW Resort Guest Services as to the most efficient route. Build in extra commuting time if you're planning to attend the Hoop-De-Doo Musical Review.

GETTING AROUND: Only vehicles bound for campsites are permit-ted beyond the guest parking lot. Fort Wilderness is serviced by an internal bus system that links all recreation areas and campsites (buses circulate at 20-minute intervals from 7 A.M. to 2 P.M.). Guests who prefer greater inde-pendence may rent bikes or elec-tric carts from the Bike Barn.

WHERE TO EAT: The Settlement Trading Post and the Meadow Trading Post stock a tiny supply of staples and prepare sand-wiches; there's also Trail's End Buffet for all-day dining.

VITAL STATISTICS: Admission is free for Disney resort guests. The Bike Barn in the Meadow Recreation Area is the place to pick up trail maps and rent bikes (about $8 per half hour, $22 per day), canoes ($6.50 per half hour, $11 per hour), rods and reels ($5.50 per hour, $9.50 per day), fishing poles ($4 per hour, about $9 per day), and electric carts (about $46 for 24 hours; reservations necessary; call 407-824-2742). Wagon rides depart twice nightly at 7 P.M. and 9:30 P.M. from Pioneer Hall and last about an hour ($6; call 407-939-7529 to confirm times).

Fort Wilderness carriage rides depart every thirty minutes, from 6 P.M. until 9:30 P.M. Each 30-minute ride begins in front of Crockett's Tavern at Pioneer Hall and costs $30 (credit cards are not accepted; Disney hotel IDs, cash, and Disney Dollars are). Tickets are sold by the carriage drivers. Small carriages fit two guests, larger ones can accommodate four. For more information, call 407-824-2734.

Guided 45-minute trail rides depart four times daily from the Tri-Circle-D Livery near the visitor lot; reservations suggested ($32; call 407-939-7529 up to 90 days ahead).

Romantic Excursions and Specialty Cruises

Breathless

Moored at the Yacht and Beach Club marina, the *Breathless* is a sleek 24-foot Chris-Craft reproduction of a 1930s mahogany runabout. The motorboat, named after the Dick Tracy character, is equipped with bench seats and fits up to seven. The boat escorts private parties on brief journeys around 25-acre Crescent Lake and adjoining waterways at speeds up to 50 miles per hour. But the most romantic outings

are its dusk IllumiNations cruises, which zip by BoardWalk, the Swan and Dolphin, and the Disney-MGM Studios en route to providing prime views of the show (from beneath the bridge at Epcot's France pavilion).

RATES: The one-hour IllumiNations cruise runs about $175. Cost is per boatload (up to seven passengers); driver is provided.

RESERVATIONS: Reservations, which can be up to 90 days, are recommended for the *Breathless*; reservations must be made at least 24 hours ahead. Call 407-WDW-PLAY (939-7529). Inquire about the length of the voyage when you book the reservation.

Grand 1

This striking 44-foot Sea Ray, completely furnished with three bedrooms, two bathrooms, kitchen, and living/dining room, is the sort of craft that escorts VIPs on private tours of the Seven Seas Lagoon and Bay Lake before nightfall, pausing in just the right spot as the Fantasy in the Sky fireworks (when available) explode above Cinderella Castle. But don't be misled: The *Grand 1* defines VIPs quite broadly, to encompass any group of up to 12 passengers lucky enough to snare a reservation. Although providing vistas of the Magic Kingdom fireworks is the *Grand 1*'s specialty, the elegant craft can be booked for most any hour, most any day. You may content yourself with feasting merely on the fireworks and the stars, or you may have your excursion catered, courtesy of chefs at the Grand Floridian. Thus, the possibilities extend from a private cruise for two, complete with dinner and champagne, to a cocktail party for 12, with as much shrimp, chips and salsa, chicken wings, beer, and wine as the boat can hold.

RATES: You'll pay $300 an hour (plus tax) to rent the *Grand 1*. Cost is per boatload (up to 12 passengers); driver and deckhand are included, refreshments are not.

RESERVATIONS: Reservations for excursions on the *Grand 1* should be made as far in advance as possible, preferably at the time you book your accommodations; they must be made 24 hours ahead. Call 407-824-2439 to book the *Grand 1*. For more information about having your affair catered, call 407-824-2578.

Pontoon Boats

No one will ever confuse a pontoon boat with a yacht, but when it comes to specialty cruises, no one's looking at the boat anyway. What matters: comfort, a great vantage point, and timing. So it is that Disney's pontoon boats, which accommodate up to ten people on private one-hour cruises, provide some of the best seats around for the fireworks and IllumiNations (when available). Fireworks cruises ply the Seven Seas Lagoon and Bay Lake, making quiet ripples on the water just outside the Magic Kingdom. IllumiNations excursions prowl the waters of Crescent Lake, where Epcot's Spaceship Earth beams like a second moon on the horizon.

RATES: Cost for Fantasy in the Sky or IllumiNations pontoon cruises, which both last about an hour, start at about $120 per boatload (up to ten passengers); a driver is provided.

RESERVATIONS: Pontoon boats must be reserved at least 24 hours ahead; advance reservations, accepted up to 90 days ahead, are strongly recommended (especially during peak times of the year). Call 407-WDW-PLAY (939-7529).

Spas

Grand Floridian Spa

Although more pocket-size than palatial, this elegant peach-and aqua-hued retreat has ample space to coddle 17 people at once—provided that there's a twosome being pummeled to contentment in the couple's treatment room. His-and-hers lounges, saunas, steam rooms, and whirlpools make worthy hangouts of the locker rooms. Signature services include baths steeped in native Floridian flowers and a deluxe facial complete with two masks and hand and foot massages. A cooling wrap incorporating lavender oil and calendula soothes the sunburned. Ultimate Relaxation pairs a traditional massage with a soak in a hydrotherapy tub that's equipped with 70 jets.

WORTH NOTING: The treatment menu includes aromatherapy; reflexology; shiatsu; Swedish, sports, and hydrotherapy massages; as well as a relaxing massage designed especially for expectant mothers. Massages last 25 to 80 minutes. Manicures, pedicures, and soothing hand and foot treatments are administered in the comfort of chairs that massage the lower back; feet are soaked in whirlpool baths. The spa offers a variety of body wraps (lavender and calendula, marine algae, clay, paraffin) and exfoliating scrubs (herbal, sea salt); an array of facials, including one especially for men; and several therapeutic and aromatherapy baths. Couples may receive side-by-side aromatherapy massages or a hands-on massage lesson in the couple's treatment room.

KNOW BEFORE YOU GO: The Grand Floridian Spa is located next to the health club at its namesake hotel, near the Magic Kingdom. Hours are from 6 A.M. to 9 P.M. (varies seasonally). Reservations may be made up to one month in advance. Call 407-824-2332.

HOW TO GET THERE: Monorail and boat transport is available to Walt Disney World resort guests from

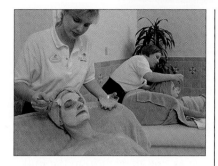

the Magic Kingdom. Similarly, guests may take the monorail from Epcot and the TTC, and buses from Downtown Disney, the Disney-MGM Studios, and Animal Kingdom.

RATES: Expect to pay about $57 for a 25-minute massage and about $110 for a facial. Prices include an 18 percent gratuity.

PACKAGES: Both half-day and full-day options are available. Packages range from the basic Spa Sampler (about $209; facial, manicure, and pedicure) to The Ultimate Day ($480; seven treatments, plus lunch).

The Spa at Disney's Saratoga Springs Resort

This sweat-free zone within Sweat Central (aka the Saratoga Springs Fitness Center) is a realm of unaffected calm, from its potted-plant accents to its teal towels and terra-cotta-colored

tiles. The ten treatment rooms couldn't feel farther removed from the clanks of weight machines and the mechanical whir of treadmills.

Services include the tingling Warm Seafoam Mud Wrap and Seaweed Hydro-Massage, a penetrating immersion in saltwater and seaweed. The locker rooms are each equipped with a steam room, sauna, and whirlpool. Ordering a spa cuisine lunch is always an option in the spa's coed lounge. Specifics may change.

WORTH NOTING: The treatment menu includes aromatherapy, reflexology, sports, and Swedish massages, as well as hydrotherapy massages that combine an aromatherapy bath in a 48-jet tub with a traditional massage. Massages last about 25 to 80 minutes. The extensive lineup of body wraps and scrubs includes several that incorporate soothing marine substances (seaweed, saltwater, sea salt, and sea mud). In addition to a large variety of specialty manicures and pedicures, the Disney Institute spa offers a diverse array of facials, from seaweed to aromatherapy.

KNOW BEFORE YOU GO: The spa is tucked within the resort's fitness

Spa Tips

- Reserve treatments well in advance; confirm your appointment before you arrive.
- Request a female or male spa therapist if you have a preference. The spa will honor your wishes, if at all possible.
- Drink plenty of water to counter the dehydrating effects of these indulgences.
- Jewelry and spa treatments don't mix. Plan ahead and leave yours in a safe at your hotel.
- Don't forget to jump in the shower before receiving a spa treatment.
- If it's a body treatment, leave underwear in the locker. Robes provided are sized for modesty, and therapists are trained to discreetly cover your most private parts during treatments.
- Bathing suits are optional for the separate men's and women's saunas and whirlpools.

center. Hours are from 8 A.M. to 8 P.M. (varies seasonally). Reservations are taken up to six months ahead. Call 407-827-4455.

HOW TO GET THERE: Buses transport WDW resort guests from the Magic Kingdom, Epcot, the Disney-MGM Studios, Animal Kingdom, and Downtown Disney. There are paved foot paths to the spa from the Downtown Disney Marketplace and West Side. (It's about a five-minute walk.)

RATES: It costs about $57 for a 25-minute massage and about $100 for a facial (plus gratuity).

PACKAGES: Choices range from the half-day Men's Programme ($175; sports massage, men's facial, and manicure) to the Full Day of Restoration ($280; four treatments, plus lunch).

The Spa at Wyndham Palace

Opposite Downtown Disney in more than location, this peaceful piece of the Wyndham Palace Resort offers a pampering repertoire that's about as deep and diverse as they come. Snazzy pedicure chairs with built-in whirlpool foot baths and back-massage capability overshadow the locker room saunas and steam rooms. Other appealing touches include lushly landscaped outdoor whirlpools and use of one-way glass to provide views from the 14 treatment rooms. An herbal bath borrowed from Germany and Shirodhara (a calming hair and scalp treatment with Asian origins) are among the more esoteric specialties. The cool-mud Theme Park Leg Relief Wrap shows the spa's lighter side. Speaking of light, spa cuisine can be delivered poolside.

Did You Know?

You're not only welcome, you are encouraged to show up at least 30 minutes before your scheduled spa service to lounge in the sauna, steam room, and whirlpool. Similarly, all three spas are linked to first-rate health clubs, which you can use before or (yeah, right) after your treatment.

WORTH NOTING: The lineup of treatments includes aromatherapy, sports, shiatsu, Swedish, deep-tissue, reflexology, and hydrotherapy massages lasting from 25 to 80 minutes. An adjoining full-service salon offers the usual (highlights to bikini wax) services; normal pedicures and manicures are eclipsed by the likes of the 80-minute Sports Pedicure, complete with whirlpool foot bath, heated mud pack, aromatherapy massage, paraffin dip, and reflexology.

The spa offers a variety of specialty baths (mineral, herbal, mud, seaweed) and a number of facials, including one designed to relieve sun-stressed skin. Its menu of body scrubs and wraps incorporates cool and warm mud, sea salt, and Asia's ancient Ayurvedic therapies.

KNOW BEFORE YOU GO: The Wyndham Palace Resort & Spa is located on Buena Vista Drive, across from the Downtown Disney Marketplace. Hours are from 6 A.M. to 9 P.M. (varies seasonally). Call 800-981-1472.

HOW TO GET THERE: The resort is a short walk from Downtown Disney, which can be reached from the Magic Kingdom, Epcot, the Disney-MGM Studios, and Animal Kingdom via bus.

RATES: A 25-minute massage runs about $60 and facials cost about $92 (including an 18 percent gratuity).

PACKAGES: The scripted half-day and full-day options range from the Royal Sampler (about $160; body scrub, hydrotherapy massage, neck and shoulder massage) to the Man's Day Away ($325; personal training session, four treatments, plus lunch). Customized packages are also available.

Spa 101

As a rule, aromatherapy massages are the lightest (and most aromatic); reflexology (all in the feet) and shiatsu involve precise pressure points rather than the (light or deep) kneading motions of Swedish massage; hydrotherapy massage (delivered by jets or a water-jet wand as you float in a tub) is as deep as it gets.

From casual to posh, Disney dining offers a delicious world of possibilities.

Dining & Entertainment

It's late in the book and we're sure you must be dying of hunger by now, so we'll begin by running through the food specials. But first, you'll be happy to hear that the outfit you are wearing at this moment, plus shoes, will be just fine for most any WDW restaurant (assuming that you didn't get all gussied up to read this chapter or that you're not in your pajamas). And second, atmosphere is a specialty of the house (you won't simply dine on seafood here, you'll do it cheek to cheek with a bustling coral reef or within the effervescent context of a New England clambake). Sampler platters include such unfamiliar cuisines as Norwegian and Moroccan. And if you're looking for some sophisticated eats, you're in luck.

In response to patrons' requests for fresher, more imaginative fare, Disney has given its chefs greater freedom. As an example of the quality of dining that can now be found at Walt Disney World, consider Artist Point restaurant, which features the likes of just-hooked king salmon, creatively prepared and served with hard-to-find pinot noirs from the Pacific Northwest. But we're getting carried away and you're hungry and need to make some decisions. Our "Restaurant Guide" will help. It cuts to the chase and describes the best dining spots for adults in the World.

Of course, you also need to be thinking about what you want to do later in the evening. Please, take your time, and when you're ready to think about after-dinner entertainment, know that this chapter's "Nightlife Guide" provides the complete scoop on Pleasure Island, the West Side, and BoardWalk, as well as compelling spots in the theme parks and resorts.

Enjoy!

RESTAURANT GUIDE

Priority Seating
To make priority seating arrangements for WDW restaurants, dial 407-WDW-DINE (939-3463).

We're happy to report that Walt Disney World has more tempting cuisine for the sophisticated palate than ever before, as behind-the-scenes improvements—from fresher, more flavorful ingredients to stronger wine lists—have quietly pushed the epicurean envelope. Healthier, more interesting grazing options in the theme parks can provide inexpensive treats that help subsidize the sit-down meals.

To ease the task of deciding among the many eateries, we've whittled the list down to the full-service restaurants and more casual noshing spots we recommend as the best adult bets. Under the heading "Standouts,"

you'll find stellar places to grab a great bite on the quick, moderately priced restaurants with exceptional flair, and extra-special havens worth every hard-earned dollar for their distinctive food and setting. Under the designation "Good Bets," we've corralled additional locales, also highly regarded, that we've come to know as fine places to have a meal. Because Disney's theme parks are unique terrain calling for both firm arrangements and flexible eating plans, we have included recommendations for fast-food and full-service options.

THEME PARKS:
Table Service
Standouts

AKERSHUS (Norway, Epcot's World Showcase): The ambience of a medieval Norwegian fortress—marked by dramatic cathedral ceilings, stone archways, and iron chandeliers—is not to be denied. Nor is the delicious novelty of the Norwegian fare. This is your

Priority Seating Explained

A system known as priority seating takes the place of reservations for all WDW restaurants, with the exception of the dinner shows. You receive a seating time but must check in at the restaurant to become eligible for the next available table. (Our advice: Arrive about 15 to 20 minutes early.)

Here's how the system works: (1) Those with priority seating will be seated at or near their assigned time, and (2) walk-ins will have a shot at any open tables. To make arrangements, call 407-WDW-DINE (939-3463) up to four months ahead. Hours are daily from 7 A.M. to 11 P.M. Because procedures tend to change, it's best to confirm policies with 407-WDW-DINE.

you think the elegant decor, with its evocative interplay of brass sconces, milk-glass chandeliers, mirrors, and leaded glass, is convincingly French, wait until you swallow your first morsel. This is hearty dining, so you might want to stroll around the promenade to walk off your escargots, rack of lamb, and chocolate soufflé.

The impressive wine list is *très* French. Priority seating suggested. **D $$$-$$$$**

chance to sample well-prepared signature dishes that don't often leave Scandinavia (appetizers are presented buffet style; entrées are served at the table; there's an extra charge for dessert). The meal washes down quite nicely with a tall draft of Ringnes beer. Wine selection is limited. Breakfast, served buffet-style, is a character affair. Priority seating suggested. **B L D $$-$$$**

BISTRO DE PARIS (France, Epcot's World Showcase): An intimate bistro that puts on romantic airs rather than the usual bustle. If

THE CRYSTAL PALACE (Main Street, Magic Kingdom): A landmark of sorts, this restaurant—one of our favorites in the Magic Kingdom—could be a Victorian garden if not for the walls and ceiling. The airy atmosphere provides a pleasant escape from the crowds on Main Street, and the

| B breakfast | L lunch | D dinner | S snacks | | $ $15 | $$ $15-$25 | $$$ $26-$46 | $$$$ $47 and up |

How to Book a Table

- In the theme parks: Priority seating is suggested for nearly all table-service restaurants in the theme parks; simply call 407-WDW-DINE (939-3463). For same-day arrangements in the Magic Kingdom, report to City Hall; in Epcot, head to Innoventions Plaza; in the Disney-MGM Studios, go to the corner of Hollywood and Sunset; in Animal Kingdom, ask at Guest Relations in The Oasis (go to Rainforest Cafe for a table at the restaurant itself). Same-day plans can also be made at all park restaurants or by dialing *88 from a pay phone within a theme park.

- In WDW resorts: Priority seating for Disney resort restaurants may be made by calling 407-WDW-DINE or by dialing *55 on any house phone.

- Elsewhere at Walt Disney World: Unless otherwise noted, reservations or priority seating arrangements at Down-town Disney and the Hotel Plaza Boulevard resorts may be made by calling 407-WDW-DINE (939-3463).

all-you-can-eat buffet is easily the most bountiful spread of any meal in the park. It's driven by fresh produce, including a salad bar, and adds carved meats, fish, and creative sides for dinner. Friends from the Hundred Acre Wood wander about during all meals. It's the ever-changing fare

that makes Crystal Palace a great spot for adults to dine in the company of characters. Priority seating suggested. B L D $$-$$$

50'S PRIME TIME CAFE (Disney-MGM Studios): In a word: cool. This good-humored retreat to the era of *I Love Lucy* is an amusing amalgam of comfort food, kitschy 1950s-style kitchen nooks, and attentive servers of the "No talking with your mouth full" ilk. Expect Mom or her favored offspring to meddle in your affairs here ("Did you wash your hands? All right, then; what color was the soap?"). And recognize that the best fun is had by doing some regressing of your own. As for the fare, it's tasty

home cooking as it used to be (heavy on the meat and potatoes), served in generous-to-the-point-of-grandmotherly portions. Most guests find that it honors their memory of fried chicken, meat loaf, s'mores, and peanut-butter-and-jelly milk shakes. A full bar is available. Priority seating suggested. L D $$-$$$

GARDEN GRILL (The Land, Future World): When your assigned priority seating time comes due at this lazy Susan-turned-dining area (it rotates slowly above the rain forest, desert, and prairie scenes visited by the Living with the Land boat ride below), you are politely informed by a "farmhand" that you have chores to do. Bessie has been milked, apparently, but the table hasn't been set. And so it is that you are seated, only to have to stand and harvest your place setting from the center of the table. Mickey and pals make the rounds at each meal. The meals, which are served family style, feature vegetables grown in The Land's greenhouses, fried fish, chicken, and grilled flank steak. Priority seating suggested. L D $$-$$$

HOLLYWOOD BROWN DERBY (Disney-MGM Studios): The Studios' most gracious dining is found at this faithful revival of the original cause célèbre, which

opened on Hollywood and Vine back in 1926. Dressed to the nines in chandeliers and celebrity caricatures, the restaurant stokes the appetite with its finely chopped signature Cobb salad and fabulous grapefruit cake. The international wine list is excellent. Priority seating is suggested. L D $$$

Note: Guests who make dining arrangements at their Disney resort or at any of the parks can take advantage of the Fantasmic! Dining Opportunity. Special seating for the evening's performance of Fantasmic! is included with a meal at no extra cost —except for tax, gratuities, and beverages, which carry an additional charge. (The Fantasmic! Dining Opportunity can—and should— be booked in advance; call 407-939-3463.)

Smoker's Alert

With the exception of designated areas, public parts of the theme parks and WDW-owned resorts are now nonsmoking. Tobacco products are not sold in the parks. Smokers may still find refuge in some Swan, Dolphin, BoardWalk, and Downtown Disney eateries.

LES CHEFS DE FRANCE (France, Epcot's World Showcase): "Bright lights, big dining room" describes this airy restaurant. With three of France's best chefs—Paul Bocuse, Roger Vergé, and pastry guru Gaston Lenôtre—keeping tabs on this nouvelle French kitchen, the broth is far from spoiled. We love the mere thought of the Lyons-style onion soup and the ways in which they fill a puff pastry. Wine pairings are suggested from the modest list. Priority seating suggested. L D $$$

L'ORIGINALE ALFREDO DI ROMA RISTORANTE (Italy, Epcot's World Showcase): Adorned with massive murals that evoke the Italian countryside, this restaurant inspires a "when in Rome" frame of mind from the outset. You suddenly hear an Italian grandma's voice in your head, urging you to "mangia." But do you go with the specialty of the house, fettuccine Alfredo? Or maybe lasagna is more to your liking? It's hard to go wrong at Alfredo's, as fresh pasta is made on the premises and Italian wines are in ready supply. This restaurant is a favorite for its atmosphere, which is at once romantic and festive. Priority seating suggested. L D $$$

Good Bets

BIERGARTEN (Germany, Epcot's World Showcase): Prepare for the best of the wurst. A buffet of traditional German cuisine (don't miss the red cabbage, spaetzle, or sauerbraten) is the main attraction in this charming makeshift courtyard. Adding to the fun are communal tables, steins of Beck's beer, a selection of German wines and liqueurs and live entertainment (at dinner only). Follow it up with apple strudel. Priority seating strongly suggested. L D $$-$$$

B breakfast L lunch D dinner S snacks $ $15 $$ $15-$25 $$$ $26-$46 $$$$ $47 and up

CINDERELLA'S ROYAL TABLE

(Cinderella Castle, Magic Kingdom): The grand renaissance setting provides a suitable backdrop for the equally grand American fare served here. Specialties have included roast prime rib, herbed chicken, and spice-crusted salmon. The majestic blue goblets, or the milady and milord salutations from our waiter always make us feel like queen and king for a day (or a meal). Long live the royal treatment! Priority seating strongly suggested for all meals, especially the daily character breakfast. (It's the toughest ticket in town. Call 60 days in advance, first thing in the morning, and keep your fingers crossed.) B L D $$$

CORAL REEF (The Living Seas,

Future World): It's all about sneaking bites of fresh fish under the watchful eyes of sea turtles, dolphins, and gargantuan groupers. Every table has a panoramic view of the living coral reef; some are right up against the glass. Menu items run the gamut from traditional seafood dishes such as broiled salmon. Grilled Black Angus rib-eye and pan-seared chicken

breast are also on the menu for those who are satisfied simply watching the fish. Priority seating suggested. L D $$$

HOLLYWOOD & VINE (Disney-MGM Studios): An Art Deco-style restaurant with Tinseltown flourishes, this restaurant now serves dinner only. Menu highlights have included citrus chicken and rotisserie turkey, as well as the catch of the day. Beer and wine are served at an additional cost.

Note: Guests who make dining arrangements at their Disney resort or at any of the parks can take advantage of the Fantasmic! Dining Opportunity. Special seating for the evening's performance of Fantasmic! is included with the meal at no extra cost—except for tax, gratuities, and beverages, which carry an extra charge. (The Fantasmic! Dining Opportunity should be booked in advance; call 407-939-3443.) D $$$

No Priority Seating?

If you're caught without priority seating arrangements in the theme parks, you can sometimes snag a place at one of these eateries (if you're willing to wait a bit):

- Hollywood Brown Derby (Disney-MGM Studios)
- Le Cellier Steakhouse (Canada, Epcot's World Showcase)
- The Plaza (Main Street, Magic Kingdom)
- Rainforest Cafe (Animal Kingdom)

LE CELLIER STEAKHOUSE (Canada, Epcot's World Showcase): We love retreating to this peaceful wine cellar-like spot, a favorite place for a hearty yet reasonably priced meal. The menu has featured stuffed filet, grilled veal chop, and New York strip steaks. Cheddar cheese soup is another specialty. Then there's potential for crème brûlée. Microbrews from Quebec and Canadian lagers are served. Priority seating suggested. L D $$-$$$

MAMA MELROSE'S RISTORANTE ITALIANO (Disney-MGM Studios): A pleasantly removed bastion of movie star photographs and thin-crust pizzas. The menu highlights Italian favorites, meats, and seafood cooked over an oak-burning oven. The wine list includes selections from California and Italy. Priority seating suggested.

Note: Guests who make dining arrangements at their Disney resort or at any of the parks can take advantage of the Fantasmic! Dining Opportunity. Special seating for the evening's performance of Fantasmic! is included with the meal at no extra cost—except for tax, gratuities, and beverages, which carry an extra charge. (The Fantasmic! Dining Opportunity should be booked in advance; call 407-939-3443.) L D $$-$$$

MARRAKESH (Morocco, Epcot's World Showcase): It's not every day that you can slip into an exquisitely tiled Moroccan palace and expect to be entertained by belly dancers and musicians as you polish off a sampler plate of distinctive Moroccan cuisine, such as couscous or kebobs. The music isn't always subtle. Priority seating suggested. L D $$$

THE PLAZA (Main Street, Magic Kingdom): Frozen desserts outnumber the fine burgers and sandwiches on the menu in this charming Main Street spot.

B breakfast   L lunch   D dinner   S snacks $ $15 $$ $15-$25 $$$ $26-$46 $$$$ $47 and up

Consider this ratio a gigantic hint to rope off some stomach space for one of the enormous sundaes or floats. Priority seating suggested. L D S $$

ROSE & CROWN PUB AND DINING ROOM (United Kingdom, Epcot's World Showcase): The menu ventures only a tad beyond (tasty) fish-and-chips, but we've never been disappointed. Outdoor tables offer a front-row view of the lagoon (and the nightly presentation of IllumiNations), and the indoor pub is downright neighborly. A pianist occasionally provides live entertainment. Priority seating suggested. L D S $$$

RAINFOREST CAFE (Animal Kingdom and Downtown Disney Marketplace): Lush (and loud) as a jungle, this place is thick with tropical vegetation and fish-filled aquariums (not to mention the occasional thunderstorm). Dishes answer to names like Mogambo (pasta with shrimp), Plant Sandwich (veggies), and Mojo Bones (barbecued ribs). Appetizers and desserts can be shared. Priority seating is suggested at the Animal Kingdom

location; the Downtown Disney locale is on a walk-up basis only. B L D S $$-$$$

SCI-FI DINE-IN THEATER (Disney-MGM Studios): The huge salads, sandwiches, and desserts here are more creative than at your average drive-in, but the food takes a backseat to the campy setting. Parking attendants lead guests their cars (the tables resemble 1950s-era convertibles). Science-fiction and horror trailers play on a large screen. Wine and beer are available. Priority seating suggested. L D $$-$$$

SAN ANGEL INN (Mexico, Epcot's World Showcase): The lights are low, the mood is romantic, and there is a smoking volcano poised tableside. If that's not enchantment enough, there's a mystical pyramid and a moonlit river. The menu? You might need to bring the table candle closer to read it, but you'll find Mexican fare from margaritas to chicken mole. Priority seating suggested. L D $$$

TEPPANYAKI DINING ROOMS (Japan, Epcot's World Showcase): It's not exactly an authentic dose of Japanese cuisine (Tempura Kiku next door gives a closer approximation with its sushi, sashimi, and tempura), but it offers a good time. Guests sit around a large teppan grill and watch as a nimble chef demonstrates just how quickly enough chicken, beef, seafood, and vegetables to feed eight people can be chopped, seasoned, and stir-fried. Entrées are sizzling and tasty. Small parties are seated together, making the meal a social affair. Priority seating suggested. L D $$$

Fast Food
Standouts

BACKLOT EXPRESS (Disney-MGM Studios): Shady and inconspicuous (it's tucked away by the Indiana Jones Epic Stunt Spectacular theater), this is a sprawling spot with both indoor and outdoor seating and unusual potential for quiet. Paint-speckled floors and movie prop debris give you an idea of the decor. Chicken Caesar salads, grilled chicken sandwiches, chili, and brownies are all available. L D S $

BOULANGERIE PATISSERIE (France, Epcot's World Showcase): The chocolate croissants, blueberry tarts, apple turnovers, and such are timeless. Follow your nose, and don't neglect to notice the sweet temptation aptly known as the Marvelous. Kronenbourg beer and French wines are also offered. S $

CANTINA DE SAN ANGEL (Mexico, Epcot's World Showcase): Forget for a moment the *churros*, the frozen margaritas, and the Dos Equis drafts: this place has south-of-the-border charm. When the weather cooperates, the outdoor lagoonside seating makes the experience even better. L D S $

COLUMBIA HARBOUR HOUSE (Liberty Square, Magic Kingdom): This spot distinguishes itself from the rest of the fast-food crowd by emphasizing things from the sea—among them, clam chowder, fried fish, salads, and harpoons (which are strictly for decor). If you get salad, request the dressing on the side (unless you *like* soggy salad). For relative privacy, take your tray to the upstairs dining room. L D S $

FOUNTAIN VIEW ESPRESSO AND BAKERY (Innoventions Plaza, Future World): This ode to pastries and coffees is a veritable oasis any time of day. Wine and beer are also available. B S $

Special Dietary Requests

Walt Disney World restaurants can accommodate special dietary requirements (vegetarian, low-sodium, lactose-free, and kosher meals, for example) if requests are made at least 24 hours in advance. Make your personal needs known when you make your priority seating arrangements by calling 407-WDW-DINE (939-3463).

KRINGLA BAKERI OG KAFE (Norway, Epcot's World Showcase): Simply a super place for a sweet fix or a light lunch. Among the tasty morsels here are open-face sandwiches (roast beef, turkey, and salmon), sweet pretzels called kringles, and vaflers (heart-shaped waffles freshly made and topped with powdered sugar and preserves). Ringnes beer is on tap. The outdoor seating area is shaded by a grass-thatched roof. L D S $

MAIN STREET BAKE SHOP (Main Street, Magic Kingdom): This dainty spot is renowned for quick breakfasts (from bagels to warm cinnamon rolls) and enormous fresh-from-the-oven cookies (we love the chocolate chip). The ice-cream cookie sandwiches make good use of flavors from the Plaza Ice Cream Parlor next door. B S $

SOMMERFEST (Germany, Epcot's World Showcase): Here, quick sustenance takes such classic forms as bratwurst, soft pretzels, Black Forest cake, German chocolates, Beck's beer, and German wine. The nicely shaded outdoor seating area sports a festive mural. L D S $

B breakfast L lunch D dinner S snacks $ $15 $$ $15-$25 $$$ $26-$46 $$$$ $47 and up

STARRING ROLLS BAKERY (Disney-MGM Studios): Have croissant and cappuccino, will travel. This is the place to get the day off to a sweet start or to take a cookie or coffee break under umbrella-shaded tables. `B` `L` `S` `$`

SUNSHINE SEASON FOOD FAIR (The Land, Future World): This bumper crop of food stands, located directly beneath the hot-air balloons on the pavilion's lower level, is the best place in Epcot to strap on the ol' feed bag and graze. For dining on the lighter side, select from fresh salads, soups, and handsomely garnished baked potatoes. Heartier fare comes in the form of pastas, sandwiches, and barbecued pork. Baked goods, ice cream, and refreshing libations round out the options. The eating's definitely more peaceful here outside prime dining hours. `B` `L` `D` `S` `$`

TUSKER HOUSE (Africa, Animal Kingdom): Wild elephants could not keep us away from this, the park's most civilized grazing option. Consider fried or rotisserie chicken, beef stew, turkey sandwiches, and grilled chicken salad in a bread bowl, and you

Cheap Eats

Our suggestions for spur-of-the-moment fast food:

- ABC Commissary (Disney-MGM Studios)
- Columbia Harbour House (Liberty Square, Magic Kingdom)
- Pecos Bill Cafe (Frontierland, Magic Kingdom)
- Sunshine Season Food Fair (The Land, Epcot's Future World)
- Tusker House (Africa, Animal Kingdom)
- Wolfgang Puck Express (Downtown Disney West Side)

may wish your safari vest came with Tupperware attachments. We dig the carved chairs inside, but somehow the Safari Amber beer tastes better out under the thatched roof. `L` `D` `S` `$-$$`

Good Bets

COSMIC RAY'S STARLIGHT CAFE (Tomorrowland, Magic Kingdom): Burgers, veggie burgers, salads, and rotisserie chicken are among the offerings here. Oddity of note: It isn't one-stop shopping. You may have to stand on several different lines to fill your order. Open seasonally. `L` `D` `S` `$`

FLAME TREE BARBECUE (Discovery Island, Animal Kingdom): Take a good gander and you'll sight fingers being licked at the riverfront tables bounding this pulled-pork and barbecued-brisket hut. Open seasonally. L D S $

PIZZAFARI (Discovery Island, Animal Kingdom): When the name of the craving is pizza, consider a spot that still prefers plain old pepperoni to funky nouveau toppings. The menu does stray a bit more than the average pizza place (with the likes of grilled chicken Caesar salad), but we like to stick to the basics. Spin on your heels for a stationary safari featuring this den's muraled menagerie. Seasonal. L D S $

PLAZA ICE CREAM PARLOR (Main Street, Magic Kingdom): Simply the park's most bountiful stash of ice cream. Head here when you'd like to have a choice of flavors. S $

YAKITORI HOUSE (Japan, Epcot's World Showcase): This pleasant spot (named for the specialty of the house, a savory skewered chicken) is set beside one of the most relaxing settings in all of Epcot for a quick and satisfying bite. Sake and Kirin beer are available. L D S $

Runnin' On Empty

Chefs at the California Grill use ingredients so fresh, there's hardly a thing in the restaurant's freezer. Except for ice cream, that is.

In the Resorts
Standouts

ARTIST POINT (Wilderness Lodge): The Pacific Northwest theme of this restaurant is announced in landscape murals, while tall red-framed windows look out to Bay Lake. The cavernous dining room is by no means intimate, but it's not without a certain charm.

Artist Point's hallmark is its knack for translating fresh seasonal ingredients from the Pacific Northwest into flavorful creations. An excellent example is the wild king salmon marinated in maple whiskey, then roasted with apples and herbs and served on a smoking cedar plank, accompanied by winter squash. If the signature tomato salad is in season, by all means give it a try.

The desserts are worth making room for, no matter how full you think you are. It's just the fork-licking finale you'd expect from a restaurant of this caliber. The wine list features some of the best pinot noirs coming out of Washington and Oregon right now. The cumulative effect is an artist's palette for the sophisticated palate. Priority seating suggested. **D $$$**

BIG RIVER GRILLE & BREWING WORKS (BoardWalk): A standout for its fresh-brewed ales alone, this unassuming place delivers huge portions of pub grub. The straightforward menu runs from burgers and steaks to lobster pot pie and yellow fin tuna.

This restaurant tends to be more low-key than the other BoardWalk eateries, and makes for a peaceful retreat during the day. Seating is available outside on the boardwalk. First-come seating. **L D S $$**

CALIFORNIA GRILL (Contemporary): The fresh, seasonal ingredients credo gets an artistic interpretation at this casual feast for the eyes (as well as the stomach) on the Contemporary resort's 15th floor. Chefs at this acclaimed restaurant keep no culinary secrets as they prepare dishes in an exhibition kitchen.

The West Coast theme shines through in such dishes as alder-

Coffee Talk

For java as main course, skip the usual cup o' automatic drip and head to one of these coffeehouses—they know double lattes from skim mocha cappuccinos.

- Sleepy Hollow (Liberty Square, Magic Kingdom)
- Fountain View Espresso & Bakery (Future World, Epcot)
- Starring Rolls Bakery (Disney-MGM Studios)
- Kusafiri Coffee Shop & Bakery (Africa, Animal Kingdom)
- Ghirardelli Soda Fountain and Chocolate Shop (Downtown Disney Marketplace)

wood-smoked salmon with whole roasted onions, and grilled-pork tenderloin with balsamic vinegar-smothered mushrooms and polenta. If there's a bit of a din in the dining room, it's partly because of unsuppressible raves and the waitstaff's collective ability to elaborate on any dish, ingredient, or wine.

The star-studded wine list is a striking mix of greatest hits and good finds. (At press time, six vintages were available by the glass, but that may change.) Also drawing a crowd: the Grill's divine California-style pizza, fine sushi bar, and a host of vegetarian choices. The goat-cheese ravioli

B breakfast　L lunch　D dinner　S snacks　　$ $15　$$ $15-$25　$$$ $26-$46　$$$$ $47 and up

appetizer is a crowd favorite.

Fresh desserts along the lines of butterscotch crème brûlée provide the finishing touches, as do sweeping views of the Magic Kingdom (from select seats). Priority seating is strongly suggested. The restaurant's only real drawback? It's usually quite chilly. Bring a sweater. D $$$-$$$$

CAPE MAY CAFE (Beach Club): The ever-popular all-you-can-eat New England-style clambake held nightly in this whimsical, beach-umbrella-decked dining area is among the best values at Walt Disney World. The tasty line-up includes mussels, fish, clams, oysters, peel-and-eat shrimp, corn-on-the-cob, ribs, red-skin potatoes, chowders, and salads; lobster is available for an extra charge. If you like, dessert can be milk and cookies. Breakfast is a (popular) character affair. Priority seating suggested. B D $$-$$$

The Inside Scoop

Hungry enough to eat Everything but the Kitchen Sink? That's what you'll get in this aptly named colossal sundae, served at Beaches & Cream Soda Shop in the Yacht and Beach Club. Expect eight scoops of ice cream smothered in every topping conceivable.

B breakfast L lunch D dinner S snacks $ $15 $$ $15-$25 $$$ $26-$46 $$$$ $47 and up

CITRICOS (Grand Floridian): From the aromas wafting from the open kitchen, it's clear that the chef has vowed to wow you with cuisine from the South of France herb by fragrant herb. Even if the kitchen were sealed off from view and scent and there were no pastry chefs at work in the dining room, no loaves of bread baking, no private party room or artful wine pairings or potential for a plate of seared jumbo sea scallops with asparagus, shiitake mushrooms, and wine butter, we'd still . . . Strike that. There's no changing the essence of Cítricos. Priority seating suggested. Closed Monday and Tuesday. `D $$$-$$$$`

snapper. The menu items vary daily, but steaks and vegetarian choices are usually offered. Make sure you save room for dessert. We were tempted to lick the plate after polishing off a chocolate-hazelnut bombe. Priority seating suggested. `D $$$`

FLYING FISH CAFE (BoardWalk): Expect an earful when you ask about the catch of the day at this compelling eatery bound and determined to serve seafood "so fresh it has an attitude." Fun, sophisticated decor from the designer of the Contemporary's California Grill elevates the appeal. As an example of the (exhibitionist) kitchen's knack for light, creatively prepared dishes, consider barbecue-glazed salmon with sweet-corn pudding and potato-wrapped yellowtail

We (Almost) Never Close

The following hotel eateries offer limited menus 24 hours a day during busy seasons (hours may change):

Captain Cook's Snack Co. (Polynesian)

Food and Fun Center (Contemporary)

Gasparilla Grill & Games (Grand Floridian)

Tubbi's (Dolphin)

Watercress Pastry Shop (Wyndham Palace)

B breakfast L lunch D dinner S snacks $ $15 $$ $15-$25 $$$ $26-$46 $$$$ $47 and up

NARCOOSSEE'S (Grand Floridian): Within the conspicuous octagonal building that looks out over Seven Seas Lagoon, you'll find a casual restaurant whose open kitchen presents such not-so-casual fare as filet mignon and garlic-stuffed Maine lobster. Yet on the seasonal menu, you may also discover wild salmon, lamb chops with garlic mashed potatoes, and penne pasta with sautéed vegetables. The food is excellent, and the international wine selection is quite good—you might even enjoy a pre-dinner glass on the veranda. Priority seating suggested. `D` `$$$`

VICTORIA & ALBERT'S (Grand Floridian): Indulgent without being too haute to handle, this is considered by many to be the grande dame of the Walt Disney World dining scene. The seven-course prix fixe menu changes daily, always offering a selection of fish, poultry, beef, veal, or lamb selections as well as a choice of soups, salads, and desserts. The $85-per-person adventure begins with the arrival of hors d'oeuvres. As an example of what could follow, consider Oriental shrimp dumplings, chicken consommé with pheasant breast,

poached Maine lobster with passion fruit butter, mixed field greens with raspberry-pinot noir vinaigrette, and a dark chocolate and strawberry soufflé. Perfect portions keep it all surprisingly manageable. The strains of a harp or violin provide a romantic backdrop. The wine list is encyclopedic. At the end of the meal, guests are presented with a souvenir menu and a red rose (ladies only). In sum, though the experience is an extremely expensive one, for many it is also quite special. Did we mention that every host and hostess at the restaurant is

Dinner in Bed

Sometimes it doesn't matter how great a restaurant's ambience is. You want the next knock on the door to be a person with a platter. Room service at Disney's deluxe hotels is as grand as you want it; ask nicely and your appetite for most anything on a house restaurant menu can be sated. With the exception of Wilderness Lodge and the Polynesian (last knock: midnight), the deluxe hotels will rustle something up around the clock. Even at moderate and value hotels, room service isn't just about breakfast; from 6 P.M. to 11 P.M. you can order sandwiches, pizza, salads, and the like. Note that deliveries generally, but not always, come within an hour.

B breakfast L lunch D dinner S snacks $ $15 $$ $15-$25 $$$ $26-$46 $$$$ $47 and up

named Victoria or Albert? Jackets are required for men. Priority seating necessary. **D $$$$**

OLIVIA'S CAFE (Old Key West): We thoroughly enjoy the Key Western manner with which Olivia's approaches its theme;

certainly, the laid-back setting and menu convey the spirit of the leisure-centric locale. Menu items include salads, conch chowder, baked mahimahi, conch fritters, and seven-layer fudge cake. Wine, beer, and cocktails are served. The menu changes seasonally. Priority seating suggested. **B L D $$**

YACHTSMAN STEAKHOUSE (Yacht Club): Quite simply, a carnivore's paradise. The generous portions begin with massive rolls and continue with the imperative spicy fried onion skillet and the Yukon Gold mashed potatoes. Of course, there's no skimping on the excellent and expertly prepared aged beef entrées (prime rib, filet

Cook Nook

You're on vacation from cooking, but you still might relish some time in the kitchen. No stirring, roasting, or chopping is required. Victoria & Albert's Chef's Table in the Grand Floridian lets you chat up the masters in the kitchen as they prepare culinary delights. To book this aromatic roost, call 407-WDW-DINE six months in advance. The Chef's Table costs $115 per person (plus tax); with wine pairings, it's $160 per person.

B breakfast L lunch D dinner S snacks $ $15 $$ $15-$25 $$$ $26-$46 $$$$ $47 and up

mignon, and chateaubriand, to name a few), so good luck finding room for crème brûlée. The menu also includes chicken and seafood dishes. This restaurant is filled with dining nooks suited for special occasions. Priority seating suggested. B L D $$$

Good Bets

BEACHES & CREAM SODA SHOP

(Yacht and Beach Club): Every inch a classic soda fountain, it's the site for egg creams, milk shakes, and ice cream and frozen yogurt, plus burgers and sandwiches. Light breakfast is offered. First-come seating. Take-out is possible. B L D S $-$$

BOATWRIGHT'S DINING HALL (Port Orleans Riverside): Reasonably

priced Southern specialties are the big draw at this unique eatery, where the centerpiece is a riverboat under construction, boat-making tools are mounted on the walls, and tables are set with condiment-filled toolboxes. Try the baby-back ribs and Cajun dirty rice. Full bar. Priority seating available. B D $$-$$$

CONCOURSE STEAKHOUSE

(Contemporary): If filet mignon stuffed with wild mushrooms speaks to you or you'd like to sample some of the best mashed potatoes in the World or you just want a quick, civilized bite one step removed from the Magic Kingdom, here you have it. The "Stickey Mickey" is a breakfast bonus; individual pizzas and salads are a good bet for lunch. The atmosphere isn't much to speak of, but the food certainly is. Priority seating suggested. B L D $$$

GRAND FLORIDIAN CAFE (Grand

Floridian): Wall-length windows incorporate the hotel's central courtyard into this inviting restaurant's potted-palm greenery. A pleasant spot any time of day, it's a reasonably priced way to check out the World's poshest resort.

Seasonal dishes feature traditional American comfort food; past selections have included fried chicken and sea bass. Try the citrus french toast with cinnamon or the crab cakes with Key lime remoulade. Excellent wine selection. Priority seating available. **B L $$$**

KIMONOS (Swan): This is the place for good sushi and tempura in a lounge styled with bamboo and kimono accents. A respectable wine selection is complemented by sake, Japanese and domestic beers, and cocktails. The calm is occasionally interrupted by a cacophony of karaoke (a big draw in the late evening). Smoking is permitted. Reservations accepted. **D S $$-$$$**

Fare Thee Well

This guide is not a comprehensive listing of the World's eateries, but a selective roundup of the best adult dining and snacking venues. Those restaurants designated as "Standouts" are dining rooms and fast-food places whose exceptional flair, distinctive fare, and/or terrific setting have earned our highest recommendation. "Good Bets" are additional locales that offer consistently rewarding dining experiences.

'OHANA (Polynesian): The beauty of 'Ohana's family-style dining experience—a South Pacific feast prepared in the restaurant's prominent open-fire cooking pit—is that the hickory-grilled skewers of turkey, pork, shrimp, chicken, and beef just keep coming. Lo mein noodles, rice, and dumplings are among the accompaniments, and the fresh pineapple dipped in caramel sauce is a fine dessert.

To make the most of 'Ohana's setting, which features exotic wood carvings under a vast thatched roof, request a table that's right up against the windows overlooking the Seven Seas Lagoon. (The number of tables there is limited, but it's worth a shot.) This puts you a comfortable distance from the grill and the route where the coconut-rolling contest is held, but still in prime position to be serenaded by Polynesian songs. Breakfast is a character affair. Priority seating suggested. **B D $$$**

PALIO (Swan): A sleek Italian trattoria that's a trusty source for imaginatively prepared homemade pasta, pizza baked in wood-fired ovens, and traditional veal and seafood dishes. (It's also

B breakfast   L lunch   D dinner   S snacks $ $15 $$ $15-$25 $$$ $26-$46 $$$$ $47 and up

one of the rare WDW spots where you'll see candles on the table.) Beers and Italian wines are also served. Priority seating available. `D $$$`

WHISPERING CANYON CAFE

(Wilderness Lodge): For savory eating that does not stop until you say "when," consider this family-style restaurant a good (if rowdy) candidate. At dinner, menu items such as apple-rosemary rotisserie chicken, barbecued pork spareribs, and smoked barbecued beef brisket are sure to satisfy. Homemade desserts come with an extra charge. (Breakfast, lunch, and dinner selections are also available à la carte.) Priority seating suggested. `B L D $$$`

Other Options in the World
Standouts

FULTON'S CRAB HOUSE (Downtown Disney Marketplace): Walk the gangplank onto this would-be riverboat and with one glance around you're prepared to book passage. Still, the polished woods, brass detailing, and nautical nostalgia of the restaurant are secondary to the fresh seafood served therein.

The extensive (albeit pricey) dinner menu changes with the day's arrivals. It's not unusual for Hawaiian albacore tuna (accompanied by, say, crab bordelaise and corn-whipped potatoes) to be seen next to Great Lakes walleye pike (with garlic chips and herb rice). Standbys include Dungeness crab cakes; cioppino, a San Francisco-style stew with seafood galore in a tomato broth; garlic chicken; crab and lobster platters; and filet mignon.

For a quicker fix, visit the ravishing raw bar at the adjoining

Scenic Cocktail Spots

Atlantic Dance
(BoardWalk)

California Grill Lounge
(Contemporary)

Cap'n Jack's Restaurant
(Downtown Disney Marketplace)

Matsu No Ma
(Japan, Epcot's World Showcase)

Narcoossee's
(Grand Floridian)

Outer Rim
(Contemporary)

Stone Crab
(Fulton's Crab House between Pleasure Island and the Marketplace)

Top of the Palace
(Wyndham Palace)

B breakfast L lunch D dinner S snacks $ $15 $$ $15-$25 $$$ $26-$46 $$$$ $47 and up

Stone Crab lounge suits. For a reasonably priced lunch, it's lounge or bust. Priority seating suggested. L D S $$$$

HOUSE OF BLUES (Downtown Disney West Side): An eclectic menu with New Orleans taste buds (think étouffée, jambalaya, barbecue, and crispy catfish nuggets) distinguishes this folk art–studded restaurant.

It's a good spot for a late-night bite. Air-conditioning-phobes will enjoy the atmospheric, lakeside Voodoo Garden. The lively Sunday gospel brunch is a winner. First-come seating. L D S $$

PORTOBELLO YACHT CLUB (between Pleasure Island and Downtown Disney Marketplace):

Menu standouts at this polished yet casual piece of nautica include thin-crust pizzas baked in a wood-burning oven, farfalle primavera, and spaghettini alla Portobello, a seafood medley served over pasta in a light tomato and wine sauce.

Portobello also offers desserts, coffees, and an impressive wine list. Smoking permitted on the patio only. Reservations, which are recommended, are available 60 days in advance. D $$$$

WOLFGANG PUCK CAFE (Downtown Disney West Side): This eatery marks the Los Angeles chef's Florida debut and brings trendy California cuisine to the fore.

There are actually three dining arenas here—an express counter, a

Knockout Views

Boma—Flavors of Africa (Animal Kingdom Lodge)	**Cinderella's Royal Table** (Magic Kingdom)	**Jiko—the Cooking Place** (Animal Kingdom Lodge)
California Grill (Contemporary)	**Coral Reef** (The Living Seas, Epcot's Future World)	**Narcoossee's** (Grand Floridian)
Cantina de San Angel (Mexico, Epcot's World Showcase)	**Fulton's Crab House** (between Pleasure Island and Downtown Disney Marketplace)	**'Ohana** (Polynesian)
Cap'n Jack's Restaurant (Downtown Disney Marketplace)	**Garden Grill** (The Land, Epcot's Future World)	**Rose & Crown Pub Dining Room** (United Kingdom, Epcot's World Showcase)

B breakfast L lunch D dinner S snacks $ $15 $$ $15-$25 $$$ $26-$46 $$$$ $47 and up

cafe, and a formal dining room on the second floor—plus a sushi bar. All feature the famous chef's signature gourmet pizzas, rotisserie chicken, and other specialties prepared in the display kitchen.

The **Wolfgang Puck Express** counter here (there's also one at the Marketplace) offers wood-fired pizzas, Chinois chicken salad, and focaccia sandwiches that defy most definitions of fast food. First-come seating. L D S $

At **Wolfgang Puck Cafe**, the menu includes (excellent) sushi, Thai chicken satay, and penne with wild shiitake and oyster mushrooms. First-come seating. L D S $$-$$$

Wolfgang Puck Cafe—The Dining Room puts hunger pangs happily to rest with such dishes as baby vegetable risotto and roast Cantonese duck with plum sauce, plus a wine list well suited to the cuisine. Priority seating suggested. D $$$ (Note that The Dining Room may undergo a name change in the near future.)

Good Bets

CAP'N JACK'S RESTAURANT (Downtown Disney Marketplace): This pretty pier house perched over Lake Buena Vista is the place to socialize over cold drafts and fresh seafood. The strawberry margarita is tops, as are the clam chowder, and crab cake starters. Or try the pan-seared Ahi tuna and seafood pasta entrées. First-come seating. L D S $$

OUTBACK (Wyndham Palace, Hotel Plaza Boulevard; 407-827-3430): Despite its similar meat-and-potatoes inclinations, this place has no relation to the chain of the same name. Go for the baby-back ribs, shrimp, and steak. Smoking is permitted. Reservations suggested. D $$

PLANET HOLLYWOOD (Downtown Disney West Side): This casual restaurant is ensconced inside a 120-foot-diameter sphere and surrounded by a three-dimensional collage of movie memorabilia. The menu has simple, creative flair and depth (consider the blackened shrimp, a Shanghai chicken salad, or the good old reliable hamburger and french fries). Priority seating suggested. L D S $$-$$$

NIGHTLIFE GUIDE

In the pages that follow, we present the best nightlife in Walt Disney World. You'll receive a thorough orientation to Pleasure Island; next, an introduction to

Downtown Disney West Side; and a briefing on the clubs found along the BoardWalk.

The final section of this guide completes the nightlife picture with our report on other recommended clubs and lounges located on WDW property. Cheers!

Downtown Disney Pleasure Island

This bustling metropolis is a six-acre island consumed entirely by clubs, stage shows, and live entertainment. Guests must be 18 or joined at the hip to a parent to be admitted to clubs, and Mannequins and BET SoundStage Club are strictly 21 and up. While the main draw here is certainly the clubs, Pleasure Island's shops are open from 11 A.M. to 1 A.M., and some of its restaurants serve lunch as well as dinner. There is no admission fee until 7 P.M., when a single cover charge of $21 (including tax; good for entry to all clubs) applies to all but restaurant-goers. Pleasure Island admission is included in Ultimate Park Hopper Tickets and an option for Park Hopper

Plus Tickets. Annual passes are available for purchase. The drinking age in Florida is 21, and a valid photo ID is required at the gate and at most clubs.

While the clubs close down at 2 A.M., that last call is sounded at about 1:30 A.M.

A Walking Tour

After exchanging your ticket for a lovely paper bracelet at the main entrance, you pass (limbo if you like) under a neon archway and into the pleasuredome itself. The first building on the left houses Mannequins, a pulsating den of special effects and techno-pop tracks that puts a unique spin on the standard club scene with a huge, rotating dance floor. Mannequins adds contemporary decor and an edgy air to its no-holds-barred scene. It takes its name from the many mannequins found throughout. Reserved strictly for patrons 21 and older, Mannequins is a club in the urban mold, and it attracts a dressed-to-impress crowd.

The music here is cranked so loud that a jet could pass through virtually unnoticed, yet somehow the place is packed all night long with revelers who actually employ verbal communication in their flirtations. If you can stand the volume, you may take pleasure in the fact that the circulating dance floor gives a little boost to your dance skills and allows for exceptionally easy scoping, whether you're dancing or on the sidelines.

As for drinks, Mannequins offers a full bar. This club is popular with locals and visitors, so be prepared to encounter a line at the door, especially on weekends.

Directly across from Mannequins you'll see a warehouselike structure. This is the site of the Pleasure Island Jazz Company. Cool, uninhibited jazz and blues are the order at this live-music venue, which runs the gamut from 1930s to contemporary tunes, and features local and

Pleasure Island Tips

- To enter Mannequins and the BET SoundStage clubs, you must be at least 21 years of age—and able to prove it. Keep your government-issued photo ID handy at all times.

- It's fun to club-hop, but you can't do it with a glass in hand. Plan ahead, and ask that your last drink be served in a plastic cup. Most places keep some by the door.

- Caught with your pockets empty? There's an ATM located out front at the Rock N Roll Beach Club.

- Adventurers Club and Comedy Warehouse are the island's only entirely nonsmoking venues.

- At the end of the night, if your feet are too tuckered to wait for a bus—consider taking a cab back to your resort. The fares for authorized cabs usually range between $10 and $20, depend-ing upon your WDW destination.

- To snag a good table at Pleasure Island Jazz Company, arrive about 20 minutes before showtime.

national talent. Good for a relaxing interlude, the place is dimly lit and dotted with small tables.

If you're up for some quality entertainment in a romantic atmosphere, if you're too pooped for anything beyond snapping your fingers, or if you're simply hankering for a jazzy libation or a nice bottle of wine, the Jazz Company will take care of you. To snag a good table, aim to arrive about 20 minutes before showtime.

Onward. When you leave the Pleasure Island Jazz Company, you're on due course for the Rock N Roll Beach Club. At the top of the surfboard stairway, you enter a rollicking dance spot that is substantially more laid-back than Mannequins (perhaps due to its surfer sensibility and live bands).

While dancing is definitely a big deal here—the dance floor is generally jam-packed with twentysomethings—there's more to do than twist and shout the night away.

Many guests enjoy the three-story club's music and casual atmosphere without so much as stepping onto the lowest level. They shoot pool, play air hockey and pinball, and hang out at tables overlooking the dance floor to people-watch and sip a cold beer. Roving souls should note that some of the specialty drinks here are available in portable 16-ounce squeeze bottles.

From the Rock N Roll Beach Club it's on to 8TRAX—a place so seventies and eighties that "YMCA" is a scheduled event (12:30 A.M.). Suffice it to say that the *Saturday Night Fever*–style dance floor is not only an extraordinarily popular destination but an infinitely

fascinating eyeful. Decor tends toward the psychedelic.

Moving along, the next club on the horizon is Pleasure Island's biggest enigma—the Adventurers Club. This elegant and eccentric parlor takes after the salons of 19th-century explorers' clubs, and is decked out with photos, trinkets, and furnishings that document the awfully far-reaching (and far-fetched) travels of its card-carrying members.

More Reasons to Go West

Downtown Disney West Side has more than just restaurants, night-clubs, and movie theaters. It's also home to interesting shops (open until 11 P.M.; see page 163 for details) and DisneyQuest (see page 215). Most notably, it has a permanent tent for a Cirque du Soleil show called La Nouba. Wipe out all thoughts of Bozo-style antics; this circus ensemble is not your typical ringmastered, big-top production. Cirque features a cast of 60 performing a mix of acrobatics and modern dance. Wild costumes and dramatic original music add to the fun. Cirque fans consider it The Greatest Show in Downtown Disney. Call 407-939-7600 for tickets (up to six months in advance).

Two for Tea

Teatime with all the trimmings—scones, tiny sandwiches, and pastries served on bone china—is 2 P.M. in the Garden View lounge at the Grand Floridian. A large selection of teas and tasty accompaniments are offered every day until 6 P.M. (priority seating recommended).

On the surface, it's a quiet place, filled with comfortable chairs. But penetrate the recesses of the Adventurers Club and you'll notice some pretty odd characters milling about, stumble upon some rather curious corners and goings-on, and, ultimately, be invited into a hideaway library (where those odd characters put on a curious show, complete with haunted organ). This is a nonsmoking venue.

Next door to the Adventurers Club is the BET SoundStage Club. This urban den for rhythm and blues and hip-hop has the cool aura of an unstoppable after-hours party.

Reserved strictly for patrons 21 and older, it's the kind of place you'd like to think Aretha Franklin might frequent, with all

due respect (pun intended). A mix of music videos keeps the energy level high and the crowd pumped to dance all night long.

Our next order of business is not a club, but a forum known as the West End Stage, which provides much of the juice for Pleasure Island's street party; live bands perform here nightly. Unless you are allergic to confetti, this is the place to be when the nightly New Year's Eve countdown reaches its pyrotechnic climax (showtime is 11:45 P.M.). Note that the New Year's Eve festivities may not be presented during your visit.

In any case, the most strategic spot to take it all in (since you'll be standing anyway) is the queue for the Comedy Warehouse located right across from the BET SoundStage Club. Get there no later than 11:30 P.M. (the last show is at 12:05 A.M.) to get a jump on any New Year's revelers who might have the same idea. The Comedy Warehouse, is the sort of club in which you prop yourself on a stool and hope to

Downtown Disney
West Side

The West Side forges with the Marketplace and Pleasure Island to make a triple-header of the distraction zone known as Downtown Disney. It's a colorful lakeside strip of restaurants, shops, and energy. Here, guests pay as they play, springing for cover charges only at places they patronize.

Puffer's alert: Smoking is permitted in designated sections of House of Blues, Bongos Cuban Cafe, and Planet Hollywood. Night owl's alert: Whereas Planet Hollywood takes orders right up to 1 A.M., Bongos and House of Blues serve until 1:30 A.M.

The easternmost spot at the West Side is the AMC Theatres complex, a colossal celebration of the silver screen (make that screens—there are 24 of them). The marquee is au courant, the seats are roomy and plush (not to mention stadium style), and the sound system, developed by George Lucas, is first-rate.

Call 407-298-4488 for showtimes, the earliest of which are about 1 P.M. And bring a sweater. The air-conditioning here is powerful, to say the least.

If you prefer a diversion with an added dimension, start a

fall off laughing. The troupe of improv comedians does funny things with suggestions from the audience. The zingers come when you least expect it.

Every improvised performance is a little bit different, but you can expect the audience to provide some pretty challenging raw material ("We need an occupation" nets the likes of "rutabaga farmer"), and count on the troupe to rise to the occasion with amusing songs and skits. The show can be hit and miss, but if the line is short, give it a whirl.

Beer, wine, and cocktails are served (only to guests older than 21 brandishing a valid photo ID); popcorn is the preferred snack. Comedy Warehouse is a non-smoking venue.

conga line and head for the three-story pineapple directly across the promenade. Bongos Cuban Cafe, created by singer Gloria Estefan and her husband, Emilio, is a bright, boisterous restaurant that parades the flavors and rhythms of Cuba and other Latin American countries.

When you've had your fill of the fruit-fly fandango, plot a moonlight stroll along the peaceful shore of Lake Buena Vista.

Melt away the Miami mentality with a dose of cool: House of Blues. It has capacity for 2,000 soul men and women. Inspired by one of America's proudest musical traditions, the club also serves up country, with an occasional mix of R & B, gospel, or rock.

You may buy tickets through TicketMaster (407-839-3900; *www.ticketmaster.com*) or at the box office up until showtime; the

After-Dark Dazzle

- The Magic Kingdom's extended curfew during busy seasons (generally summers and holiday periods) means the relaxed atmosphere and romance of the park in the early-evening hours are more accessible. After-dark also means nightly fireworks and performances of the nighttime parade.

- The fireworks show is a pyrotechnics display worthy of a Fourth of July finale. And the evening parade is not to be missed; if there are two performances, aim for the later one, when the prime viewing spots (anywhere on Main Street) are easier to snare, thanks to the little ones' need to go beddie-bye.

- Epcot's World Showcase, which stays open until at least 9 P.M. year-round, assumes a sparkling beauty at night. For this reason, Disney presents a special show, IllumiNations. This simulation of our planet's evolution features a three-story globe, intense fireworks, and stirring music. The 13-minute show, typically ignited at closing time, is visible from any point along the promenade.

- Sure to top the after-dark A-list is Fantasmic!, served up in an amphitheater behind The Twilight Zone Tower of Terror at the Disney-MGM Studios. The 26-minute show takes you inside Mickey's dreams as he conducts dancing fountains, swirling stars, and a delightful musical score. Animation projected onto water screens on the lake helps tell the story, which climaxes with a visit from Disney villains. A battle powered by flaming special effects leads to a character-filled finale.

- The Electrical Water Pageant, a 1,000-foot-long string of illuminated floating creatures, makes its way around Bay Lake each night. You can usually view the pageant at 9 P.M. from the Polynesian, 9:15 P.M. from the Grand Floridian, 9:35 P.M. from Wilderness Lodge, 9:45 P.M. from Fort Wilderness, and 10:05 P.M. from the Contemporary. Times may change.

cost is $5 to $30, depending on the act.

BoardWalk

While merely strolling the boards of this nostalgic entertainment district a short walk from Epcot provides a delightful escape to simpler times, the temptations en route are tough to resist. Cotton candy vendors, savory dining, and surrey bike rides aside, BoardWalk gives the World things it has long needed—a sports bar, a brewpub, a sing-along piano bar, and more. In addition to being an appealing resort (see *Checking In* for a complete description), Board-Walk is a great adult hangout. Although there's no general admission fee, Jellyrolls charges a cover (usually about $5), as does Atlantic Dance (about $5),

Information, Please

For more on Downtown Disney happenings—from retail to concerts to the AMC 24 movie lineup—call 407-WDW-2-NITE (939-2648).

and you must be 21 or older to enter both venues. Valet parking ($6) is available on Friday and Saturday. All of the bars and clubs described below stay open until 2 A.M. Smoking is permitted in many spots.

High on the hit list is ESPN Club, a sports bar so over-the-top it practically has referees. Between the live sports commentators, the ballpark fare, and the more than 100 televisions (some in the restrooms) broadcasting any number of games, no unnecessary time-outs are taken. Professional athletes tend to drop by on occasion to engage in a little Q&A with diners (from a

stage, with a moderator; no auto-
graphs, please). Ask a host
what's on the lineup for your
stay. And try those hot wings.

Several first downs away, the
Big River Grille & Brewing
Works invites you to bend the
ol' elbow right under the brew-
master's nose. Five specialty ales,
including two that change with
the seasons, are crafted on the
premises. It's a tough job, but
someone's got to polish off the
beer bread and raise a glass to
the brew maestro. After trying
the beer sampler (tastes of all
five ales for $4.75), we heartily
waved on the Tilt Pale Ale house
brew. Hot beer pretzels and other
appetizers from the restaurant
menu are available at the bar
until the kitchen closes around
11 P.M., providing fitting accompaniments to tastings.

Walk a few short strides into
the dueling-pianist realm of
Jellyrolls and you're soon croon-
ing and swaying along with the
rest of the congregation to songs
from the 1970s to the present. As
an example of the musicians' ver-
satility, consider this sampling of
one set: "King of the Road," "Joy
to the World," and a rousing med-
ley of TV theme songs—including odes to *The Brady Bunch* and
The Jeffersons. The music comes

uninterrupted (except by the wise-
cracking pianists themselves).
Soon you're wondering how you
got so hoarse.

So you head next door to
Atlantic Dance, an elegant club
which is perpetually reinventing
itself. A deejay supplies a sound
track to groove to, with a live
band filling in on auspicious
nights. You're free to dance,
order hors d'oeuvres or desserts,
and, if you like, enjoy a specialty
drink on a balcony overlooking
the water. From this perspective,
the game highlights on ESPN
Club's monitors seem miles
away. But they're not, and so,
when your mood shifts, you can
easily venture back to check the
scores. Such is an evening at
BoardWalk.

Virgin Daiquiri, Anyone?

Soft drinks, fruit juices, and tasty
specialty drinks *sans* alcohol are
available at all Walt Disney World
clubs. Just ask the bartender.

Other World Options

Standouts

CALIFORNIA GRILL LOUNGE
(Contemporary): The tiny (and
ever-shrinking) companion
lounge to the California Grill
restaurant offers what amounts to
box seats for the Magic
Kingdom fireworks. You can
order from the California Grill
menu, too. Doors close: 1 A.M.

CREW'S CUP (Yacht Club): When
it comes to beer, the Crew's Cup
runneth over with 35 international brews. Consider the warm
copper-accented decor, the scin-
tillating aromas wafting in from
the neighboring Yachtsman
Steakhouse, and the potential for
four-cheese garlic bread and New
England clam chowder, and you
have an even better idea of why

we are putty in this lounge's
hands. Doors close: midnight.

**THE LAUGHING KOOKABURRA GOOD
TIME BAR** (Wyndham Palace,
Buena Vista Drive): At "The
Kook," a band plays Top 40
music Wednesday through Saturday for a crowd in the 25 to 40
age range. If you'd rather not
dance, snag a spot in one of four
seating areas. Some 80 beers are
on hand. Daily happy hour.
Doors close: 2 A.M.

MARTHA'S VINEYARD (Beach
Club): Although appetizers and
desserts are served, the main
reason you're here is the wine.
Selections from a real Martha's
Vineyard winery, as well as those
from California, Long Island,
and European vineyards, make
for tough decisions, but it helps
to know that wine can be ordered

in sample sizes, as well as full glasses. Doors close: 11 P.M.

MATSU NO MA (Japan, Epcot's World Showcase): A quiet setting where—in addition to sake, beer, cocktails, and green tea—you can drink in a stunning vista of Epcot. Sushi and edamame are among the items served. Doors close: at park closing.

ROSE & CROWN PUB (United Kingdom, Epcot's World Showcase): We've always loved this cheeky classic—for its polished-wood and brass decor; its rich Irish, Scottish, and British drafts; and its neighborly feel. So we weren't too surprised during one of many visits to overhear a gentleman asking a fellow behind the bar to please let Jerry (a bartender not present) know that he was sorry he'd missed him. "Next time," he said hopefully. You needn't be a fan of shandies or black and tans to appreciate that. Doors close at park closing. Note that specifics are apt to change.

STONE CRAB (Fulton's Crab House, Downtown Disney Marketplace): Like the local heartthrob who happens to be loaded, this gorgeous riverboat bar stacks the odds even more in its favor with an excellent raw bar, prime water views, and a honey-wheat house brew. It doesn't just make Bloody Marys from scratch (as in hand-squeezed tomatoes and fresh horseradish), it garnishes them with shrimp. Doors close: 2 A.M.

TERRITORY (Wilderness Lodge): This scenic spot is marked by wood-carved grizzlies and a muraled map of the western frontier that "unfolds" over the ceiling.

While this spot can be swamped with diners-in-waiting during prime mealtimes, it more often inspires lingering. Appetizers and

DisneyQuest: A Virtual Toy Box

Call it a virtual-reality check. An ode to flippers and joysticks. A bumper-car blast from your arcade past. DisneyQuest at Downtown Disney West Side is five stories of rampant interactivity that could test the supple wrists of The Who's Pinball Wizard. A sampling: You paddle a buoyant raft around rugged rocks, not to mention dinosaurs, on the Virtual Jungle Cruise. After rediscovering Centipede, you ride a simulated self-made roller coaster—a hair-raising excuse for a Virtual Makeover at Magic Mirror. DisneyQuest is open from 11:30 A.M. to 11 P.M. Sunday through Thursday, 11:30 A.M. to midnight Friday and Saturday. One-day admission is about $31, including tax (prices may change).

snacks add to the appeal. But the true toast of the Territory is Lodge House Brew, a micro-brewed light beer with a hint of honey that's a Wilderness Lodge exclusive. Doors close: midnight.

TUNE-IN LOUNGE (Disney-MGM Studios): This Formica-laden spot, the family den to 50's Prime Time Cafe, serves Dad's Super Snacks and spirits from Dad's Liquor Cabinet, while vintage television sets show clips from the decade's most popular sitcoms (all food related). A baby-boomer's paradise, it's a great spot to cool off and regroup. Doors close: at park closing.

Good Bets

CAP'N JACK'S RESTAURANT

(Downtown Disney Marketplace): This pier house jutting out over Lake Buena Vista scores with a convivial atmosphere and strawberry margaritas. It also offers reasonably priced sunsets and beautiful seafood (or is it the reverse?). If there's a line for a table, sit at the bar. Doors close: 10:30 P.M.

RIVER ROOST (Port Orleans Riverside): This one's nothing fancy. Just your average, unassuming nook that happens to

have a fireplace and ready access to chicken wings and spicy Cajun onion straws. Drinks stop at midnight.

MIZNER'S (Grand Floridian): If you look past the house orchestra that sets up shop nightly outside this second-floor alcove, you'll find a mahogany bar with fine ports, brandies, and appetizers. It's popular with the business set. Doors close: 1 A.M.

NARCOOSEE'S (Grand Floridian): You've got to love a lounge that's thoroughly steeped in Victoriana on the inside, and framed by a lake that lies like a picnic blanket beneath the Magic Kingdom fireworks on the veranda. Worldly wines by the glass, as well as traditional cocktails and specialty drinks. Doors close: 10 P.M.

RAINFOREST CAFE (Two locations: Downtown Disney Marketplace and Disney's Animal Kingdom. The latter has two entrances: one outside the park entrance, and another inside the turnstiles. It generally keeps later hours than the park itself.): When the restaurant is mobbed, we like to take in the thunderstorms and waterfalls from the central mushroom-capped bar. We simply saddle an unwitting zebra or giraffe (the animal bar stools are strictly hooves-to-hips) and chase our tails. There's nothing quiet about this joint, but its festive "natural" ambience is intoxicating. Doors close: 11 P.M., weekdays; midnight, weekends.

SHULA'S (Dolphin): Enjoy your cocktail of choice in either the bar or cozy lounge areas of this restaurant that proclaims itself to be "one of the Top 10 steakhouses in America." Who are we to argue? Former Miami Dolphins coach Don Shula scores big with appetizers ranging from barbecued shrimp to steak soup. There's a TV in each room, too. Expect the big sporting event du jour to be playing. Note that the smoking of cigars is not discouraged in these parts. Doors close: 11 P.M.

Dinner Shows

If you're looking for a side of entertainment to complement your meal, consider a Disney dinner show. Reservations are required and may be booked up to two years in advance by calling 407-WDW-DINE (939-3463). Special dietary requests are honored with advance notice. Cancellations must be made at least 48 hours prior to showtime to avoid paying full price. Prices are subject to change.

The most popular of the lot is the Hoop-Dee-Doo Musical Revue, held in Pioneer Hall at Fort Wilderness. The show incorporates whoopin', singin', dancin', and audience participation in a frontier hoedown. Country vittles include ribs, fried chicken, salad, corn, and strawberry shortcake. There are three seatings, at 5 P.M., 7:15 P.M., and 9:30 P.M.; adults pay $49.01, including tax and tip.

At the Polynesian resort, Disney's new Spirit of Aloha Dinner Show—complete with hula skirts, ukuleles, and fire dancers takes guests on a whirlwind journey from New Zealand to Samoa. The meal is served family-style and features, roast chicken, spareribs, rice, and a tropical fruit dessert. The festive outdoor show is presented in Luau Cove. It is a rain or shine affair and is canceled only when temperatures drop below 50 degrees. Adults pay $47.80, including tax and tip.

It's not a dinner show per se, but the nightly Oktoberfest celebration at the Biergarten restaurant in the Germany pavilion at Epcot's World Showcase makes for an entertaining dining experience. It features performers in lederhosen or dirndls yodeling and playing everything from accordions to cowbells. Seating here is family-style (eight to a table), and guests have full run of a buffet that includes bratwurst, rotisserie chicken, homemade spaetzle, red cabbage, and German potato salad.

Adults pay $18.99 for dinner, plus tax and tip; desserts cost extra, as does beer (Beck's only). The cost for lunch is $13.99. Note that entertainment comes with dinner only.

A lower profile dinner show, Mickey's Backyard Barbecue, is one of our favorites. Think of it as a Fourth of July-type picnic, fortified by live entertainment. As an instructor gives line-dance lessons, a country band whoops it up Nashville-style. Disney characters kick up their heels on the dance floor. For couples, it makes for an entertaining night out. For groups, it's a full-out party. The hearty chow includes chicken and ribs, corn-on-the-cob, baked beans, corn bread, and other savory reminders of summer, plus as many cold drafts as you need to wash it all down. This seasonal show, presented at Fort Wilderness, costs $38 for adults (including tax and tip). For reservations, call 407-939-3463 up to a year in advance.

For the Love of Chocolate

When only a chocolate fix will do, the Ghirardelli Soda Fountain and Chocolate Shop makes a sweet retreat—the perfect place to pause between shops at the Marketplace for a root-beer float, a malt, or a peek at the chocolate-making equipment. On the West Side, try the southern-style confections at the Candy Cauldron, or smoothies and desserts at Wetzel's Pretzels. On Pleasure Island, D-Zertz is the sweetest solution.

10% OFF

GOLF REGULAR DAY VISITOR RATES

Receive 10% OFF Regular Day Visitor Rates at all 5 of the *Walt Disney World* championship golf courses.

Subject to terms and conditions on reverse side

10% OFF

AT PLANET HOLLYWOOD

food, non-alcoholic beverage, or merchandise (excludes taxes, gratuities, and alcoholic beverages) at Planet Hollywood at DOWNTOWN DISNEY® West Side.

Subject to terms and conditions on reverse side

How to take advantage: Tee times at this rate are limited and may be made 14 days in advance by calling 407-WDW-GOLF (939-4653). This offer is valid for the coupon holder and up to 3 guests. Guest must present coupon at the pro-shop check-in to receive discount.

Offer is valid through 12/31/04. ©Disney.

Offer valid at Planet Hollywood restaurant in DOWNTOWN DISNEY® West Side.

Not valid with any other offers.
PH Tracking Code: 10170000649

Valid through 12/31/04